A Centaur's Life

14

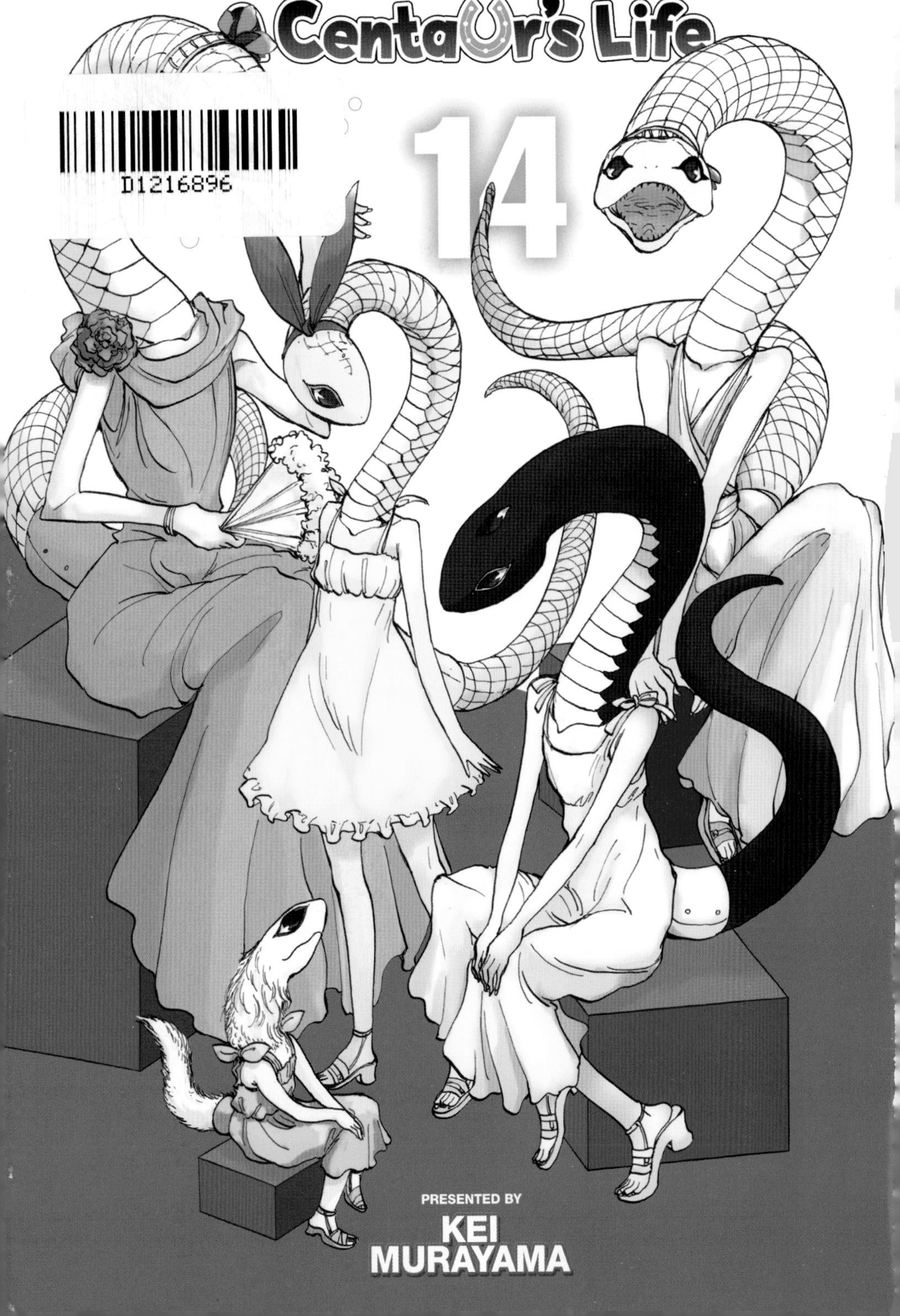

PRESENTED BY

KEI MURAYAMA

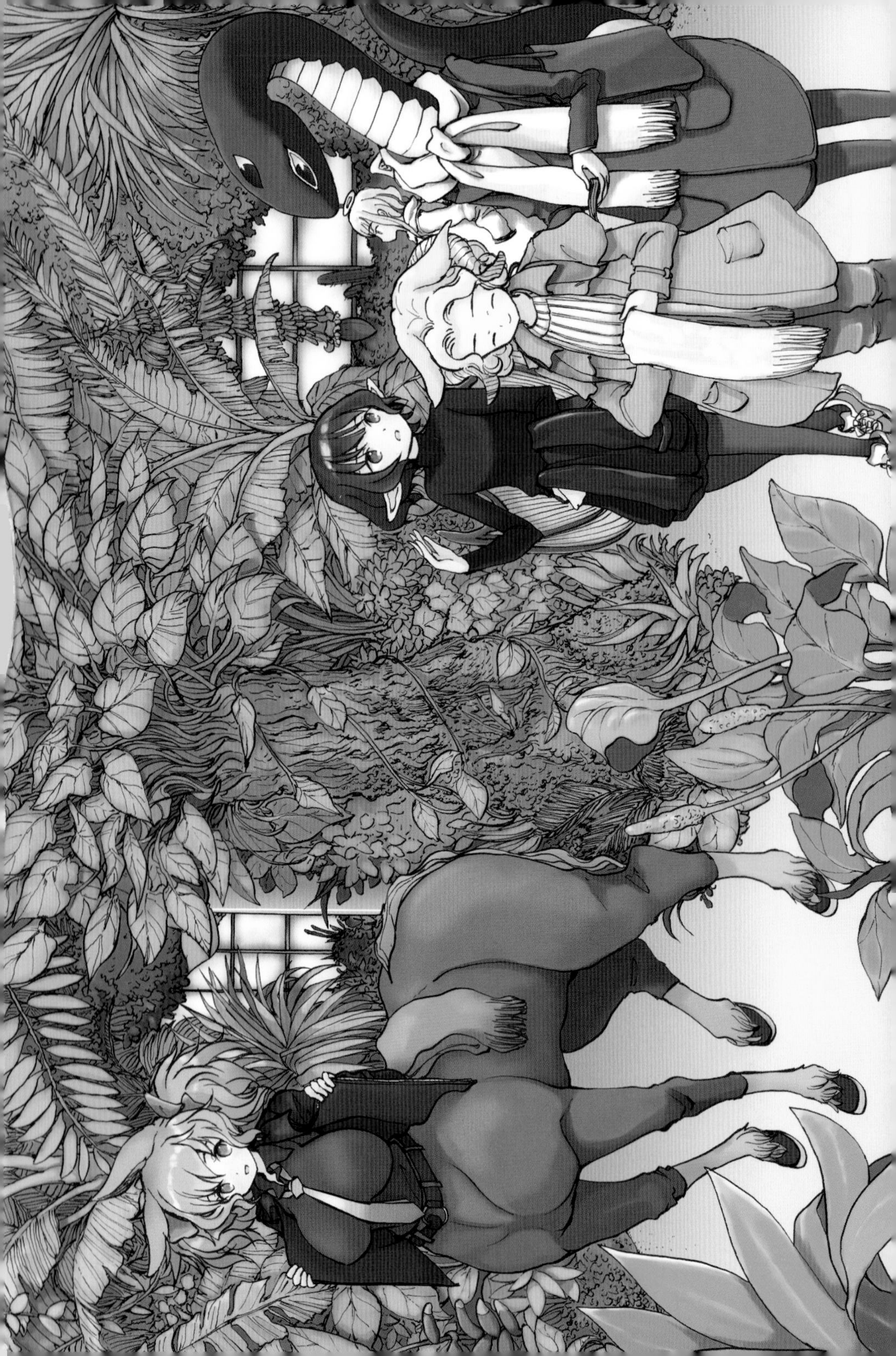

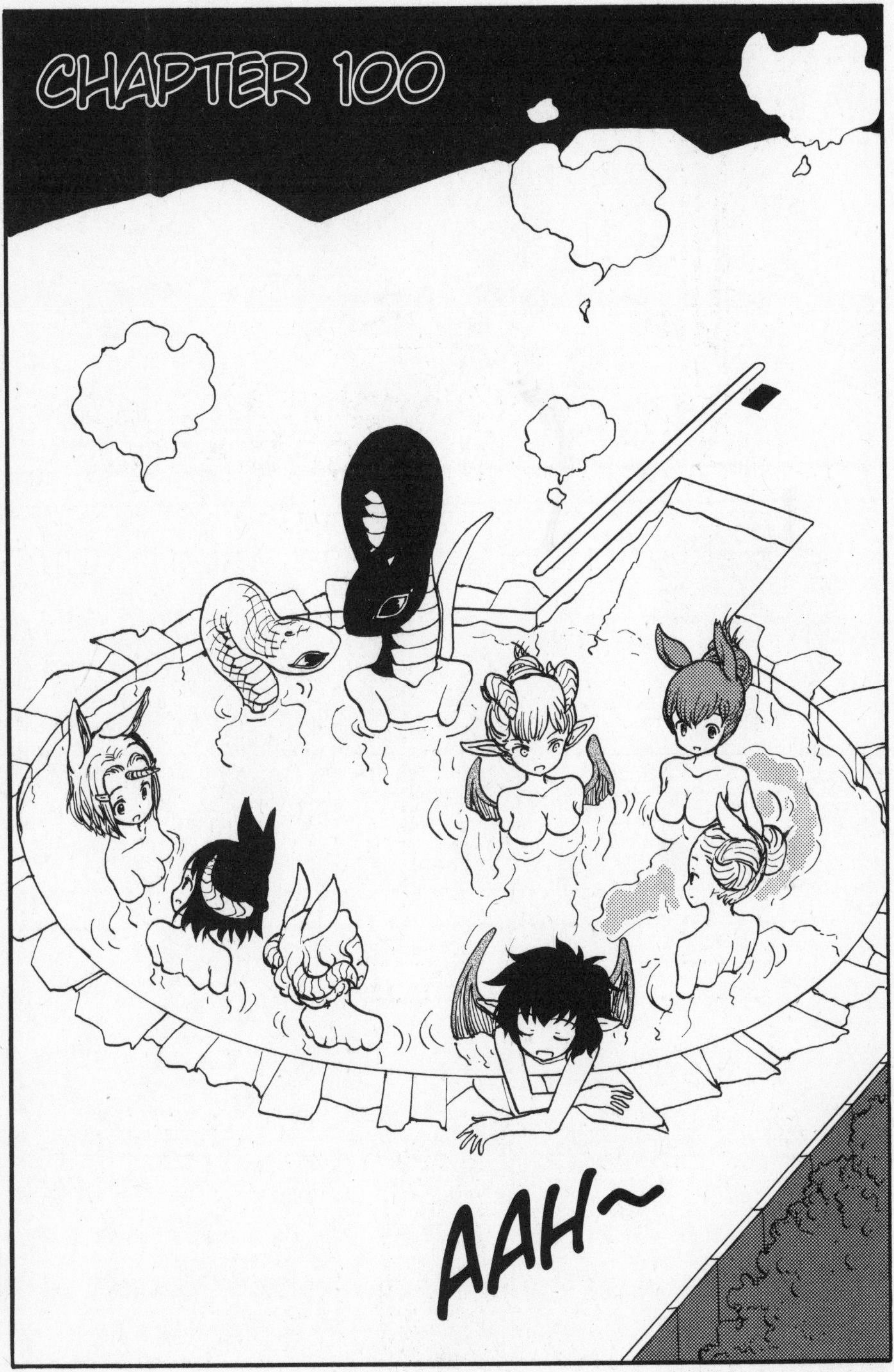
CHAPTER 100
AAH~

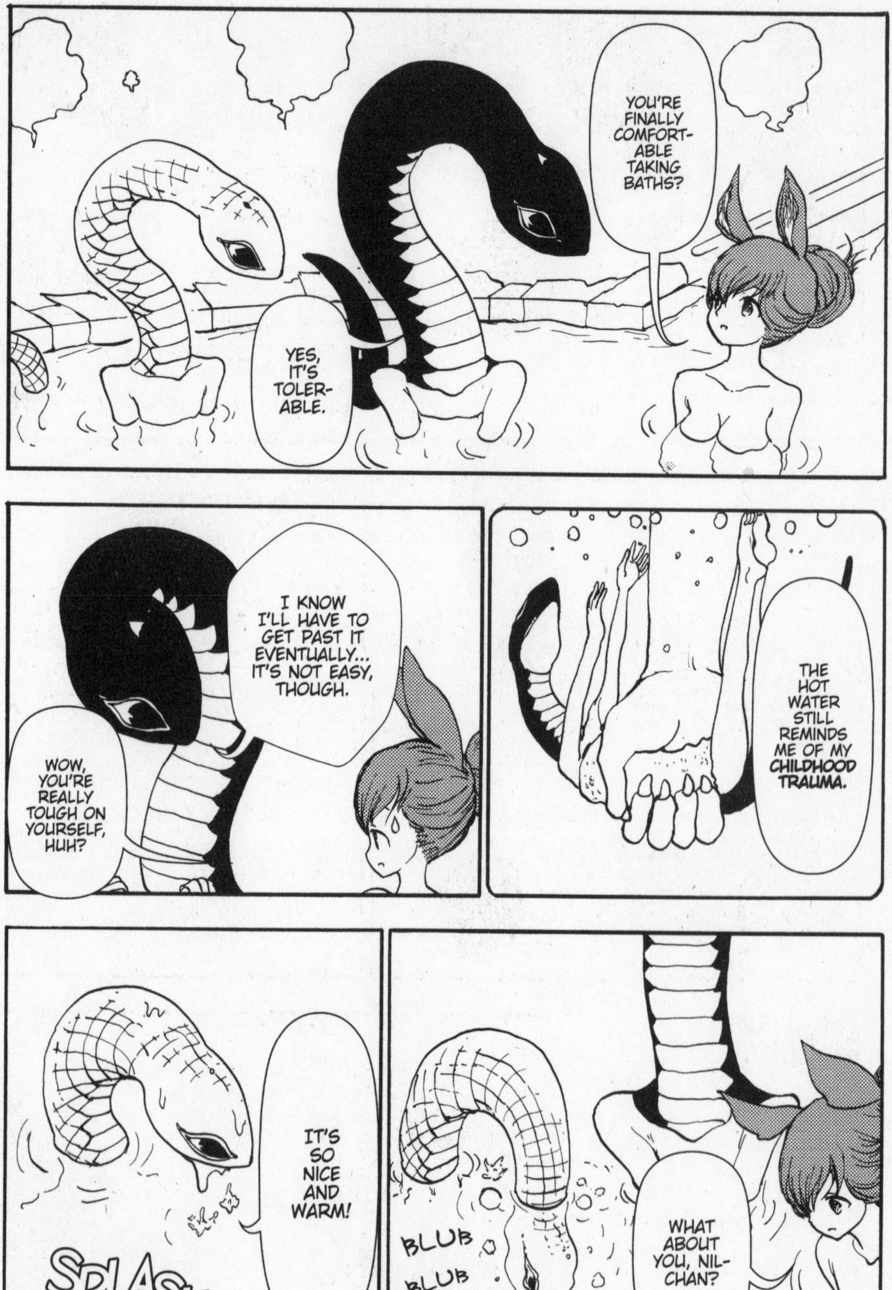
YOU'RE FINALLY COMFORTABLE TAKING BATHS?
YES, IT'S TOLERABLE.
THE HOT WATER STILL REMINDS ME OF MY **CHILDHOOD TRAUMA.**
I KNOW I'LL HAVE TO GET PAST IT EVENTUALLY... IT'S NOT EASY, THOUGH.
WOW, YOU'RE REALLY TOUGH ON YOURSELF, HUH?
WHAT ABOUT YOU, NIL-CHAN?
BLUB
BLUB
BLUB
IT'S SO NICE AND WARM!
SPLASH

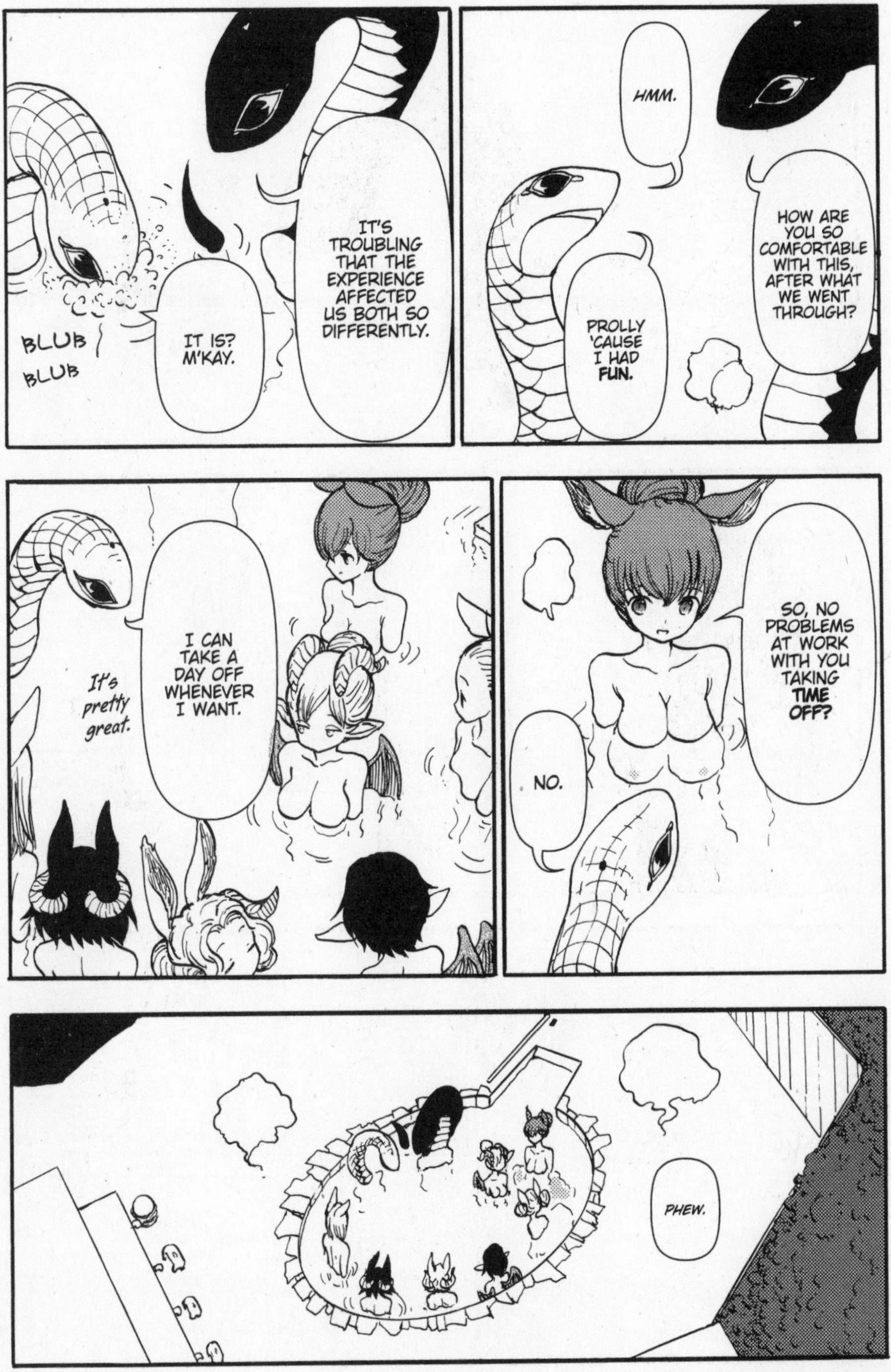
HMM.
HOW ARE YOU SO COMFORTABLE WITH THIS, AFTER WHAT WE WENT THROUGH?
PROLLY 'CAUSE I HAD **FUN.**
IT'S TROUBLING THAT THE EXPERIENCE AFFECTED US BOTH SO DIFFERENTLY.
IT IS? M'KAY.
BLUB
BLUB
SO, NO PROBLEMS AT WORK WITH YOU TAKING **TIME OFF?**
NO.
I CAN TAKE A DAY OFF WHENEVER I WANT.
It's pretty great.
PHEW.

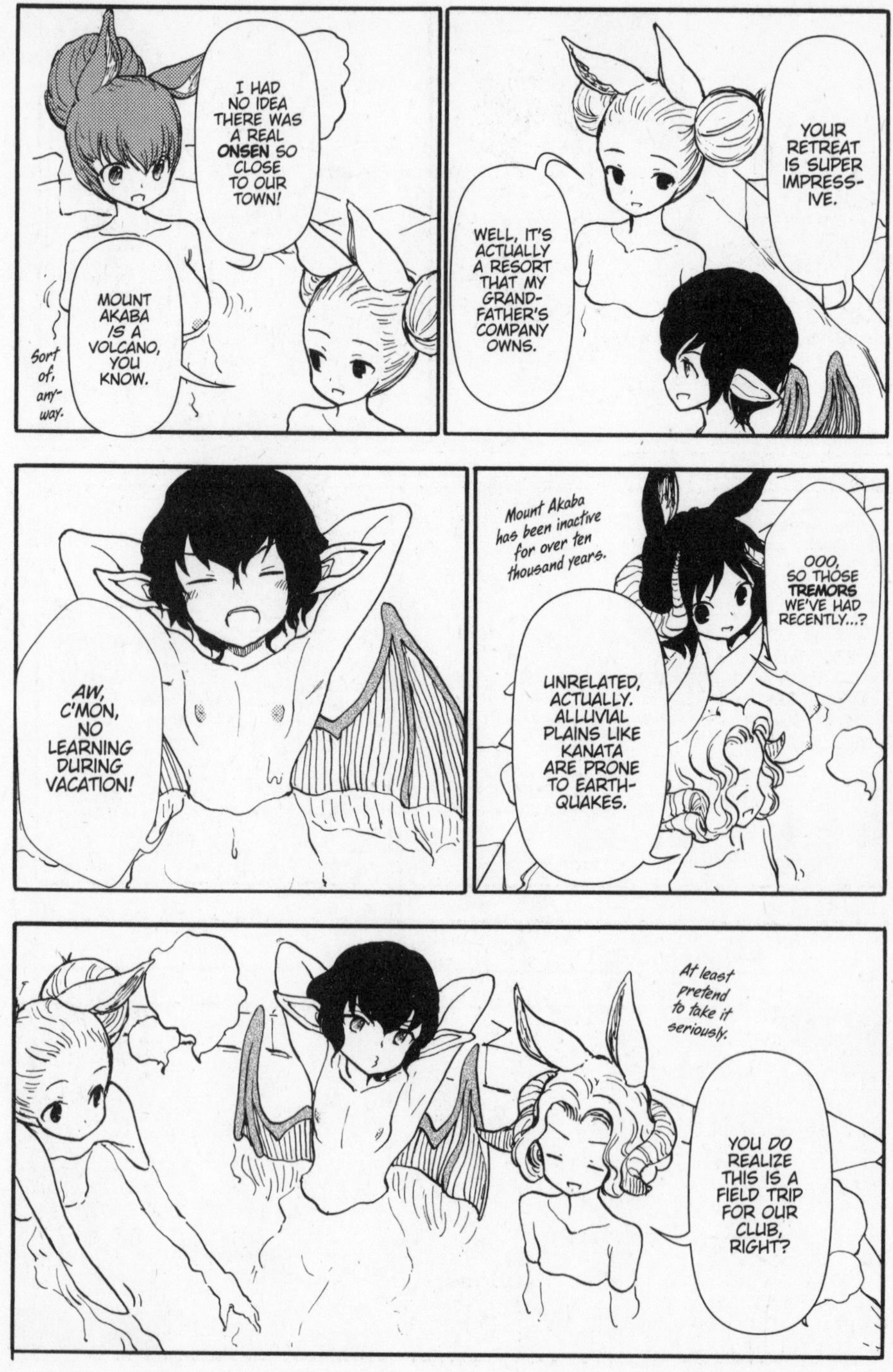
YOUR RETREAT IS SUPER IMPRESSIVE.
WELL, IT'S ACTUALLY A RESORT THAT MY GRANDFATHER'S COMPANY OWNS.
I HAD NO IDEA THERE WAS A REAL ONSEN SO CLOSE TO OUR TOWN!
MOUNT AKABA IS A VOLCANO, YOU KNOW.
Sort of, anyway.
OOO, SO THOSE TREMORS WE'VE HAD RECENTLY...?
Mount Akaba has been inactive for over ten thousand years.
UNRELATED, ACTUALLY. ALLUVIAL PLAINS LIKE KANATA ARE PRONE TO EARTHQUAKES.
AW, C'MON, NO LEARNING DURING VACATION!
YOU DO REALIZE THIS IS A FIELD TRIP FOR OUR CLUB, RIGHT?
At least pretend to take it seriously.

WHO SAYS WE CAN'T RELAX ON A FIELD TRIP?
HERE, HAVE A DRINK.
AH, THANK YOU.
YOINK
A DRINK, HUH?
Where did that come from?
ARE YOU KIDDING ME? THIS IS REAL ALCOHOL!
SNIFF SNIFF
NOPE.
AWW~!
ARE YOU REALLY THAT UPTIGHT, KYOKO-SENPAI?

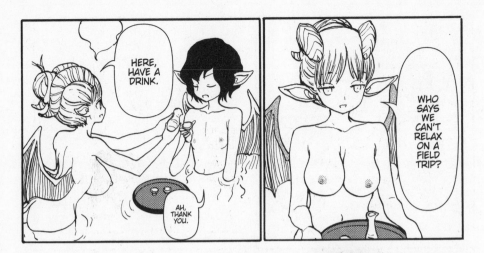

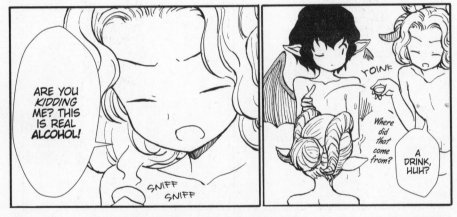

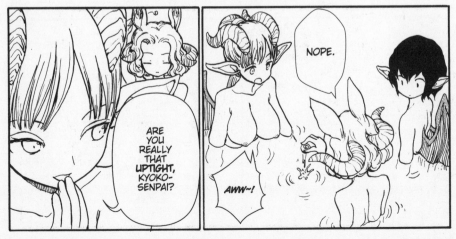

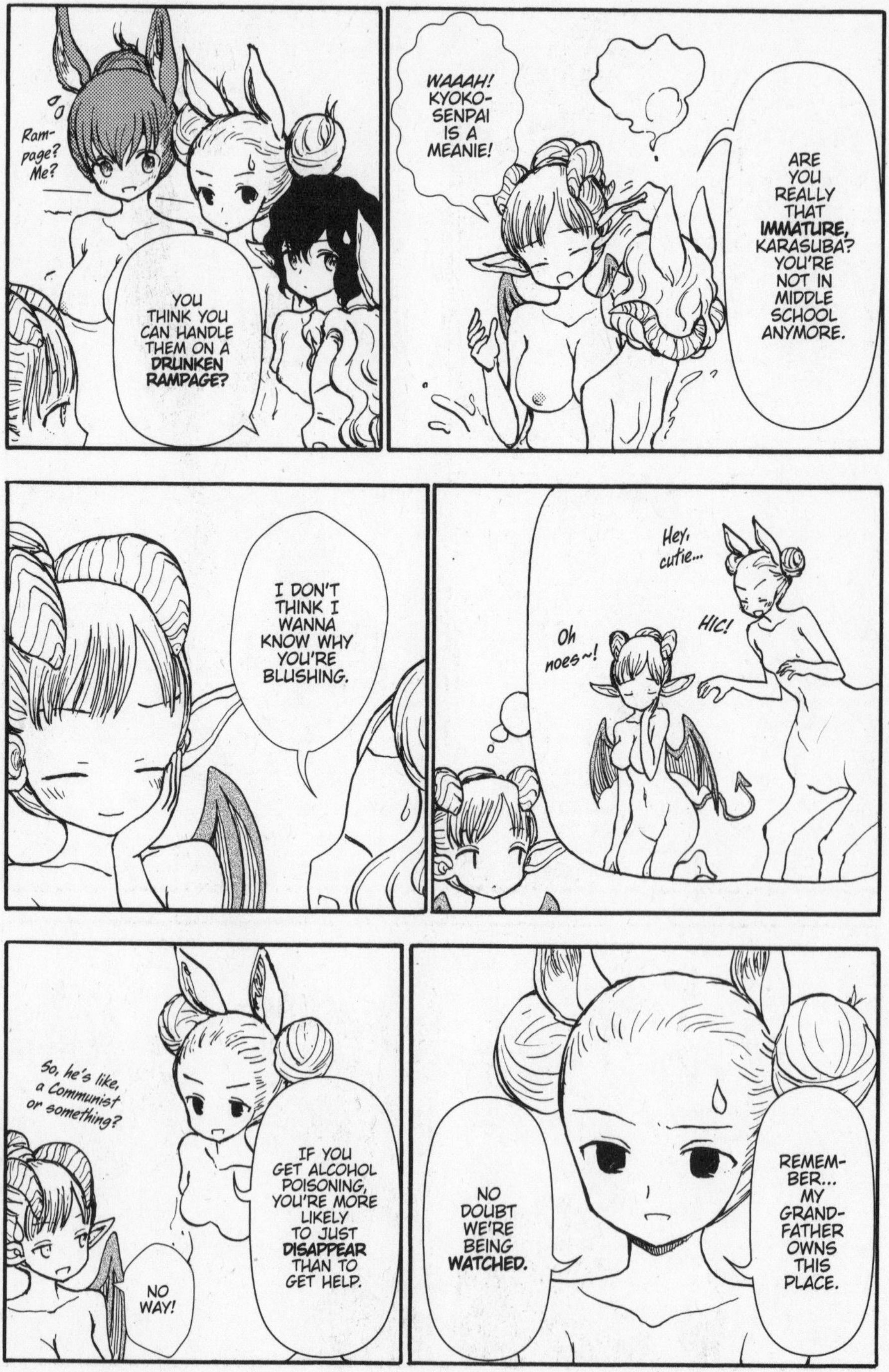
ARE YOU REALLY THAT **IMMATURE,** KARASUBA? YOU'RE NOT IN MIDDLE SCHOOL ANYMORE.
WAAAH! KYOKO-SENPAI IS A MEANIE!
YOU THINK YOU CAN HANDLE THEM ON A **DRUNKEN RAMPAGE?**
Ram-page? Me?
Hey, cutie...
HIC!
Oh noes~!
I DON'T THINK I WANNA KNOW WHY YOU'RE BLUSHING.
REMEMBER... MY GRAND-FATHER OWNS THIS PLACE.
NO DOUBT WE'RE BEING **WATCHED.**
So, he's like, a Communist or something?
IF YOU GET ALCOHOL POISONING, YOU'RE MORE LIKELY TO JUST **DISAPPEAR** THAN TO GET HELP.
NO WAY!

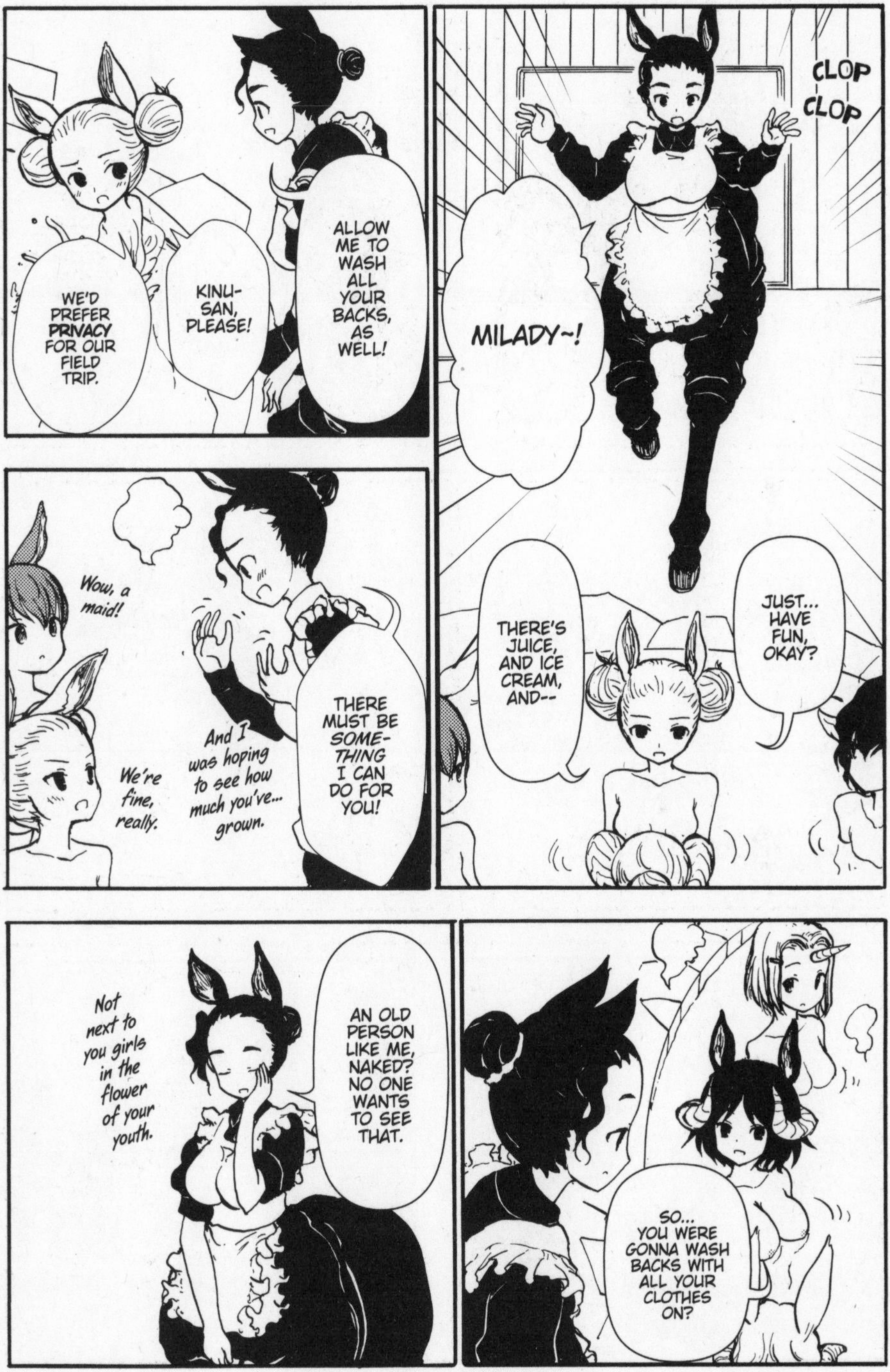
CLOP
CLOP
MILADY~!
THERE'S JUICE, AND ICE CREAM, AND--
JUST... HAVE FUN, OKAY?
ALLOW ME TO WASH ALL YOUR BACKS, AS WELL!
KINU-SAN, PLEASE!
WE'D PREFER PRIVACY FOR OUR FIELD TRIP.
THERE MUST BE SOME-THING I CAN DO FOR YOU!
And I was hoping to see how much you've... grown.
Wow, a maid!
We're fine, really.
SO... YOU WERE GONNA WASH BACKS WITH ALL YOUR CLOTHES ON?
AN OLD PERSON LIKE ME, NAKED? NO ONE WANTS TO SEE THAT.
Not next to you girls in the flower of your youth.

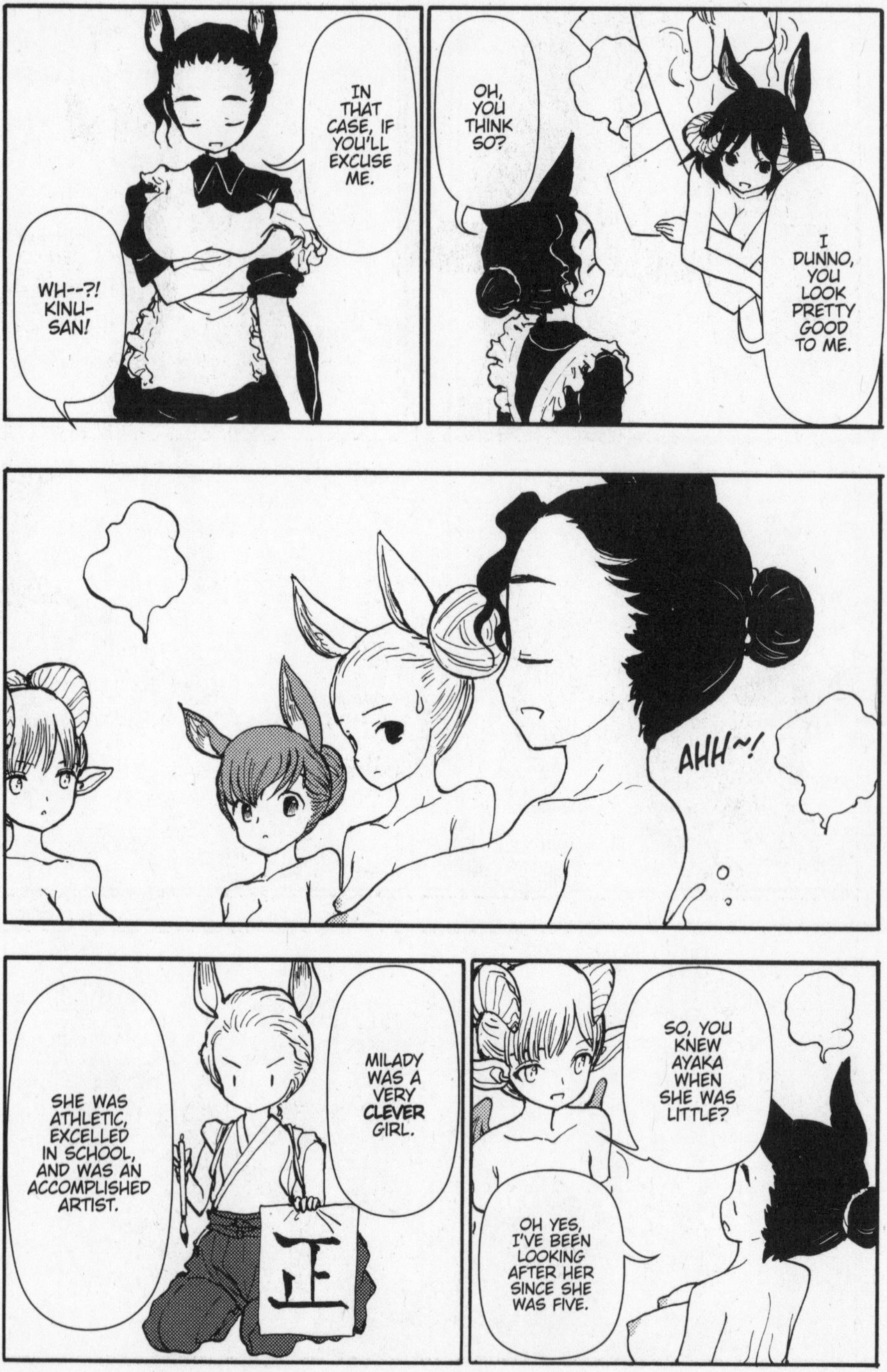
I DUNNO, YOU LOOK PRETTY GOOD TO ME.
OH, YOU THINK SO?
IN THAT CASE, IF YOU'LL EXCUSE ME.
WH--?! KINU-SAN!
AHH~!
SO, YOU KNEW AYAKA WHEN SHE WAS LITTLE?
OH YES, I'VE BEEN LOOKING AFTER HER SINCE SHE WAS FIVE.
MILADY WAS A VERY CLEVER GIRL.
SHE WAS ATHLETIC, EXCELLED IN SCHOOL, AND WAS AN ACCOMPLISHED ARTIST.
正

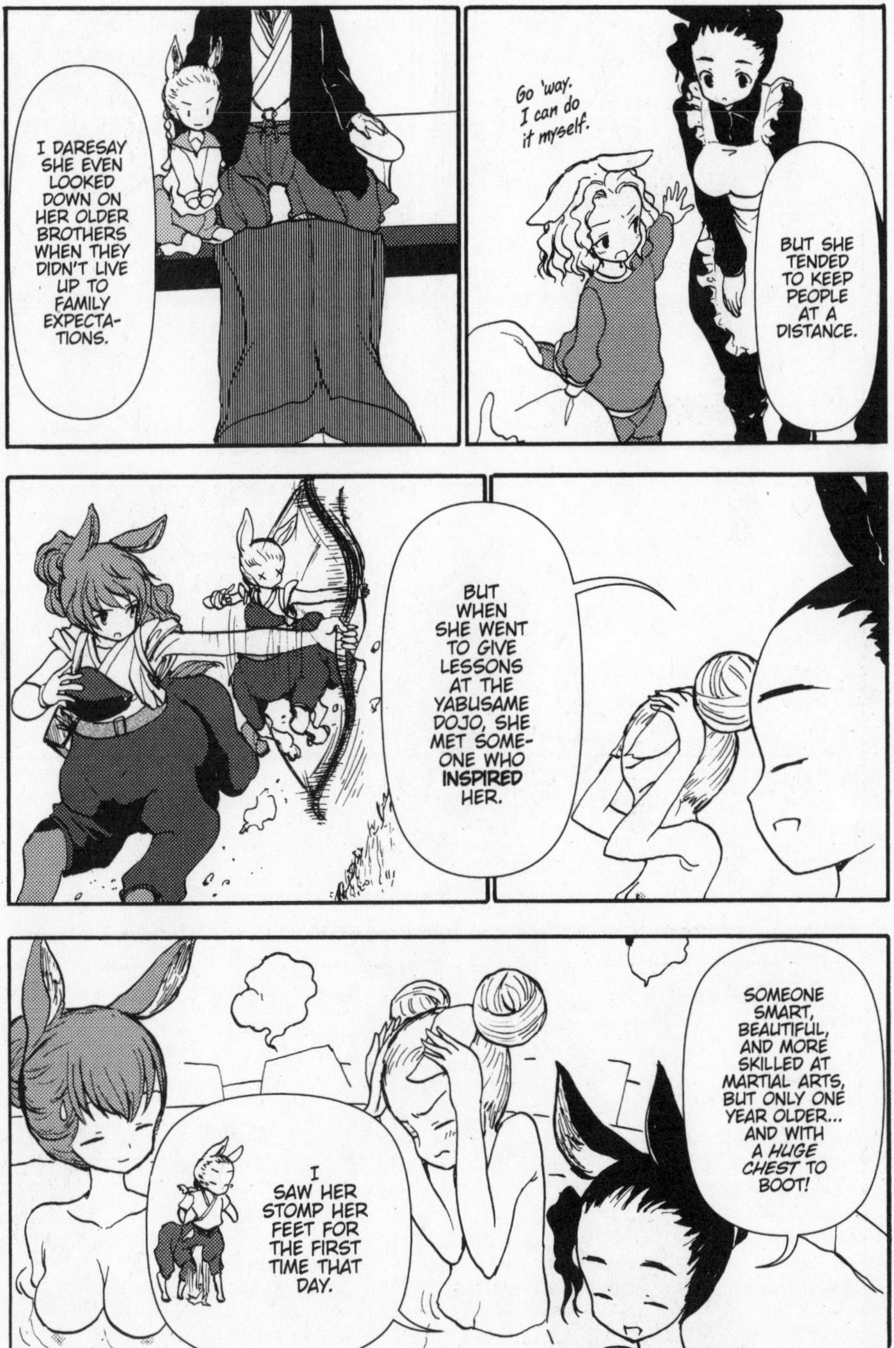
Go 'way. I can do it myself.
BUT SHE TENDED TO KEEP PEOPLE AT A DISTANCE.
I DARESAY SHE EVEN LOOKED DOWN ON HER OLDER BROTHERS WHEN THEY DIDN'T LIVE UP TO FAMILY EXPECTATIONS.
BUT WHEN SHE WENT TO GIVE LESSONS AT THE YABUSAME DOJO, SHE MET SOMEONE WHO **INSPIRED** HER.
SOMEONE SMART, BEAUTIFUL, AND MORE SKILLED AT MARTIAL ARTS, BUT ONLY ONE YEAR OLDER... AND WITH *A HUGE CHEST* TO BOOT!
I SAW HER STOMP HER FEET FOR THE FIRST TIME THAT DAY.

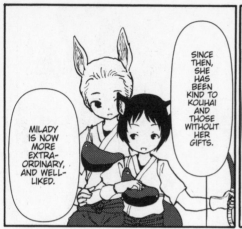

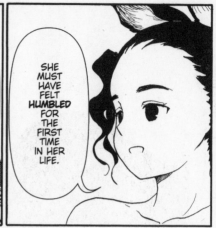

SHE MUST HAVE FELT **HUMBLED** FOR THE FIRST TIME IN HER LIFE.
SINCE THEN, SHE HAS BEEN KIND TO KOUHAI AND THOSE WITHOUT HER GIFTS.
MILADY IS NOW MORE EXTRA-ORDINARY, AND WELL-LIKED.
So, she just likes to brag on Ayaka.
Just like a doting parent.
Can you not?
Huh?
SO, MIGHT *YOU* BE THE RED-HEADED, BIG-CHESTED GIRL WHO BESTED MILADY?
YES, YOU LOOK LIKE THE TYPE THAT WOULD INSENSITIVELY DEFEAT A SMART, HARD-WORKING PERSON.
Eh?!
Okinu!
AH, I MUST GO.
Finally! Get out!

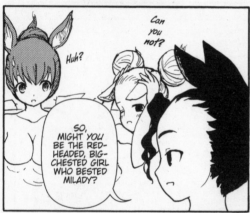

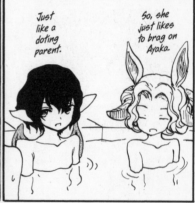

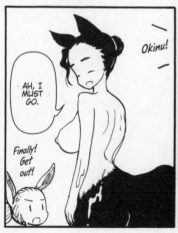

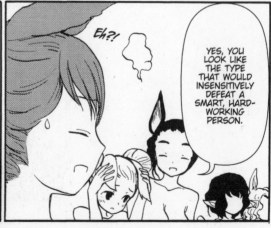

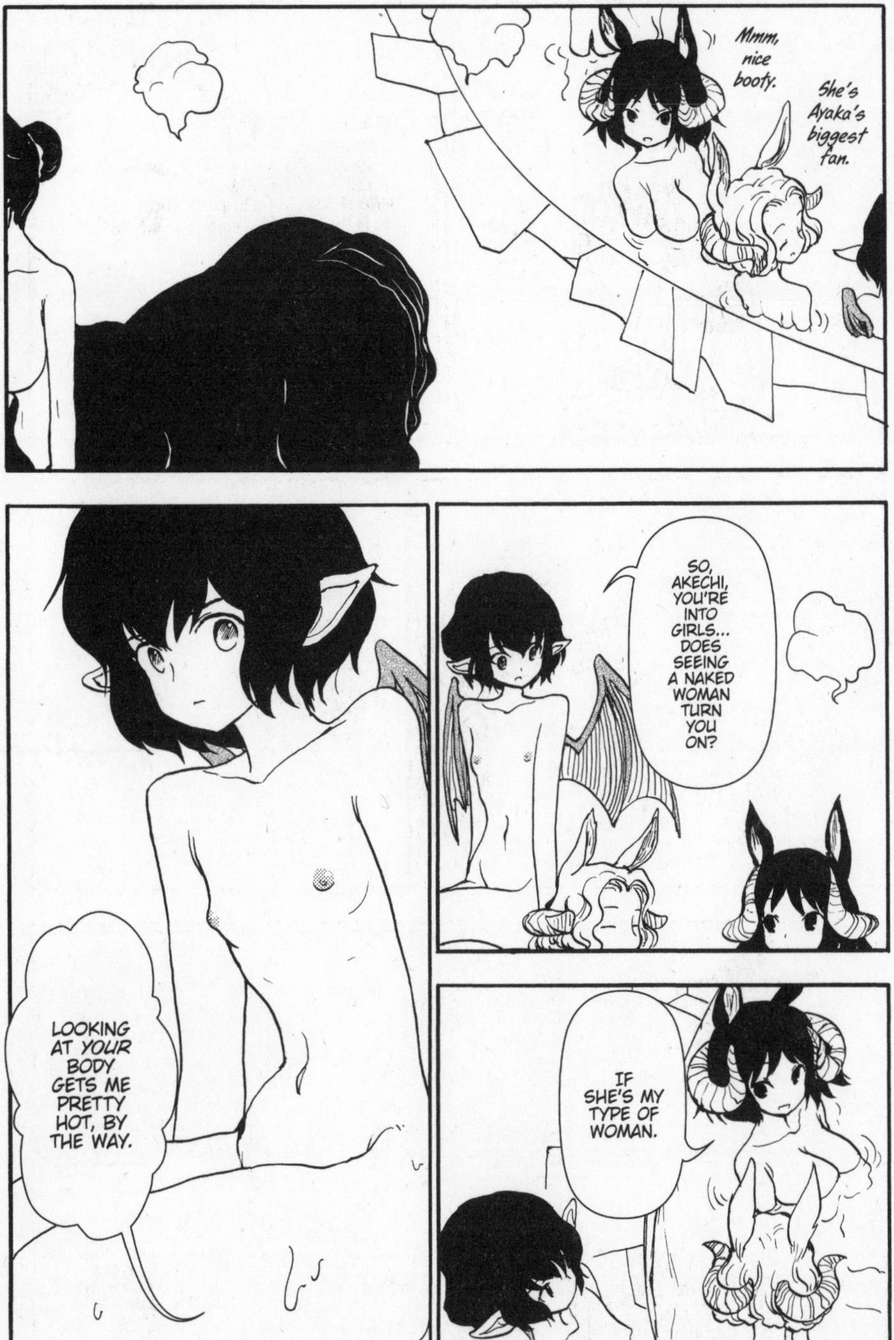
Mmm, nice booty.
She's Ayaka's biggest fan.
SO, AKECHI, YOU'RE INTO GIRLS... DOES SEEING A NAKED WOMAN TURN YOU ON?
IF SHE'S MY TYPE OF WOMAN.
LOOKING AT *YOUR* BODY GETS ME PRETTY HOT, BY THE WAY.

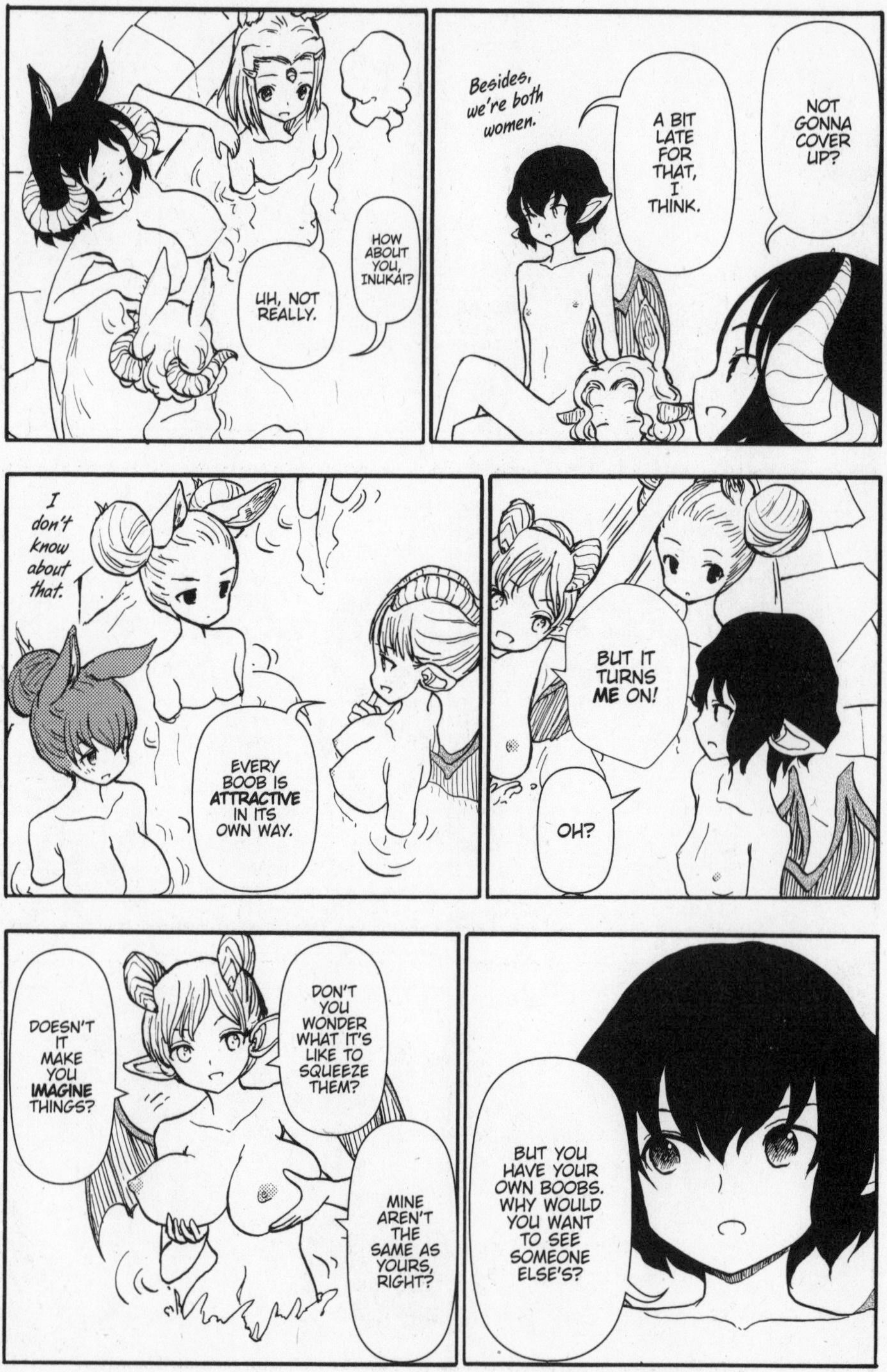
NOT GONNA COVER UP?
A BIT LATE FOR THAT, I THINK.
Besides, we're both women.
HOW ABOUT YOU, INUKAI!?
UH, NOT REALLY.
BUT IT TURNS ME ON!
OH?
EVERY BOOB IS ATTRACTIVE IN ITS OWN WAY.
I don't know about that.
BUT YOU HAVE YOUR OWN BOOBS. WHY WOULD YOU WANT TO SEE SOMEONE ELSE'S?
MINE AREN'T THE SAME AS YOURS, RIGHT?
DON'T YOU WONDER WHAT IT'S LIKE TO SQUEEZE THEM?
DOESN'T IT MAKE YOU IMAGINE THINGS?

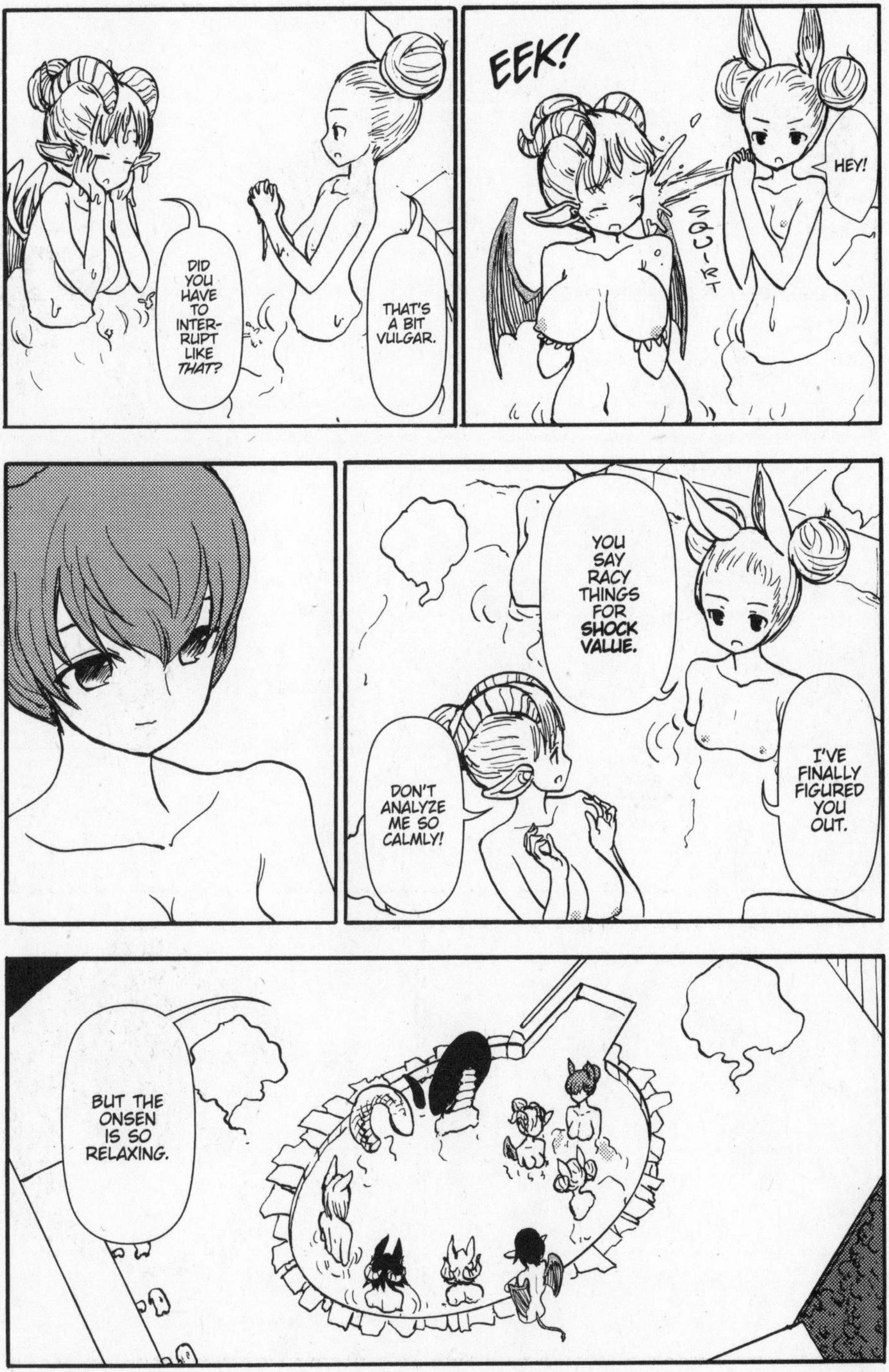
EEK!
HEY!
SQUIRT
THAT'S A BIT VULGAR.
DID YOU HAVE TO INTERRUPT LIKE *THAT*?
I'VE FINALLY FIGURED YOU OUT.
YOU SAY RACY THINGS FOR **SHOCK VALUE.**
DON'T ANALYZE ME SO CALMLY!
BUT THE ONSEN IS SO RELAXING.

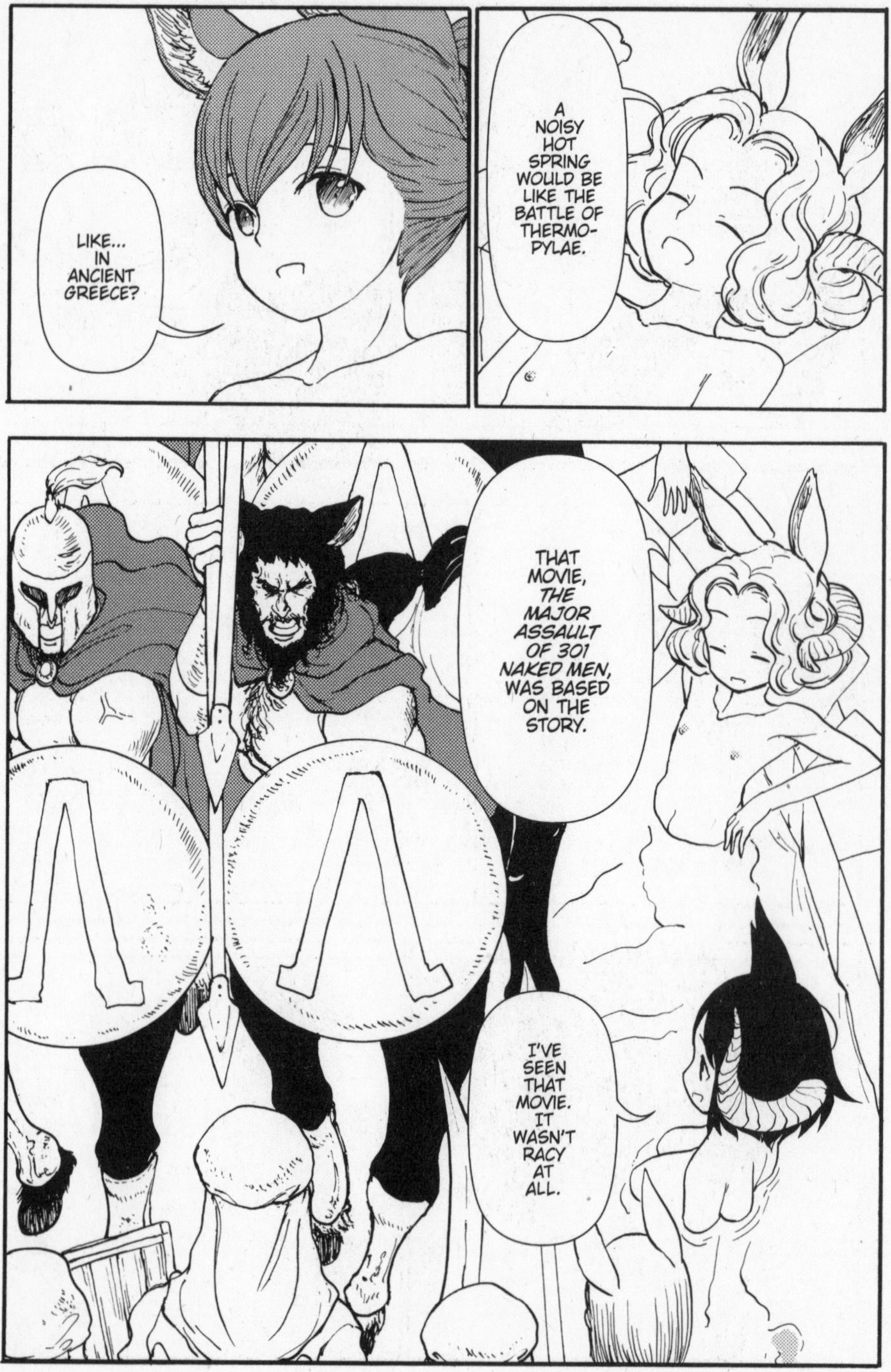
A NOISY HOT SPRING WOULD BE LIKE THE BATTLE OF THERMO-PYLAE.
LIKE... IN ANCIENT GREECE?
THAT MOVIE, *THE MAJOR ASSAULT OF 301 NAKED MEN*, WAS BASED ON THE STORY.
I'VE SEEN THAT MOVIE. IT WASN'T RACY AT ALL.

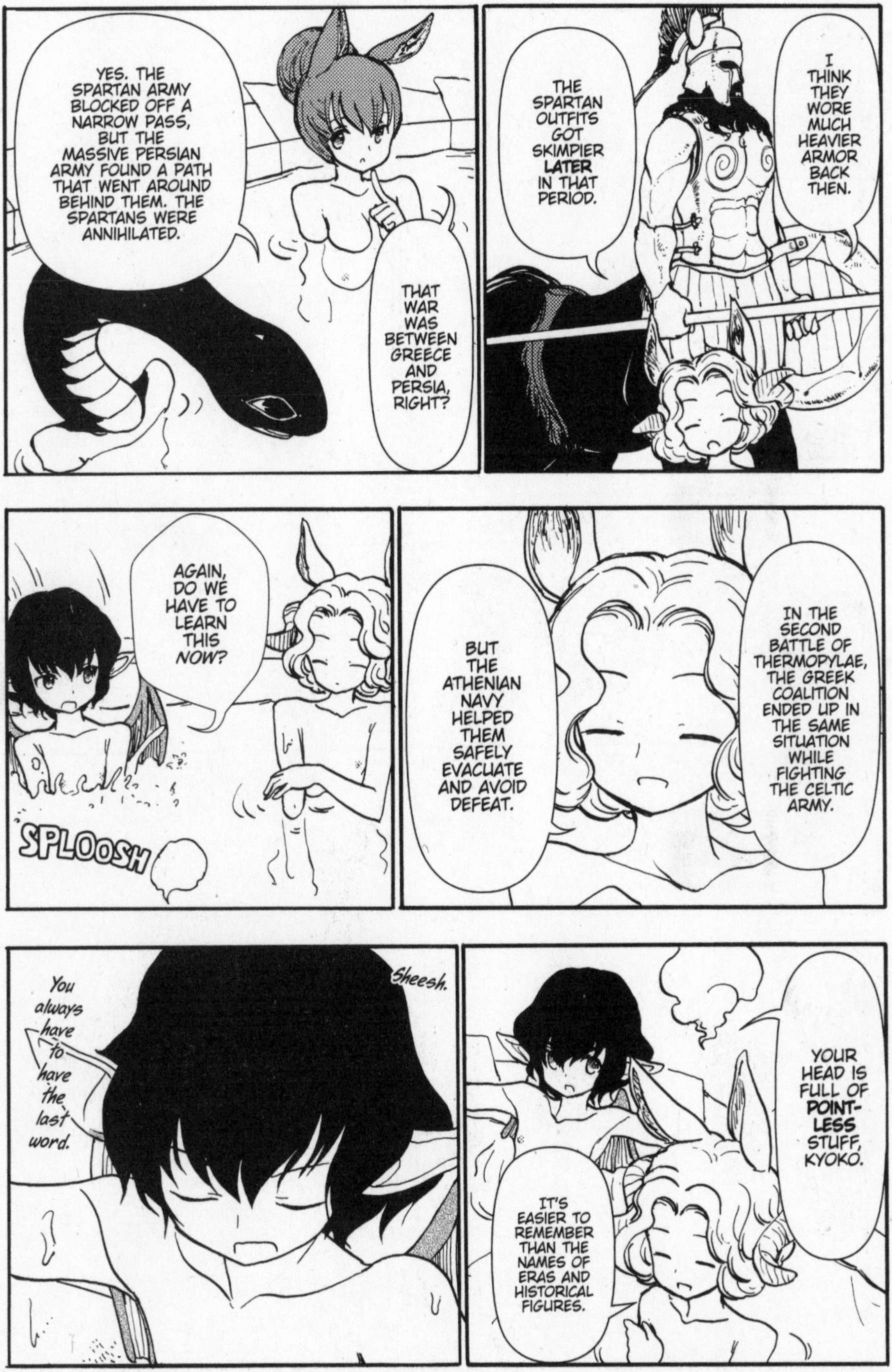
I THINK THEY WORE MUCH HEAVIER ARMOR BACK THEN.
THE SPARTAN OUTFITS GOT SKIMPIER **LATER** IN THAT PERIOD.
THAT WAR WAS BETWEEN GREECE AND PERSIA, RIGHT?
YES. THE SPARTAN ARMY BLOCKED OFF A NARROW PASS, BUT THE MASSIVE PERSIAN ARMY FOUND A PATH THAT WENT AROUND BEHIND THEM. THE SPARTANS WERE ANNIHILATED.
IN THE SECOND BATTLE OF THERMOPYLAE, THE GREEK COALITION ENDED UP IN THE SAME SITUATION WHILE FIGHTING THE CELTIC ARMY.
BUT THE ATHENIAN NAVY HELPED THEM SAFELY EVACUATE AND AVOID DEFEAT.
AGAIN, DO WE HAVE TO LEARN THIS *NOW*?
SPLOOSH
YOUR HEAD IS FULL OF **POINTLESS** STUFF, KYOKO.
IT'S EASIER TO REMEMBER THAN THE NAMES OF ERAS AND HISTORICAL FIGURES.
Sheesh.
You always have to have the last word.

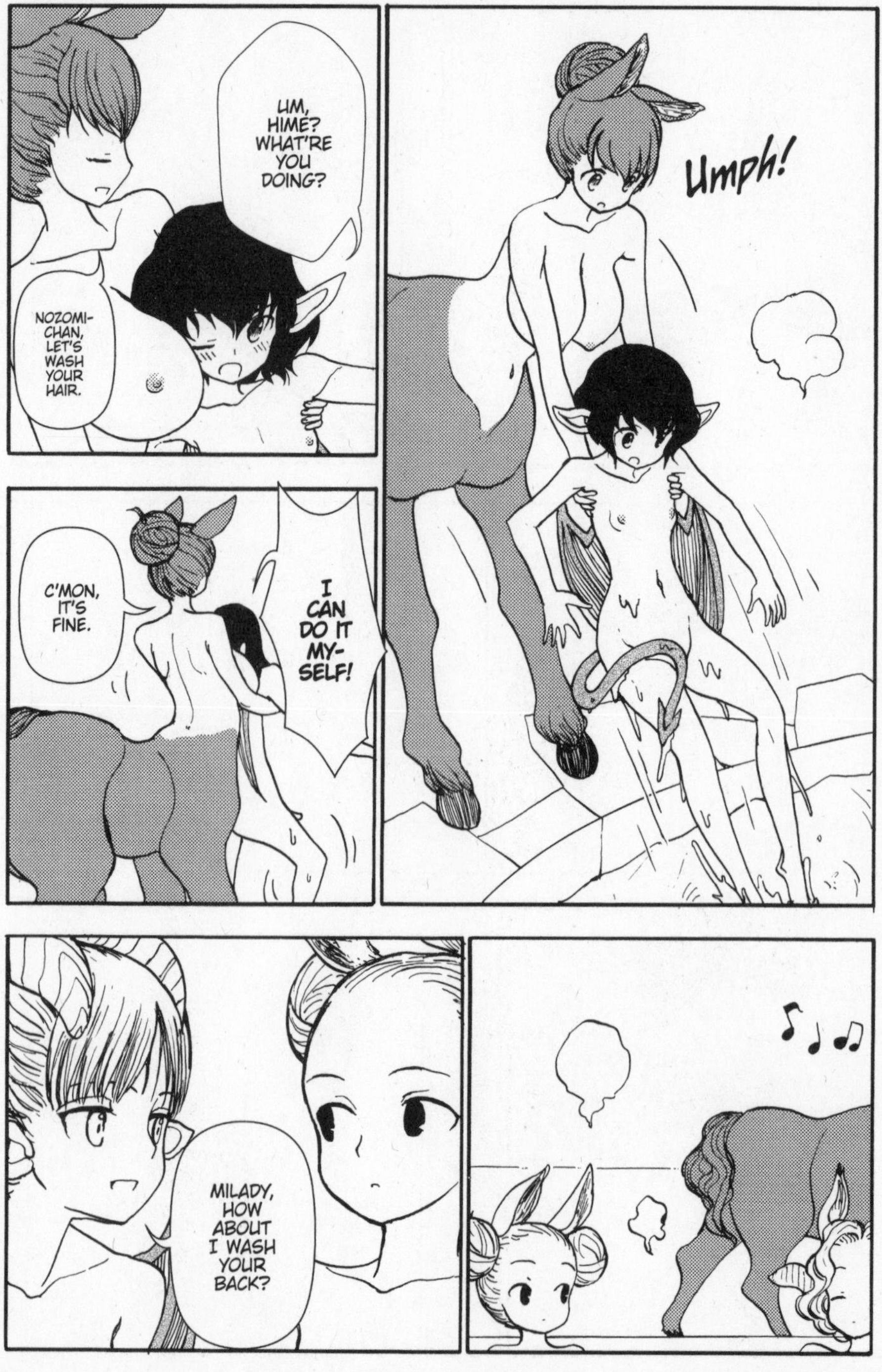
NOZOMI-CHAN, LET'S WASH YOUR HAIR.
UM, HIME? WHAT'RE YOU DOING?
C'MON, IT'S FINE.
I CAN DO IT MY-SELF!
Umph!
MILADY, HOW ABOUT I WASH YOUR BACK?

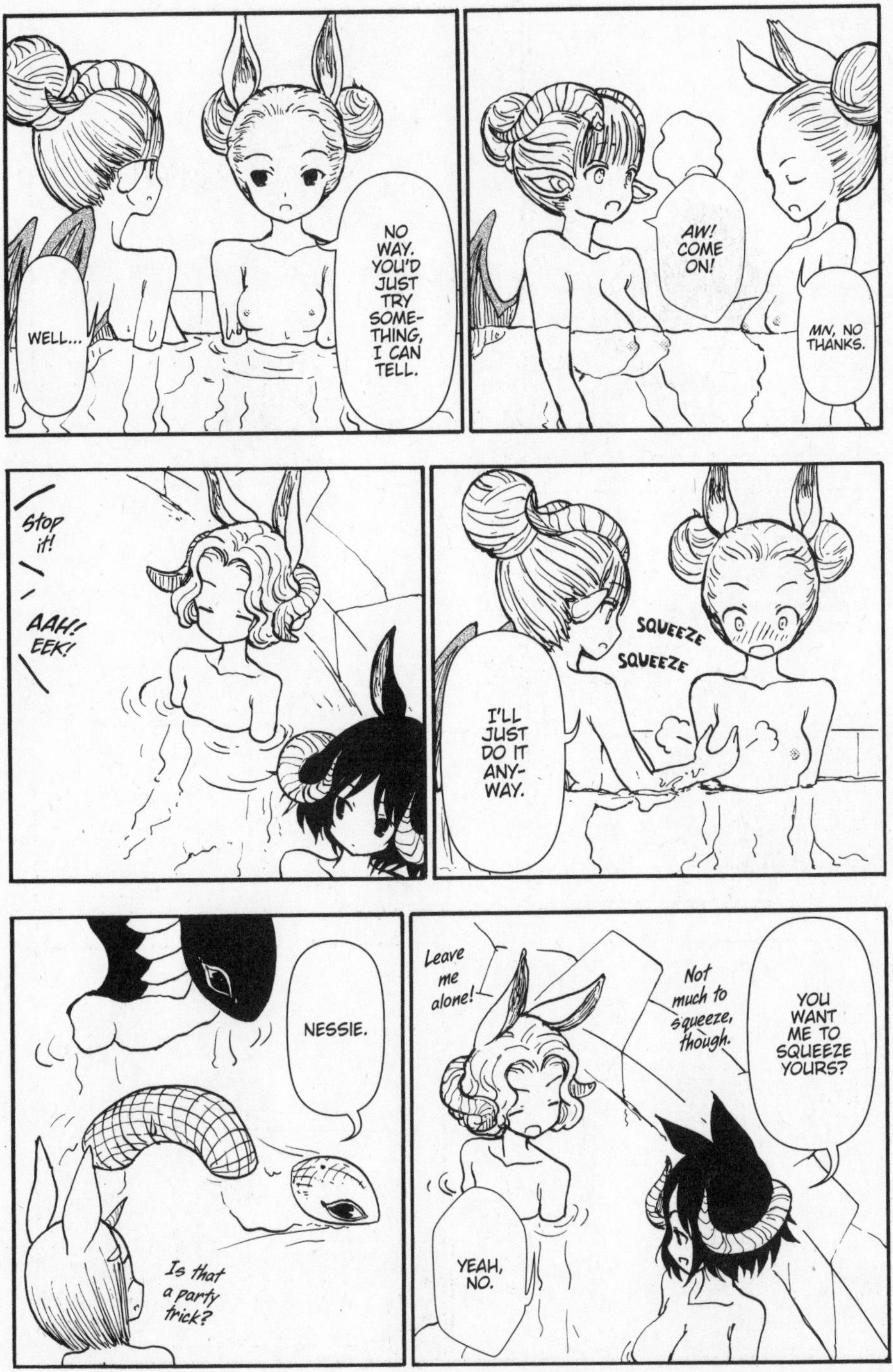
AW! COME ON!
MN, NO THANKS.
NO WAY. YOU'D JUST TRY SOME-THING, I CAN TELL.
WELL...
I'LL JUST DO IT ANY-WAY.
SQUEEZE SQUEEZE
Stop it!
AAH! EEK!
YOU WANT ME TO SQUEEZE YOURS?
Not much to squeeze, though.
Leave me alone!
YEAH, NO.
NESSIE.
Is that a party trick?

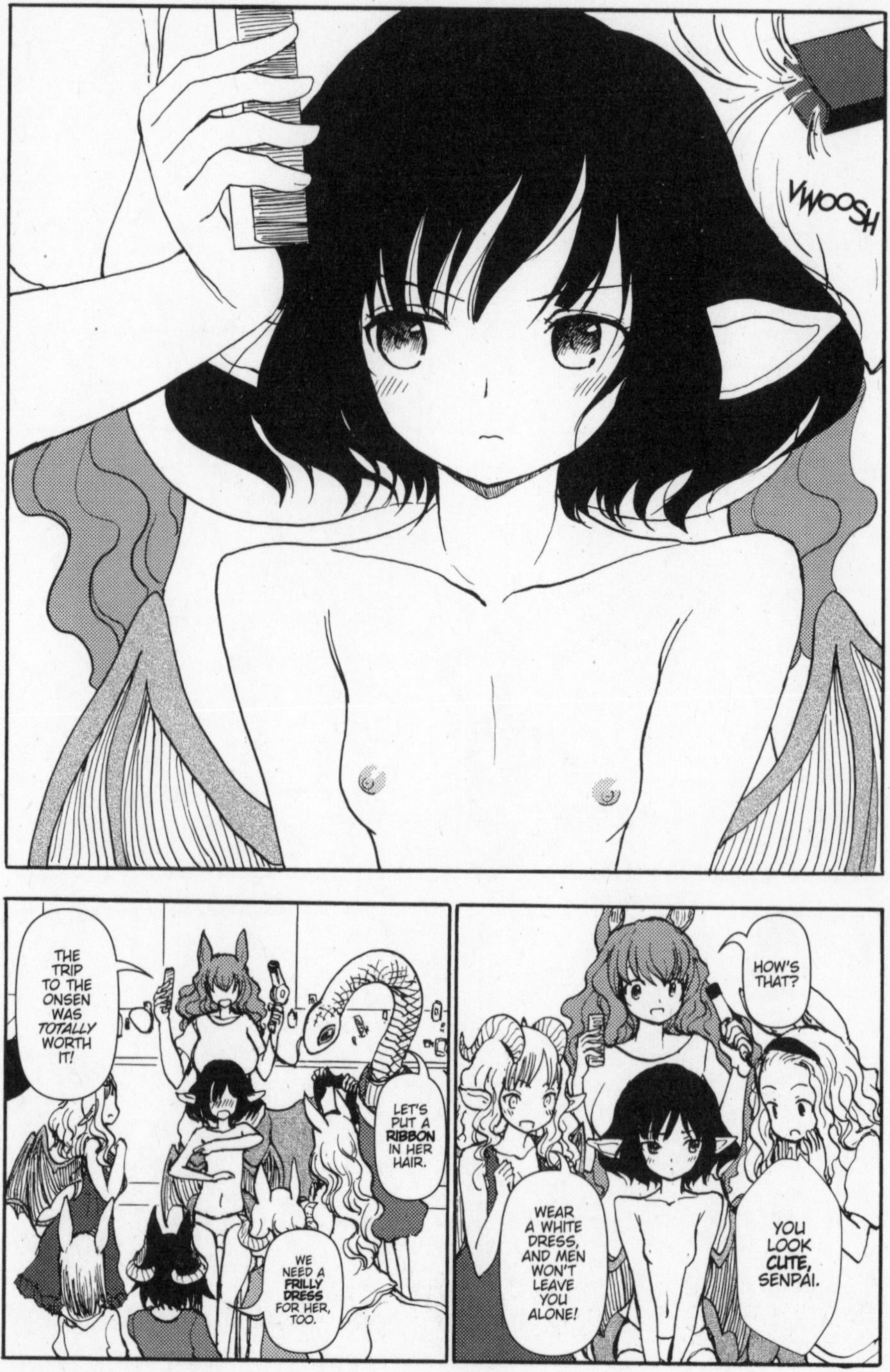
VWOOSH
THE TRIP TO THE ONSEN WAS *TOTALLY* WORTH IT!
LET'S PUT A **RIBBON** IN HER HAIR.
WE NEED A **FRILLY DRESS** FOR HER, TOO.
HOW'S THAT?
YOU LOOK **CUTE,** SENPAI.
WEAR A WHITE DRESS, AND MEN WON'T LEAVE YOU ALONE!

A Centaur's Life

SOLDIERS AROUND THE WORLD:

THE SUMERIAN CHARIOT

WE WERE ONCE CERTAIN THAT WILD ANIMALS DIDN'T KILL MEMBERS OF THEIR OWN SPECIES FOR ANY REASON OTHER THAN CONSUMPTION, BUT THESE DAYS, WIDESPREAD REPORTS OF ANIMALS KILLING OTHERS TO GAIN TERRITORY OR PROTECT THEIR YOUNG ARE BRINGING THAT BELIEF INTO QUESTION. THE SIMILARITIES BETWEEN ANIMALS AND HUMANS GO EVEN FURTHER IN SOME CASES; CHIMPANZEES, FOR EXAMPLE, EXHIBIT COMPLEX SOCIAL STRUCTURES BY FORMING COALITIONS WITH OTHER INFLUENTIAL CHIMPANZEES, RELENTLESSLY ATTACKING ENEMIES, OVERTHROWING LEADERS, AND ELIMINATING INDIVIDUALS WHO GO AGAINST SOCIAL NORMS. AS IS CHARACTERISTIC OF A SPECIES CAPABLE OF ABSTRACT THOUGHT, A MEMBER THAT DISAGREES WITH A SOCIAL GROUP'S DECISION-- SUCH AS WAR--STILL FOLLOWS THE GROUP REGARDLESS. SUCH GROUPS TEND TO HAVE SUPERIOR WEAPONS AND SKILLS.

THE SUMERIAN CIVILIZATION, THE FIRST IN THE WORLD, WAS CONSTANTLY AT WAR. THEIR ETHNICITY AND LINGUISTIC GENEALOGY ARE UNKNOWN, BUT WE DO KNOW THAT THEIR CITIES (INCLUDING UR, URUK, AND LAGASH) ROSE IN SOUTHERN MESOPOTAMIA AROUND 3500 BCE. THEY WERE NOT UNITED DURING THIS EARLY PERIOD, HOWEVER, AND ENGAGED IN TRADE AND WAR WITH ONE ANOTHER.

THE ABOVE ILLUSTRATION DEPICTS A CHARIOT USED BY SUMERIANS, THE WHEELS OF WHICH WERE SIMPLY BUT HEAVILY CONSTRUCTED FROM TWO PIECES OF WOOD. THE CHARIOTS WERE DRAWN BY DONKEYS; PRIOR TO BREEDING, HORSES WERE UNFIT FOR RIDING OR EVEN DRAWING CHARIOTS.

IN THE 24TH TO 23RD CENTURY BCE, SUMER BECAME A UNIFIED STATE UNDER KING LUGAL-ZAGE-SI, WHO WAS DEFEATED SOON AFTER (AND, IT IS SAID, CHAINED TO THE GATE LIKE A DOG) BY SARGON OF AKKAD OF THE NORTH. A SUMERIAN RULING DYNASTY KNOWN AS THE THIRD DYNASTY OF UR AROSE LATER, AFTER THE FALL OF AKKADIAN AND GUTIAN RULE. ITS KING PRIDED HIMSELF IN BEING LITERATE IN AKKADIAN AS WELL AS SUMERIAN, WHICH BECAME OBSOLETE AS A SPOKEN LANGUAGE.

CHAPTER 101

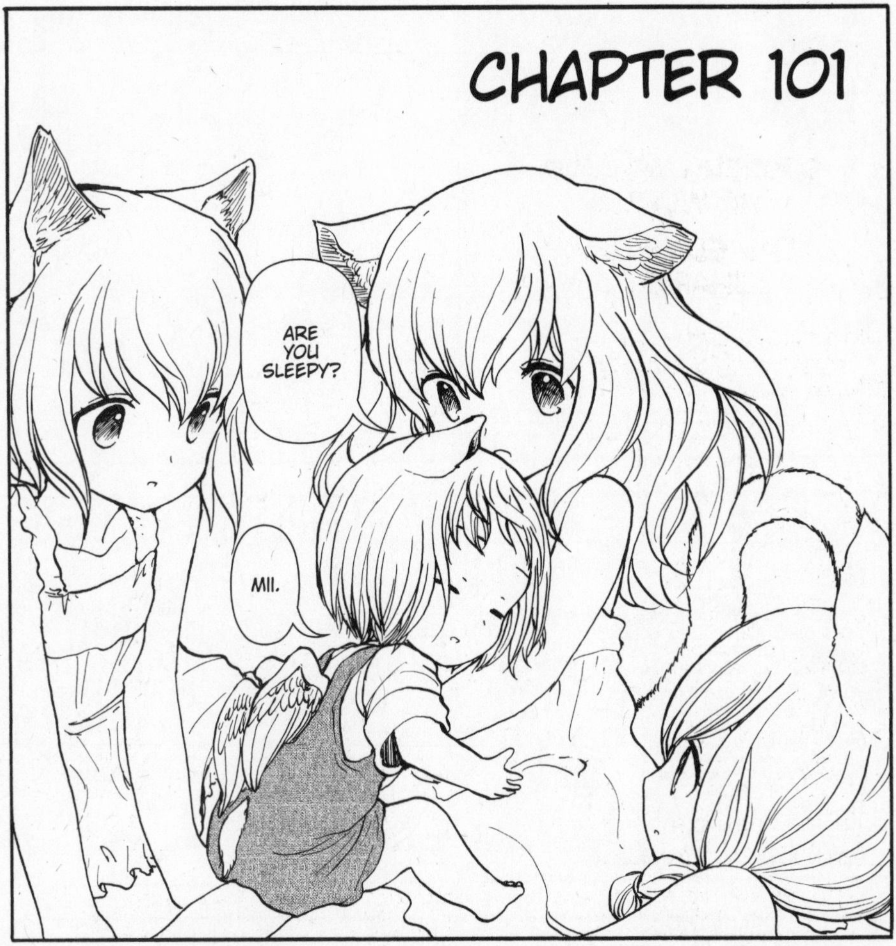
ARE YOU SLEEPY?
MII.

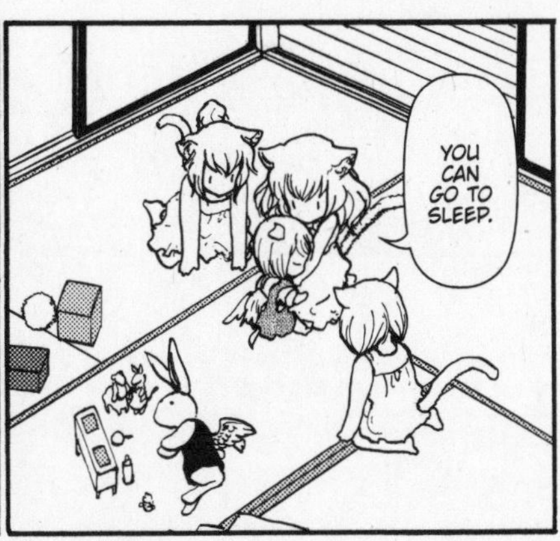
YOU CAN GO TO SLEEP.

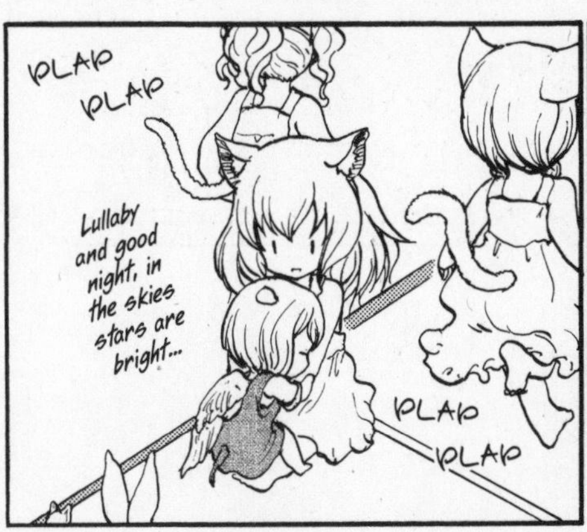
PLAP PLAP
Lullaby and good night, in the skies stars are bright...
PLAP
PLAP

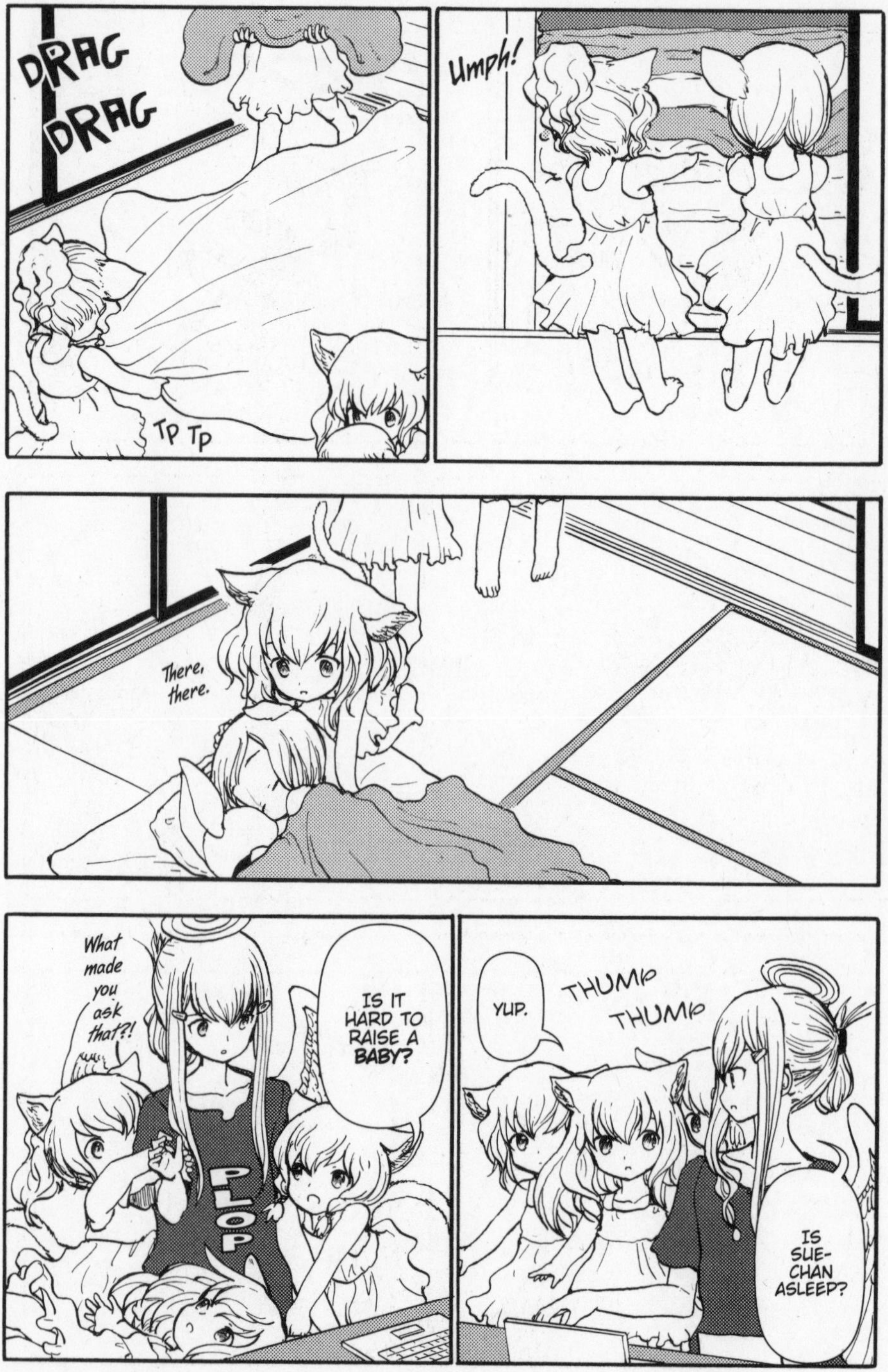
Umph!
DRAG
DRAG
Tp Tp
There, there.
THUMP
THUMP
IS SUE-CHAN ASLEEP?
YUP.
IS IT HARD TO RAISE A BABY?
What made you ask that?!
PLOP

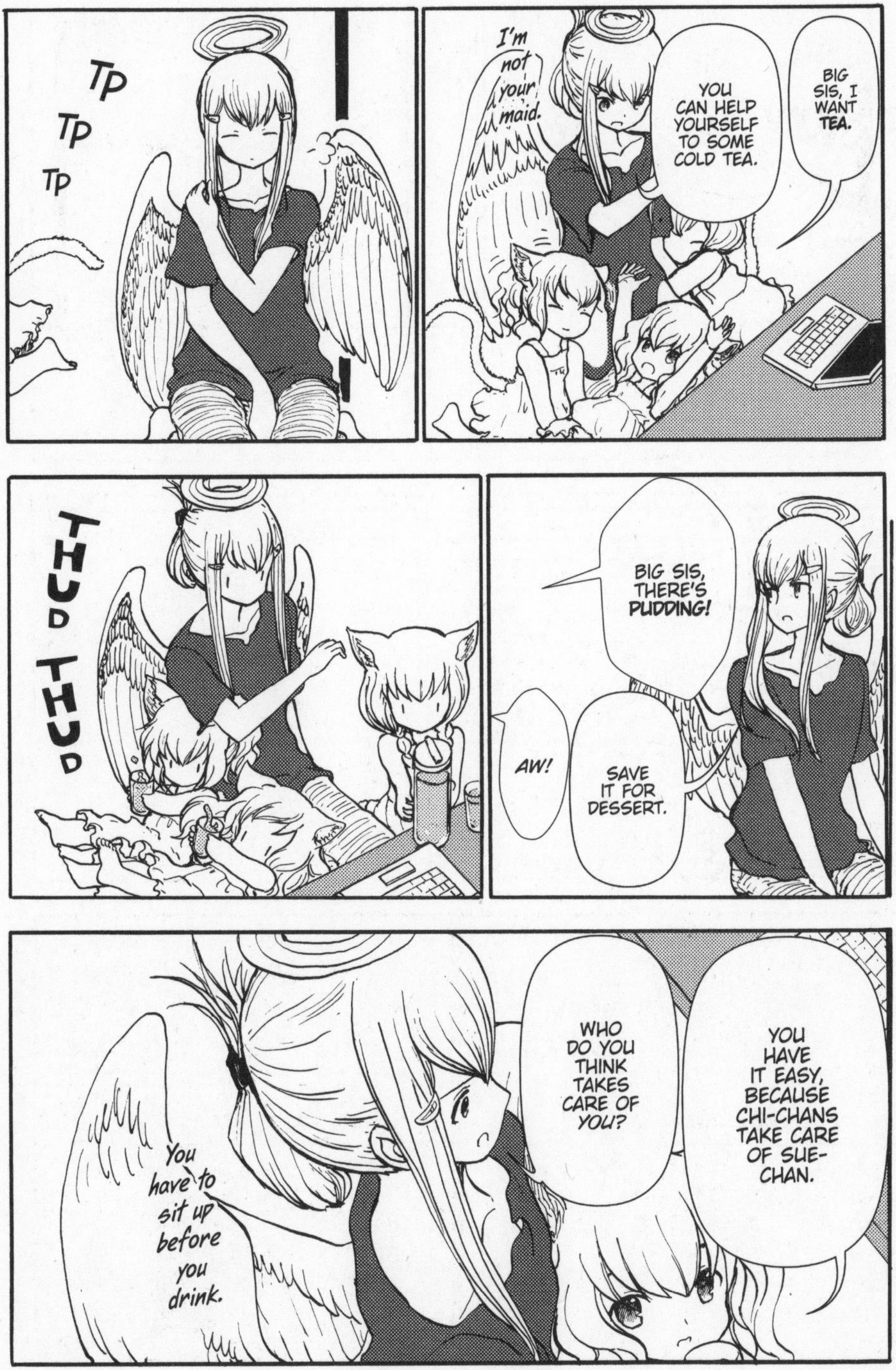
BIG SIS, I WANT **TEA.**
YOU CAN HELP YOURSELF TO SOME COLD TEA.
I'm not your maid.
TP TP TP
BIG SIS, THERE'S **PUDDING!**
SAVE IT FOR DESSERT.
AW!
THUD THUD
YOU HAVE IT EASY, BECAUSE CHI-CHANS TAKE CARE OF SUE-CHAN.
WHO DO YOU THINK TAKES CARE OF YOU?
You have to sit up before you drink.

YOU'VE BEEN A **HANDFUL** SINCE THE DAY YOU WERE BORN.

YEAH, RIGHT.

CHI-CHANS ARE BEING GOOD GIRLS.

THEY'RE BEING BORN VERY PREMATURELY.

OH NO! THEY MIGHT NOT MAKE IT?!

PLEASE, GOD...

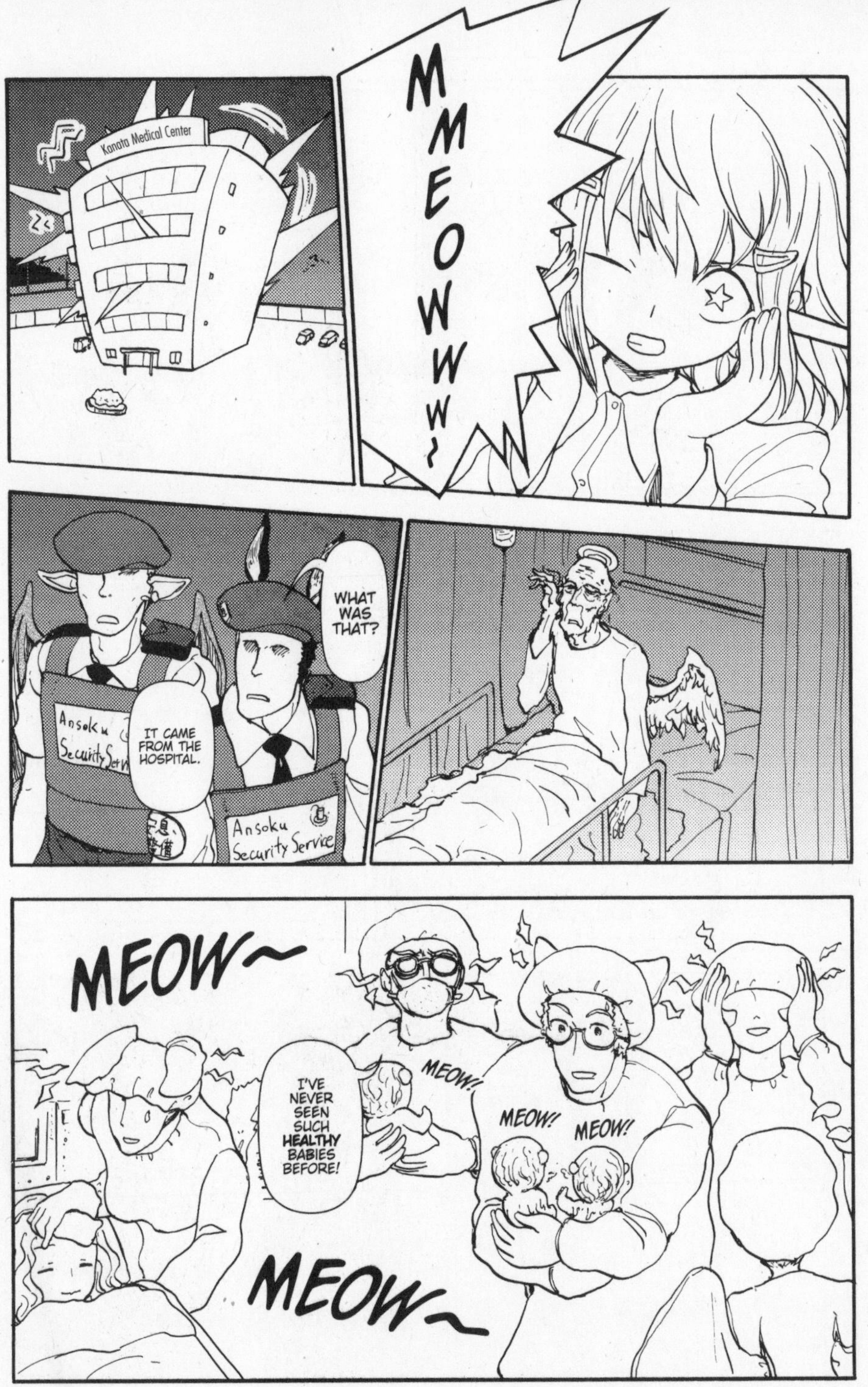
MMEOWWWW~
Kanata Medical Center
WHAT WAS THAT?
IT CAME FROM THE HOSPITAL.
Ansoku Security Service
Ansoku Security Service
MEOW!
MEOW!
MEOW!
I'VE NEVER SEEN SUCH **HEALTHY** BABIES BEFORE!
MEOW~
MEOW~

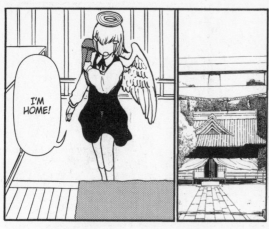

WEREN'T YOU GLAD THAT WE WERE HEALTHY?
THERE'S A LIMIT TO EVERYTHING.
But I was relieved.
I'M HOME!
They wake upon sensing their sister.
Kind, meticulous, and attentive.
MEOW!
MEOW!
MEOW!
Kind, but rough and inattentive.
MII!
THERE, THERE.
MII!
DAD, THEY DON'T NEED DIAPER CHANGES. THEY'RE HUNGRY.
IT'S OKAY. IT'S OKAY. YOUR BOTTLES ARE COMING.
Don't suck on my uniform.
MII!
MII!
MII!

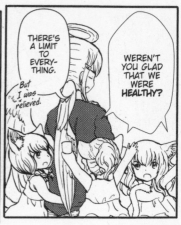

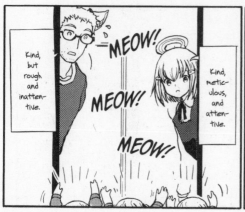

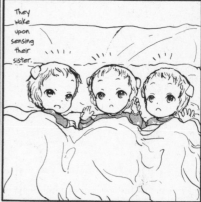

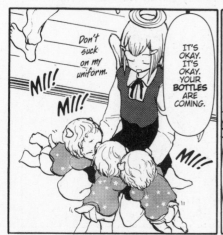

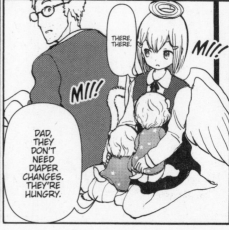

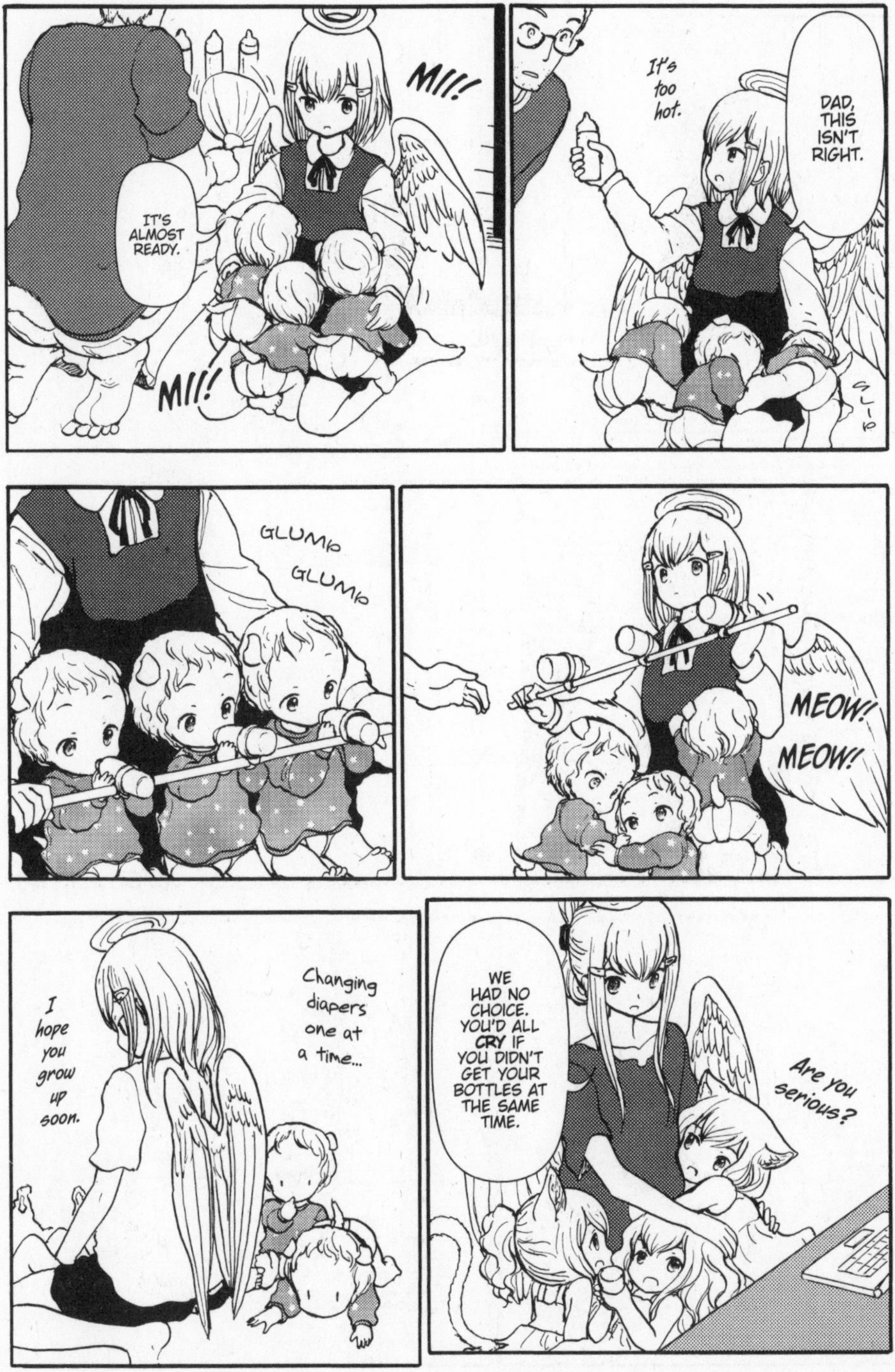
DAD, THIS ISN'T RIGHT.
It's too hot.
MII!
IT'S ALMOST READY.
MII!
MEOW! MEOW!
GLUMP GLUMP
WE HAD NO CHOICE. YOU'D ALL CRY IF YOU DIDN'T GET YOUR BOTTLES AT THE SAME TIME.
Are you serious?
Changing diapers one at a time...
I hope you grow up soon.

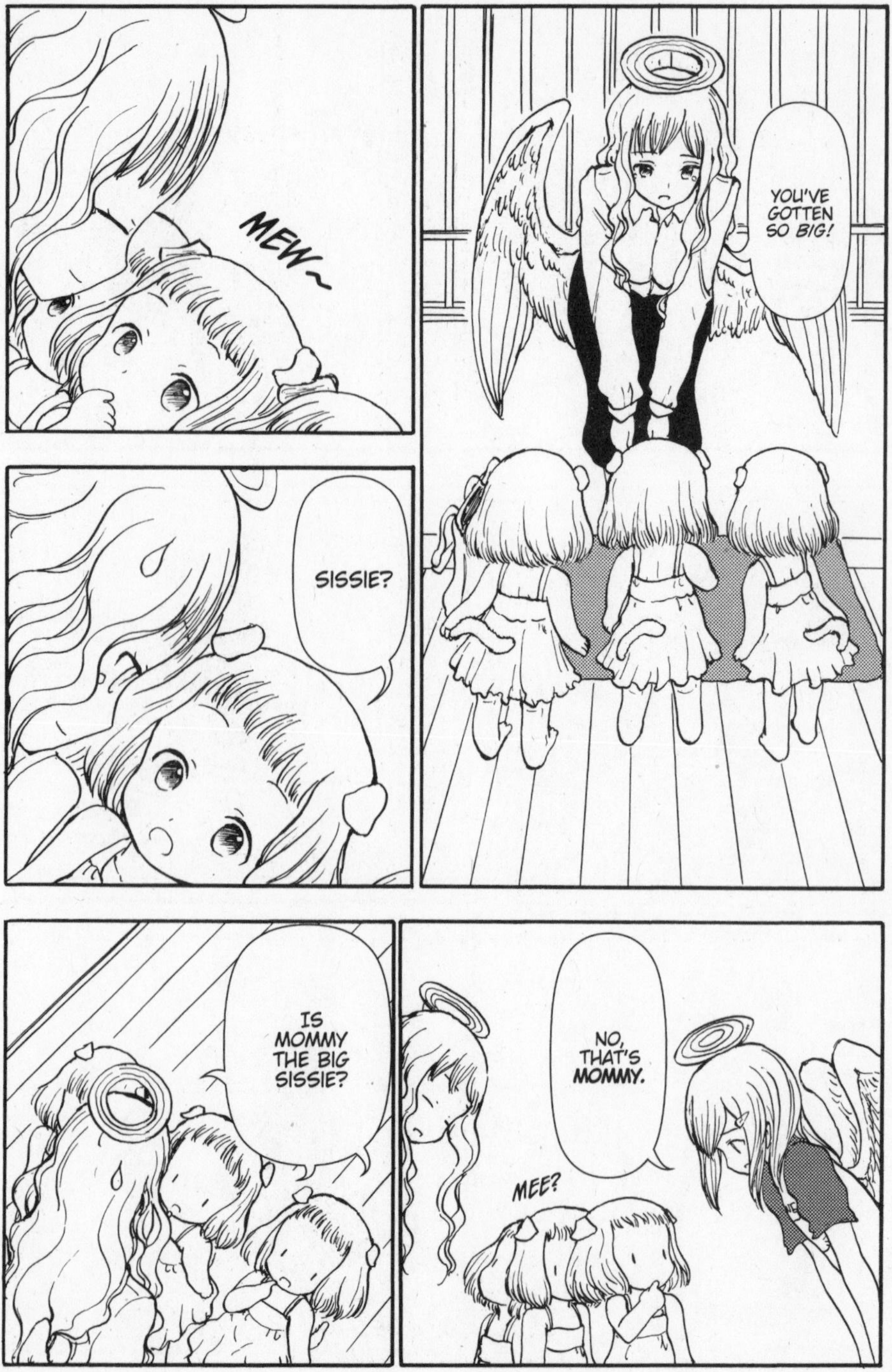
YOU'VE GOTTEN SO BIG!
MEW~
SISSIE?
NO, THAT'S MOMMY.
MEE?
IS MOMMY THE BIG SISSIE?

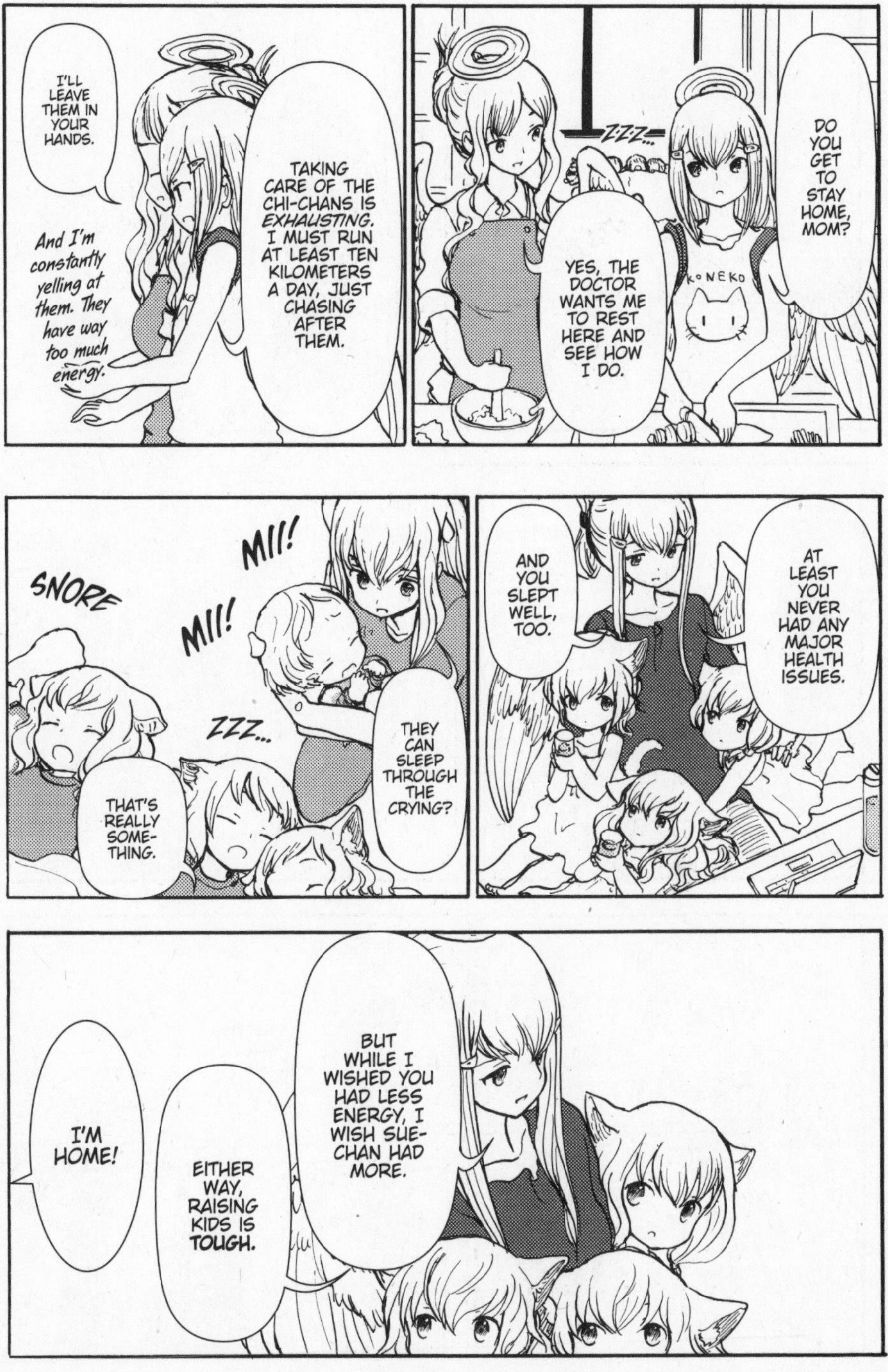
DO YOU GET TO STAY HOME, MOM?
Z-Z-Z...
YES, THE DOCTOR WANTS ME TO REST HERE AND SEE HOW I DO.
KONEKO
TAKING CARE OF THE CHI-CHANS IS *EXHAUSTING.* I MUST RUN AT LEAST TEN KILOMETERS A DAY, JUST CHASING AFTER THEM.
I'LL LEAVE THEM IN YOUR HANDS.
And I'm constantly yelling at them. They have way too much energy.
AT LEAST YOU NEVER HAD ANY MAJOR HEALTH ISSUES.
AND YOU SLEPT WELL, TOO.
MII!
MII!
SNORE
THEY CAN SLEEP THROUGH THE CRYING?
ZZZ...
THAT'S REALLY SOME-THING.
BUT WHILE I WISHED YOU HAD LESS ENERGY, I WISH SUE-CHAN HAD MORE.
EITHER WAY, RAISING KIDS IS **TOUGH.**
I'M HOME!

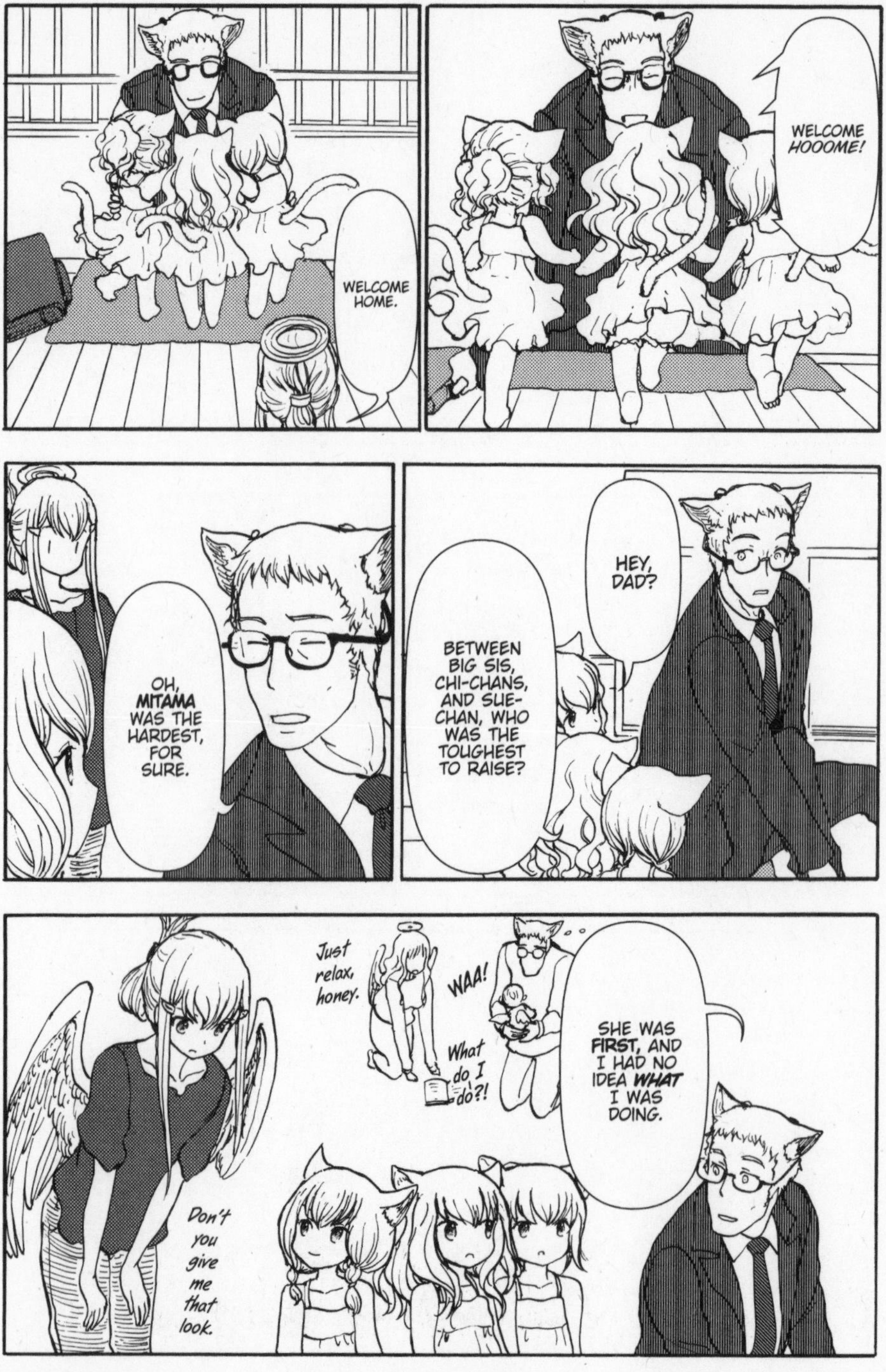
WELCOME HOOOME!
WELCOME HOME.
HEY, DAD?
BETWEEN BIG SIS, CHI-CHANS, AND SUE-CHAN, WHO WAS THE TOUGHEST TO RAISE?
OH, MITAMA WAS THE HARDEST, FOR SURE.
SHE WAS FIRST, AND I HAD NO IDEA WHAT I WAS DOING.
WAA!
What do I do?!
Just relax, honey.
Don't you give me that look.

A CentaUr's Life

SOLDIERS AROUND THE WORLD:
GREEK HEAVY INFANTRY

THE KINGDOMS OF MYCENAE AND TIRYNS BOASTED CITIES THAT WERE TRANSFORMED INTO IMPRESSIVE CITADELS, THE HOMES OF THE WARRIORS ON CHARIOTS DEPICTED IN HOMER'S ILIAD; DESPITE THESE DEFENSES, THESE KINGDOMS WHERE DESTROYED BY THE "SEA PEOPLES." THE GREEK CITY-STATES DID NOT BEGIN TO FORM AGAIN UNTIL AROUND THE 8TH CENTURY BCE. ALTHOUGH TRADE WAS COMMON AMONG THE CITY-STATES, THEY REMAINED DIVIDED AND WARRED AMONGST THEMSELVES.

THE CITY-STATES WERE DEMOCRACIES RATHER THAN KINGDOMS, AND SOME CITIZENS PROVIDED THEIR OWN EQUIPMENT AND FOUGHT AS HEAVY FOOT SOLDIERS IN MASS INFANTRY FORMATIONS, DESPITE THEIR LACK OF MILITARY TRAINING. THESE SOLDIERS TYPICALLY USED LARGE ROUND SHIELDS TO PROTECT THEMSELVES AND ADJACENT ALLIES WHILE ATTACKING WITH SPEARS. AS DEFENSIVE SHIELD TECHNIQUES WERE PERFECTED, SOLDIERS EXCHANGED THEIR HEAVY BRONZE ARMOR FOR ARMOR MADE OF MORE LIGHTWEIGHT BUT LESS PROTECTIVE MATERIAL, SUCH AS CLOTH. FOR THESE CITIZENS, IT WAS CONSIDERED THE HIGHEST HONOR TO FIGHT AS A HEAVY INFANTRYMAN.

ATHENS AND SPARTA, THE TWO LARGEST CITY-STATES, SUCCESSFULLY FOUGHT OFF AN INVASION FROM THE NEIGHBORING EMPIRE OF PERSIA. OTHER LARGE CITY-STATES CLASHED WITH ONE ANOTHER AND FELL. THE GREEK CITY-STATES, DIMINISHED BY WAR AND UNABLE TO QUICKLY INCREASE THEIR POPULATIONS DUE TO STRICT CITIZENSHIP REQUIREMENTS, ULTIMATELY ACCEPTED THEIR FATE AND WERE CONQUERED AND CONSUMED BY THE GROWING ROMAN EMPIRE.

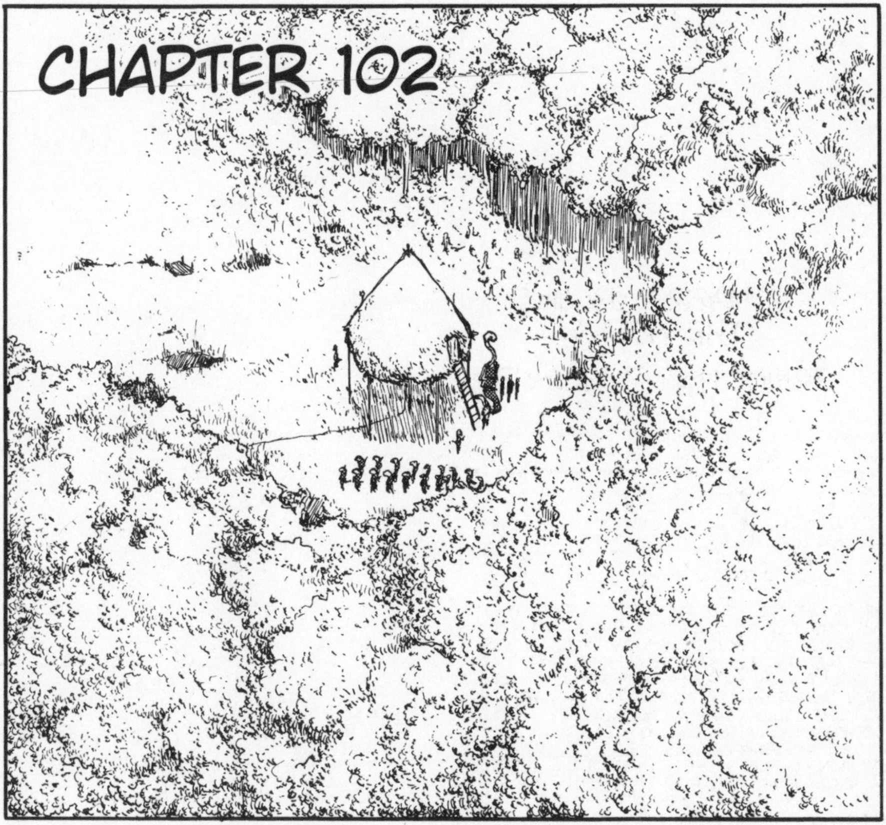
CHAPTER 102

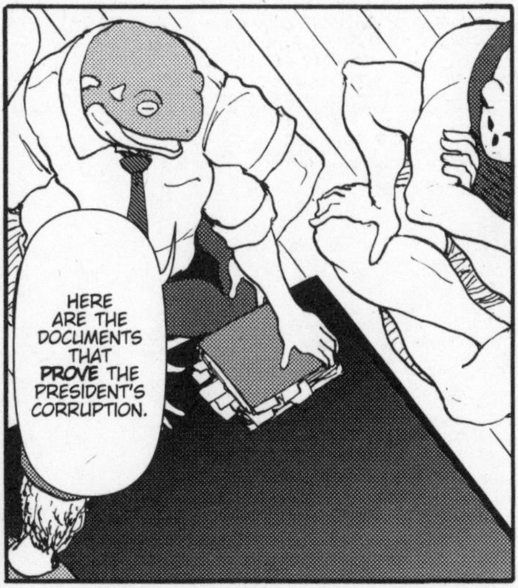
HERE ARE THE DOCUMENTS THAT **PROVE** THE PRESIDENT'S CORRUPTION.

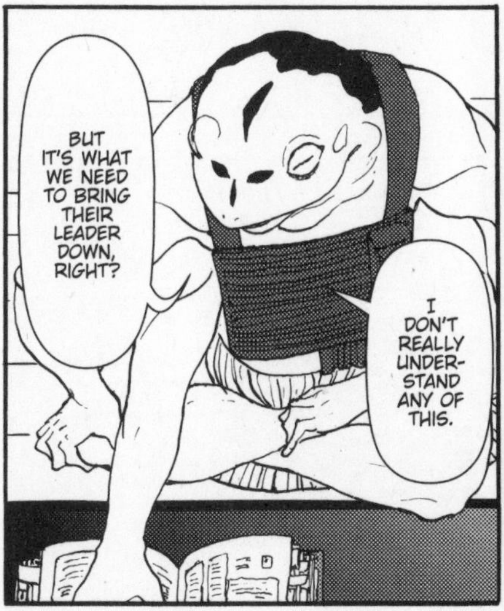
I DON'T REALLY UNDER-STAND ANY OF THIS.
BUT IT'S WHAT WE NEED TO BRING THEIR LEADER DOWN, RIGHT?

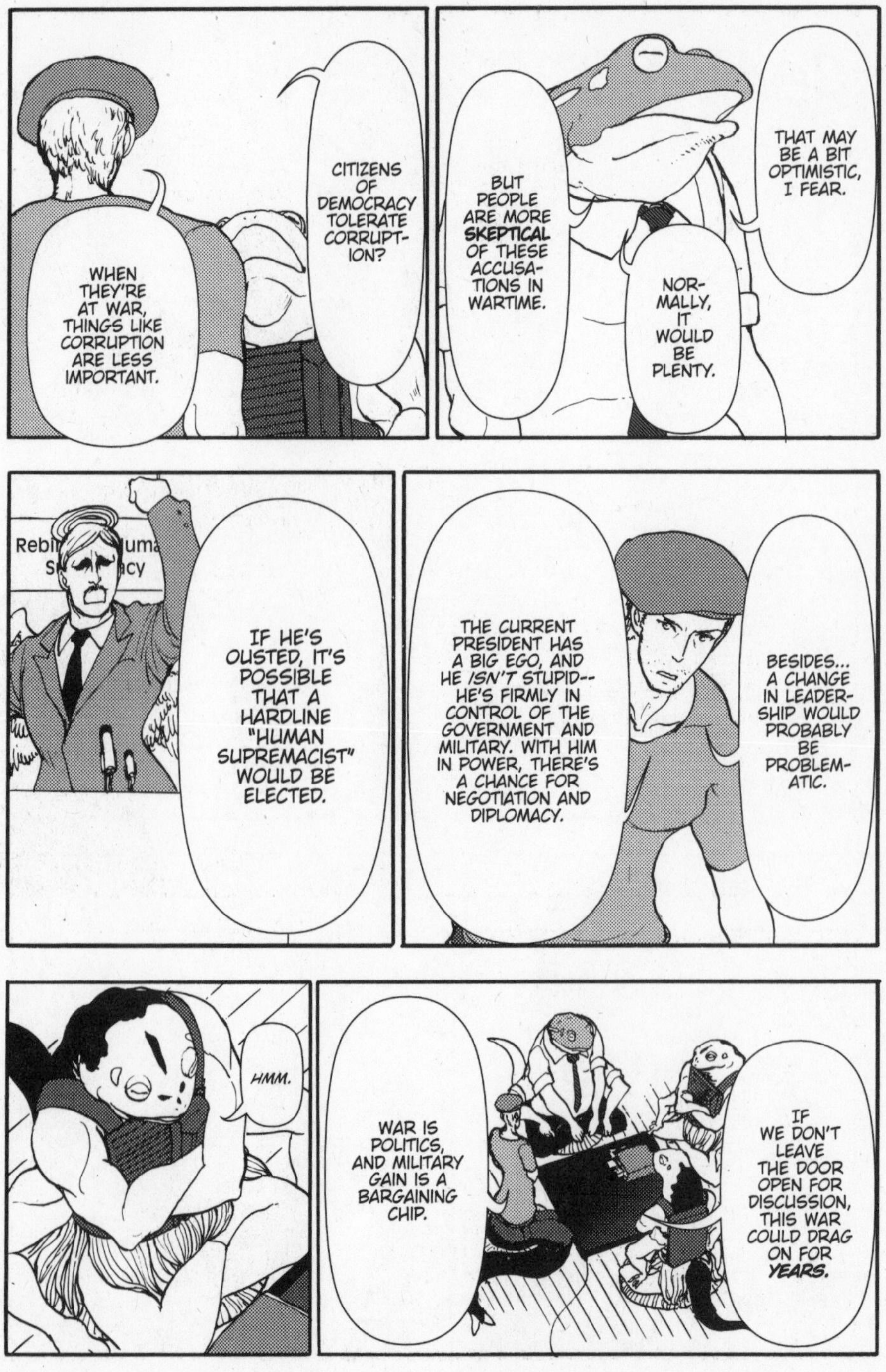
THAT MAY BE A BIT OPTIMISTIC, I FEAR.
NOR-MALLY, IT WOULD BE PLENTY.
BUT PEOPLE ARE MORE **SKEPTICAL** OF THESE ACCUSA-TIONS IN WARTIME.
CITIZENS OF DEMOCRACY TOLERATE CORRUPT-ION?
WHEN THEY'RE AT WAR, THINGS LIKE CORRUPTION ARE LESS IMPORTANT.
BESIDES... A CHANGE IN LEADER-SHIP WOULD PROBABLY BE PROBLEM-ATIC.
THE CURRENT PRESIDENT HAS A BIG EGO, AND HE *ISN'T* STUPID-- HE'S FIRMLY IN CONTROL OF THE GOVERNMENT AND MILITARY. WITH HIM IN POWER, THERE'S A CHANCE FOR NEGOTIATION AND DIPLOMACY.
IF HE'S OUSTED, IT'S POSSIBLE THAT A HARDLINE "HUMAN SUPREMACIST" WOULD BE ELECTED.
IF WE DON'T LEAVE THE DOOR OPEN FOR DISCUSSION, THIS WAR COULD DRAG ON FOR ***YEARS.***
WAR IS POLITICS, AND MILITARY GAIN IS A BARGAINING CHIP.
HMM.

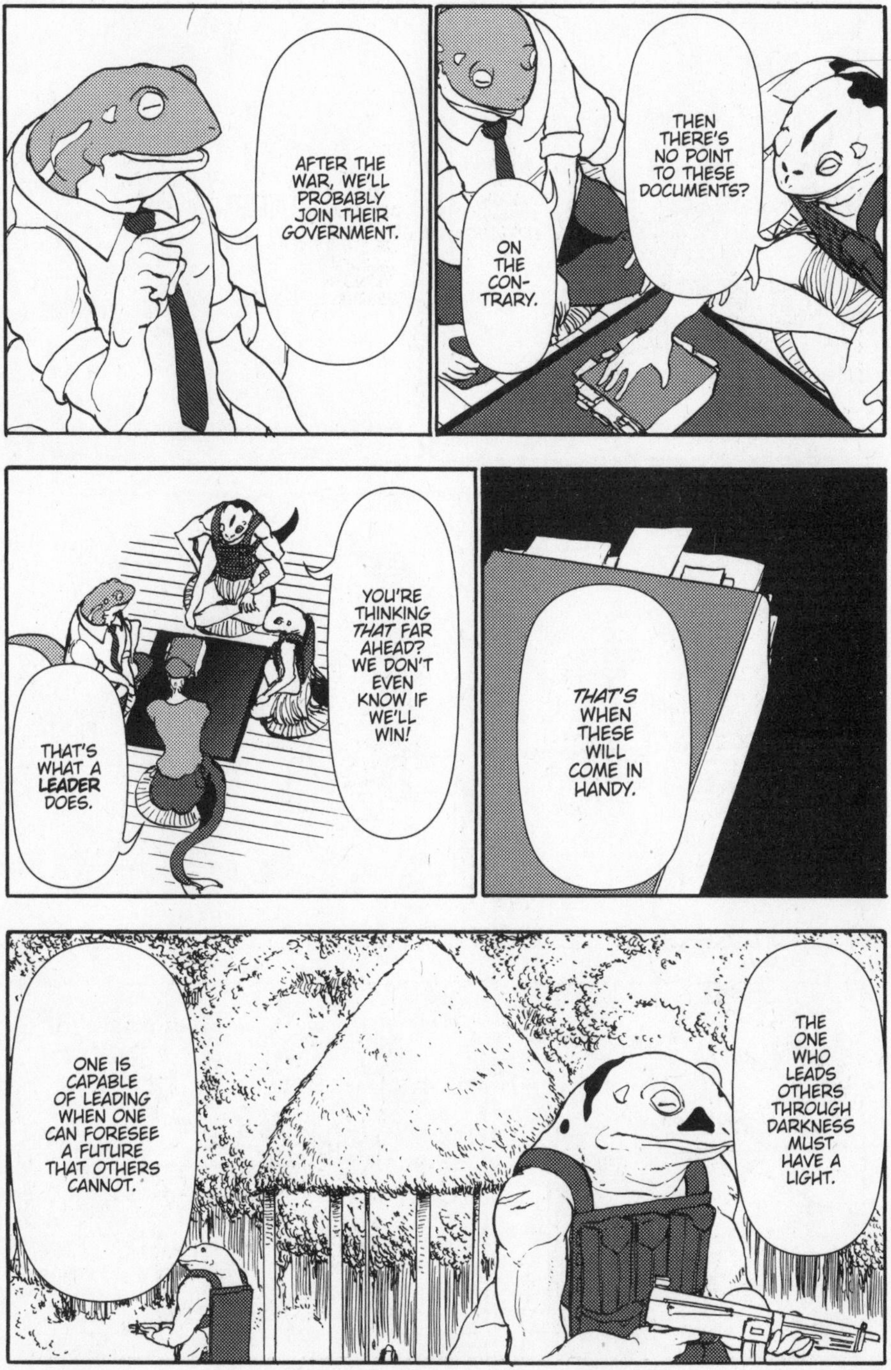
THEN THERE'S NO POINT TO THESE DOCUMENTS?
ON THE CONTRARY.
AFTER THE WAR, WE'LL PROBABLY JOIN THEIR GOVERNMENT.
THAT'S WHEN THESE WILL COME IN HANDY.
YOU'RE THINKING *THAT* FAR AHEAD? WE DON'T EVEN KNOW IF WE'LL WIN!
THAT'S WHAT A **LEADER** DOES.
THE ONE WHO LEADS OTHERS THROUGH DARKNESS MUST HAVE A LIGHT.
ONE IS CAPABLE OF LEADING WHEN ONE CAN FORESEE A FUTURE THAT OTHERS CANNOT.

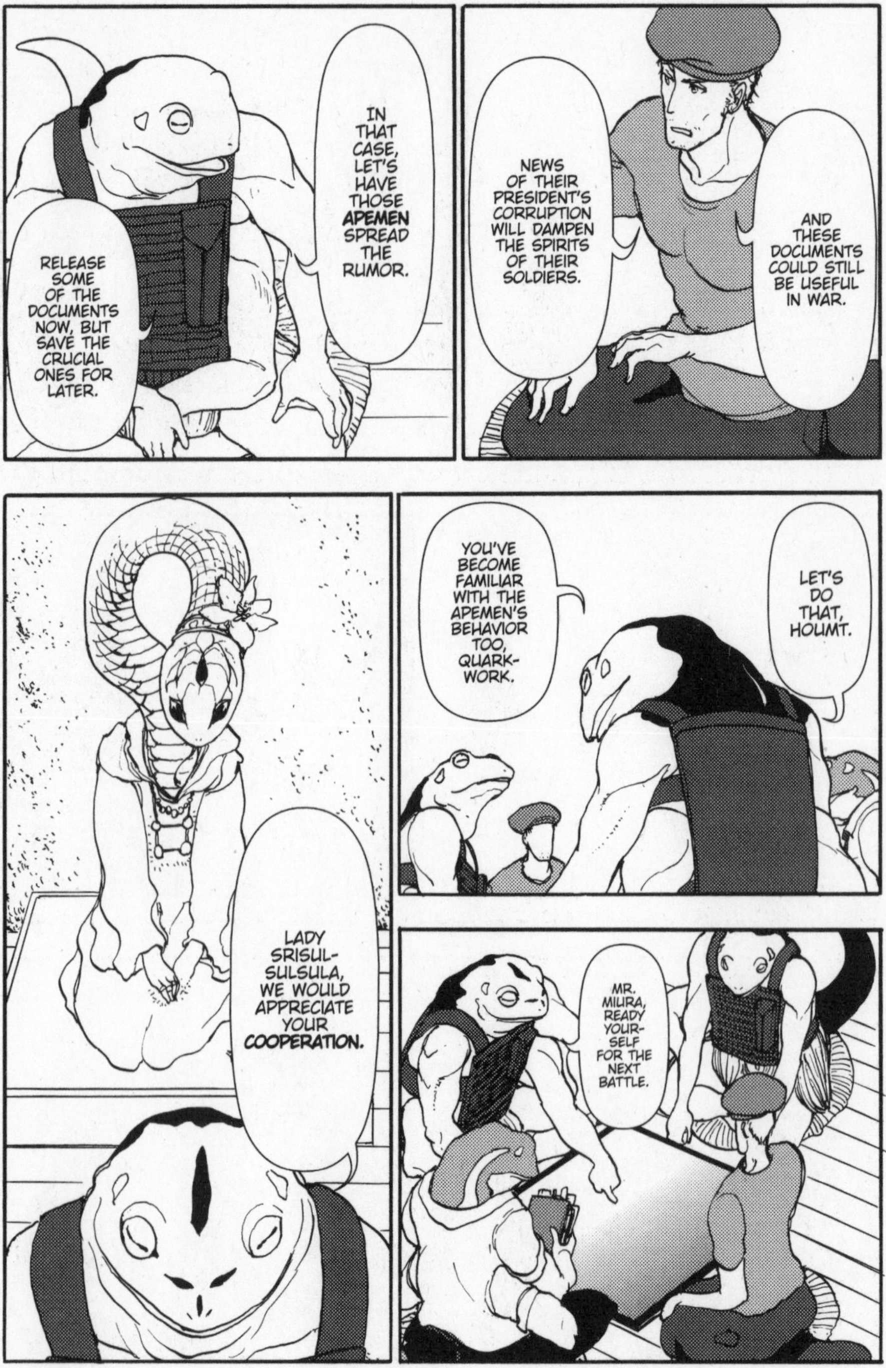
NEWS OF THEIR PRESIDENT'S CORRUPTION WILL DAMPEN THE SPIRITS OF THEIR SOLDIERS.
AND THESE DOCUMENTS COULD STILL BE USEFUL IN WAR.
IN THAT CASE, LET'S HAVE THOSE **APEMEN** SPREAD THE RUMOR.
RELEASE SOME OF THE DOCUMENTS NOW, BUT SAVE THE CRUCIAL ONES FOR LATER.
LET'S DO THAT, HOUMT.
YOU'VE BECOME FAMILIAR WITH THE APEMEN'S BEHAVIOR TOO, QUARK-WORK.
MR. MIURA, READY YOUR-SELF FOR THE NEXT BATTLE.
LADY SRISUL-SULSULA, WE WOULD APPRECIATE YOUR **COOPERATION.**

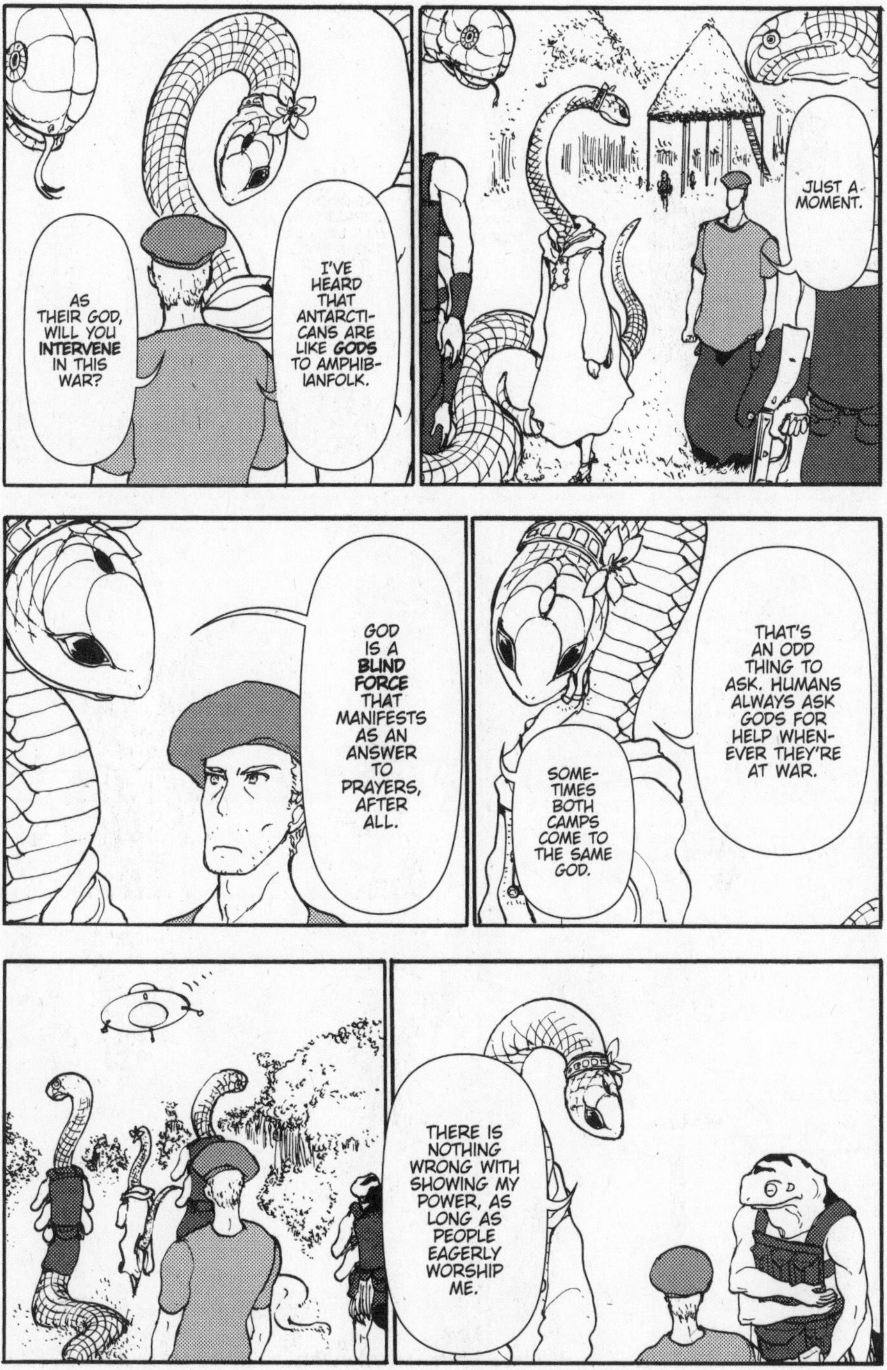
JUST A MOMENT.
I'VE HEARD THAT ANTARCTI-CANS ARE LIKE **GODS** TO AMPHIB-IANFOLK.
AS THEIR GOD, WILL YOU **INTERVENE** IN THIS WAR?
THAT'S AN ODD THING TO ASK. HUMANS ALWAYS ASK GODS FOR HELP WHEN-EVER THEY'RE AT WAR.
SOME-TIMES BOTH CAMPS COME TO THE SAME GOD.
GOD IS A **BLIND FORCE** THAT MANIFESTS AS AN ANSWER TO PRAYERS, AFTER ALL.
THERE IS NOTHING WRONG WITH SHOWING MY POWER, AS LONG AS PEOPLE EAGERLY WORSHIP ME.

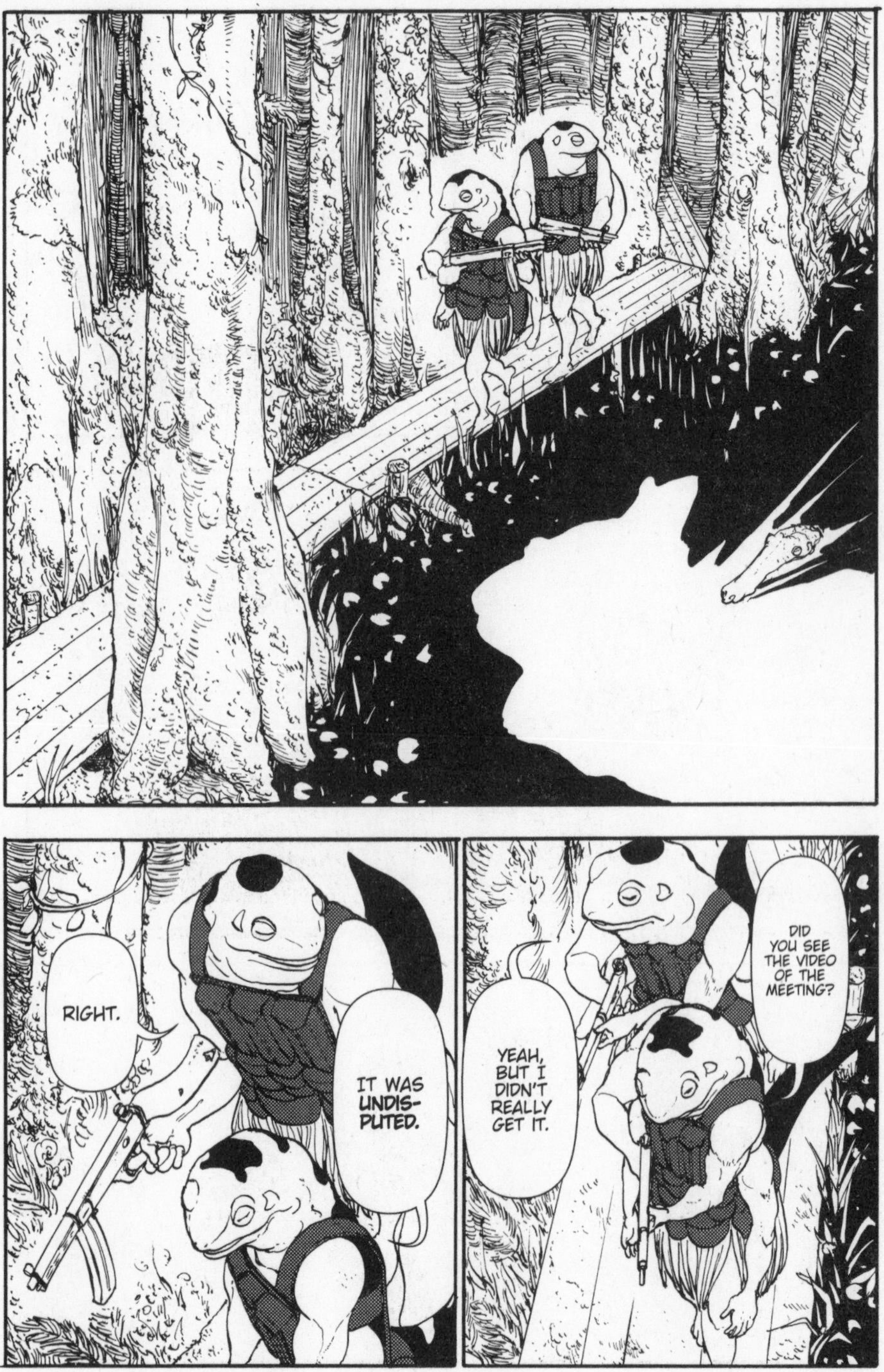
DID YOU SEE THE VIDEO OF THE MEETING?
YEAH, BUT I DIDN'T REALLY GET IT.
IT WAS **UNDISPUTED.**
RIGHT.

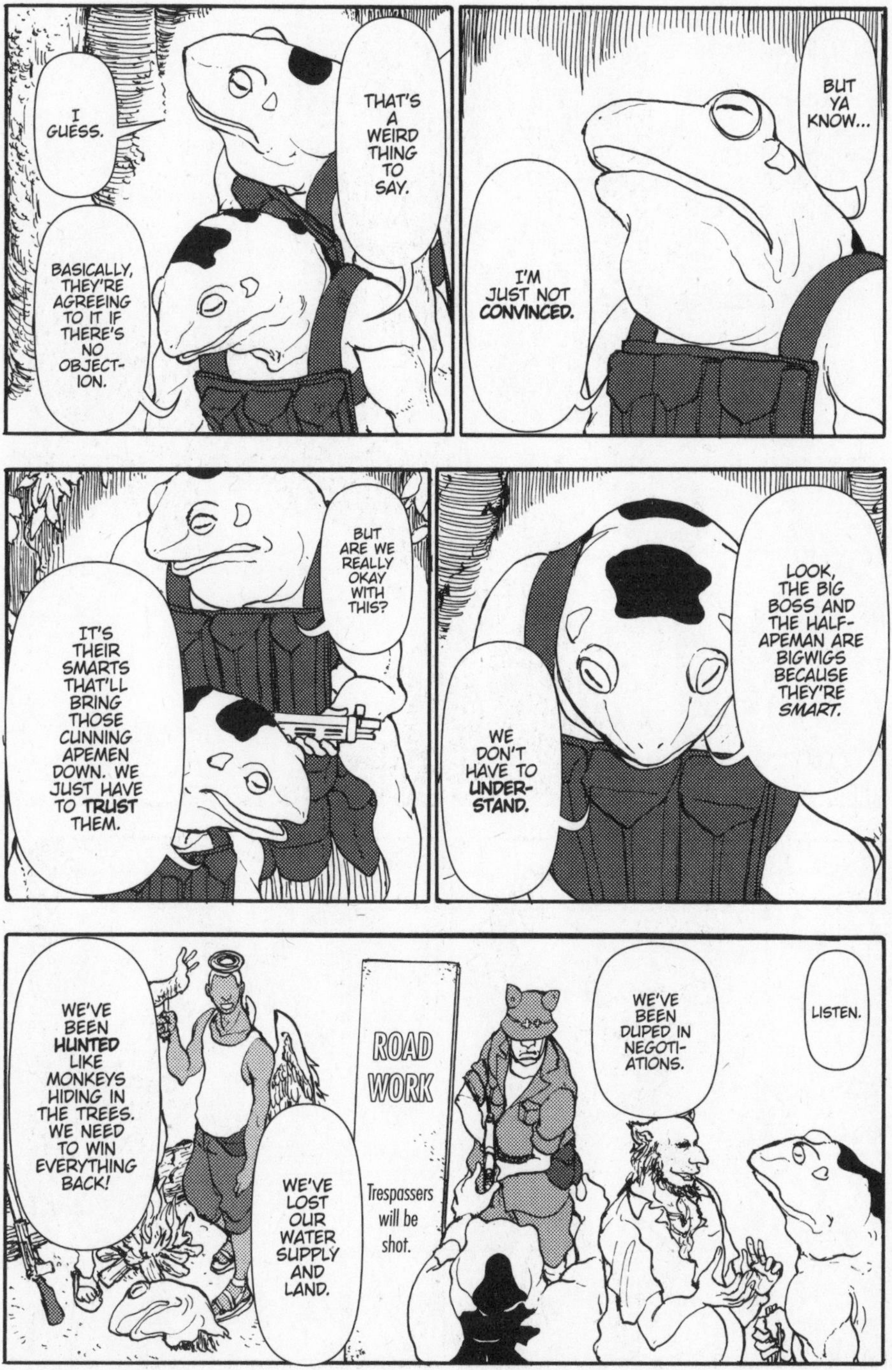
BUT YA KNOW...
I'M JUST NOT CONVINCED.
THAT'S A WEIRD THING TO SAY.
I GUESS.
BASICALLY, THEY'RE AGREEING TO IT IF THERE'S NO OBJECTION.
LOOK, THE BIG BOSS AND THE HALF-APEMAN ARE BIGWIGS BECAUSE THEY'RE *SMART.*
WE DON'T HAVE TO **UNDERSTAND.**
BUT ARE WE REALLY OKAY WITH THIS?
IT'S THEIR SMARTS THAT'LL BRING THOSE CUNNING APEMEN DOWN. WE JUST HAVE TO **TRUST** THEM.
LISTEN.
WE'VE BEEN DUPED IN NEGOTIATIONS.
ROAD WORK
Trespassers will be shot.
WE'VE LOST OUR WATER SUPPLY AND LAND.
WE'VE BEEN **HUNTED** LIKE MONKEYS HIDING IN THE TREES. WE NEED TO WIN EVERYTHING BACK!

HOW ARE WE DIFFER-ENT FROM MONKEYS?
KIII KIII
HOW ARE WE DIFFERENT FROM APEMEN?
WHAT'S UP WITH YOU? ARE YOU SICK?
WE'RE... AN INTELLIGENT TRIBE.
WE DO WHAT WE MUST TO **SURVIVE.**
SO, WE PROSECUTE ANY MURDERERS AND DEFEND OURSELVES FROM THE APEMEN. THAT'S WHAT JUSTICE IS!
YOU'RE JUST REPEATING WHAT THE BIGWIGS SAY.
I FEEL LIKE WE'RE LETTING THEM **MANIPULATE** US.
YOU'RE NOT EDUCATED. LEAVE IT ALONE.
PU-KLUNK
DOES THIS GUN WORK?
SHOULDN'T WE **MOURN** HIM IF HE'S FROM AN INTELLIGENT TRIBE, TOO?
WHAT'S THE POINT OF PRAYING FOR AN APEMAN?

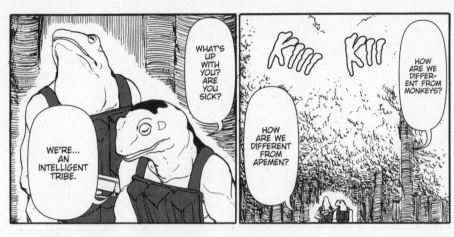

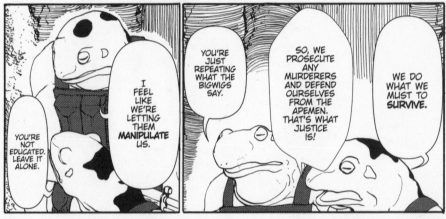

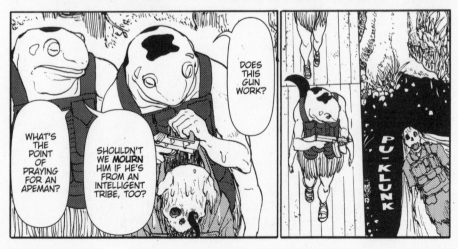

A Centaur's Life

SOLDIERS AROUND THE WORLD:

MONGOLIAN LIGHT TROOPS

IT IS BELIEVED THAT THE ORIGINALLY IDYLLIC AND COMMUNISTIC LIFESTYLE OF NOMADS CHANGED DRASTICALLY WITH THE INTRODUCTION OF A CARNIVOROUS DIET. THIS DIETARY CHANGE NECESSITATED THE CONSUMPTION OF TEA TO TREAT THE RESULTING VITAMIN DEFICIENCY, BUT THE NOMADS COULD ONLY ACQUIRE TEA VIA TRADE. THE TRADING OF GOODS CREATED ECONOMIC INEQUALITY, AND THE GAP BETWEEN THE RICH AND THE POOR LED TO A FINANCIAL BLOODBATH.

GENGHIS KHAN WAS BORN ON THE MONGOLIAN PLATEAU DURING TURBULENT TIMES. DESPITE LOSING HIS FATHER AT AN EARLY AGE, GENGHIS KHAN RULED THE NOMADIC TRIBES WITH EXCELLENT LEADER-SHIP. HE INVADED SURROUNDING COUNTRIES WITH HIS WARRIORS AND BUILT A MASSIVE EMPIRE IN EURASIA.

THE MONGOL ARMY HAD MANY ADVANTAGES, INCLUDING THE SUPERIOR MOBILITY AND PERFECT STRUCTURE EMBODIED IN CENTAURS. THEIR STRATEGY WAS TO NIMBLY MANEUVER IN RESPONSE TO SIGNALS AND LURE ENEMIES INTO AN AMBUSH, SLAUGHTERING THEM WITH A HAIL OF ARROWS. NO OTHER MILITARY TACTICS OF THE TIME COULD COUNTER THEIR PRECISION. BUT THIS SEEMINGLY UNSTOPPABLE FORCE, EVEN WITH NEW TECHNOLOGY SUCH AS FIREARMS AND SIEGE WEAPONS, COULDN'T DEFEAT SUCH FOES AS TROPICAL DISEASE, TYPHOONS, AND GUERILLA FIGHTERS IN THE MOUNTAINS. THE ULTIMATE DOWNFALL OF THE MONGOLS, HOWEVER, WAS A PROBLEM OF SUCCESSION. THEIR EMPIRE'S CUSTOM OF A SINGLE POWERFUL RULER OVER THEIR VAST DOMINION OF CONQUERED LANDS MADE THEM MORE VULNERABLE TO INTERNAL STRIFE.

CHAPTER 103

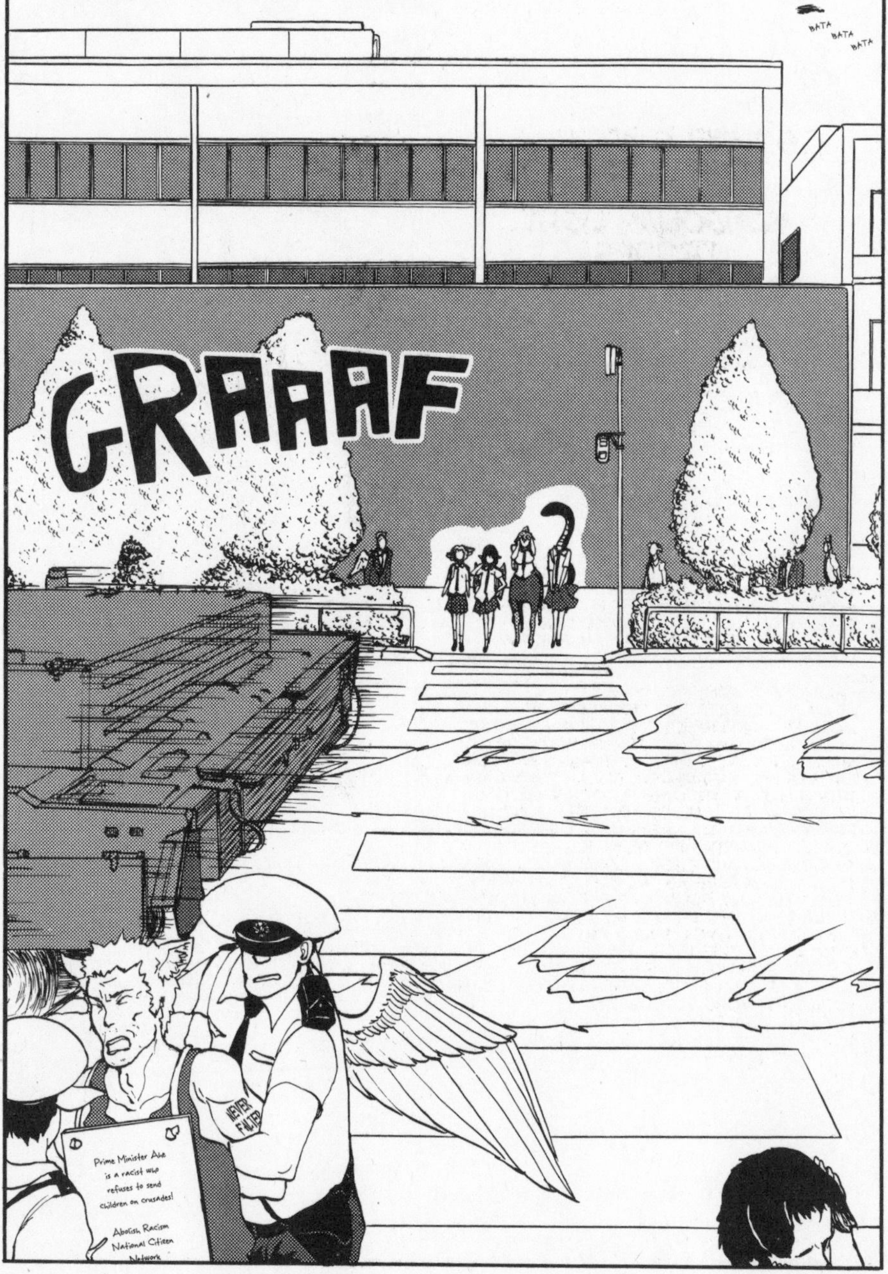
BATA BATA BATA
GRAAAF
NEVER FALTER
Prime Minister Ahe is a racist who refuses to send children on crusades!
Abolish Racism National Citizen Network

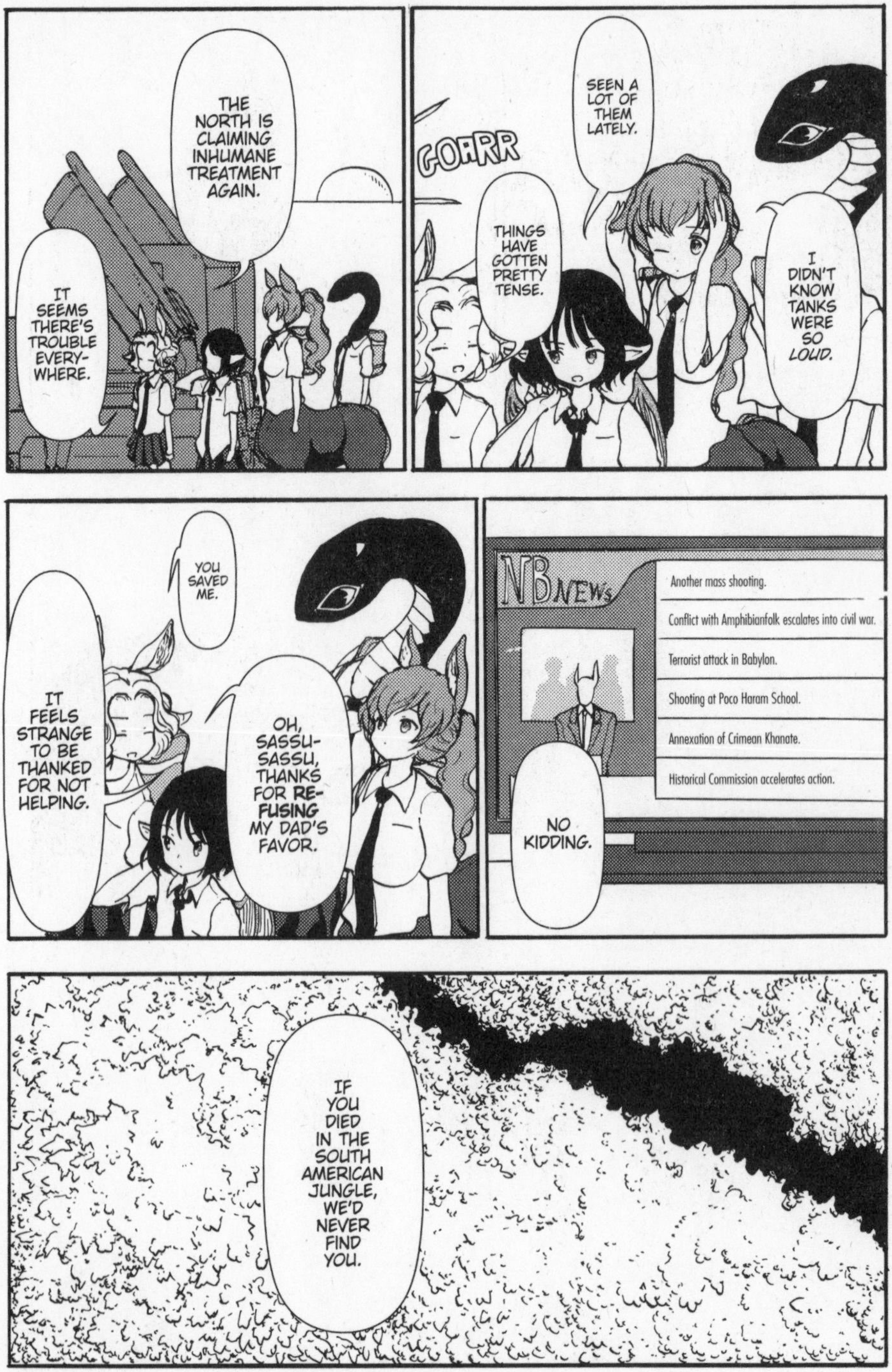
I DIDN'T KNOW TANKS WERE SO *LOUD.*
SEEN A LOT OF THEM LATELY.
GOARR
THINGS HAVE GOTTEN PRETTY TENSE.
THE NORTH IS CLAIMING INHUMANE TREATMENT AGAIN.
IT SEEMS THERE'S TROUBLE EVERY-WHERE.
NB NEWS
Another mass shooting.
Conflict with Amphibianfolk escalates into civil war.
Terrorist attack in Babylon.
Shooting at Poco Haram School.
Annexation of Crimean Khanate.
Historical Commission accelerates action.
NO KIDDING.
YOU SAVED ME.
OH, SASSU-SASSU, THANKS FOR **RE-FUSING** MY DAD'S FAVOR.
IT FEELS STRANGE TO BE THANKED FOR NOT HELPING.
IF YOU DIED IN THE SOUTH AMERICAN JUNGLE, WE'D NEVER FIND YOU.

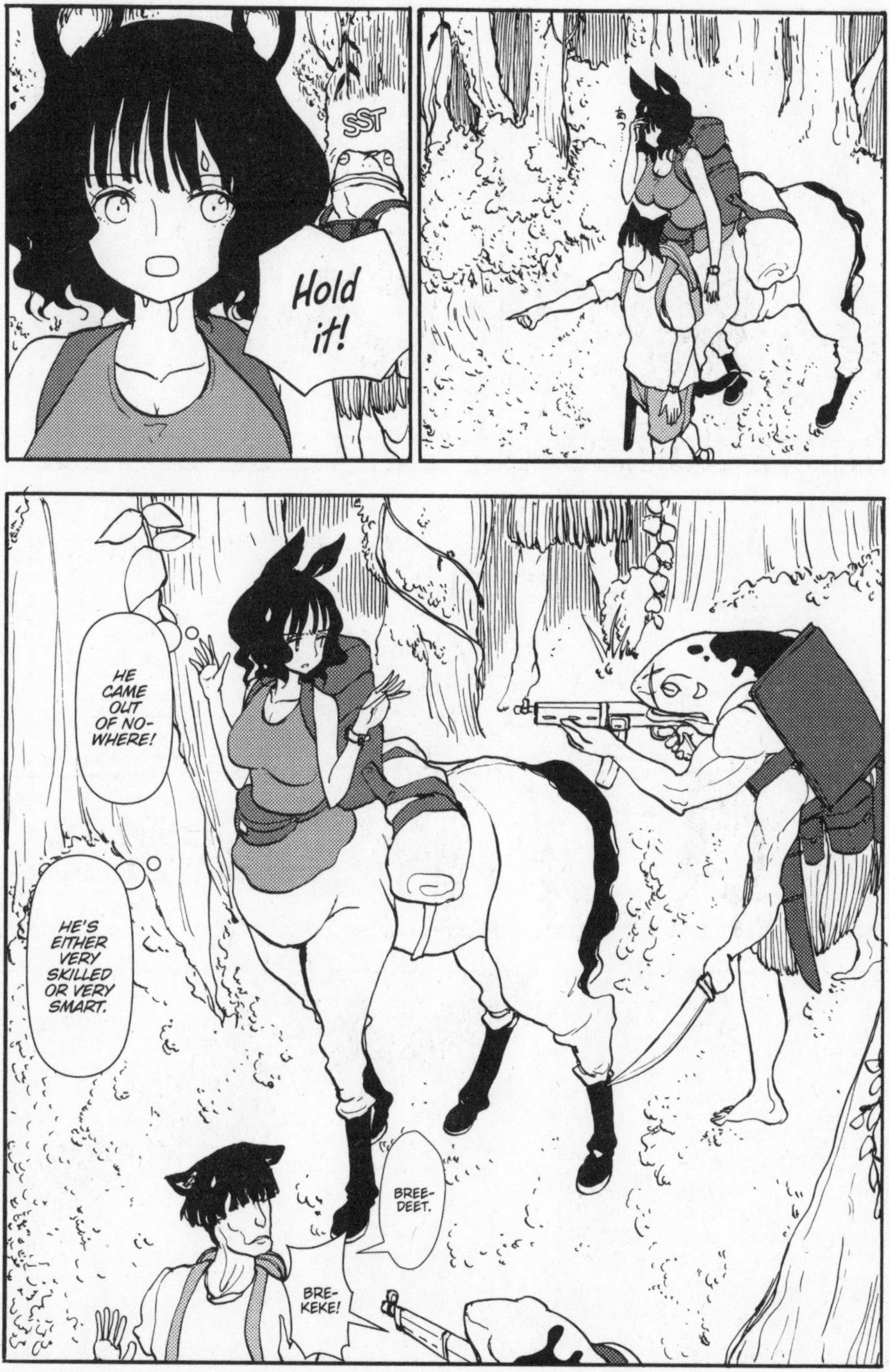
SST
Hold it!
HE CAME OUT OF NO-WHERE!
HE'S EITHER VERY SKILLED OR VERY SMART.
BREE-DEET.
BREKEKE!

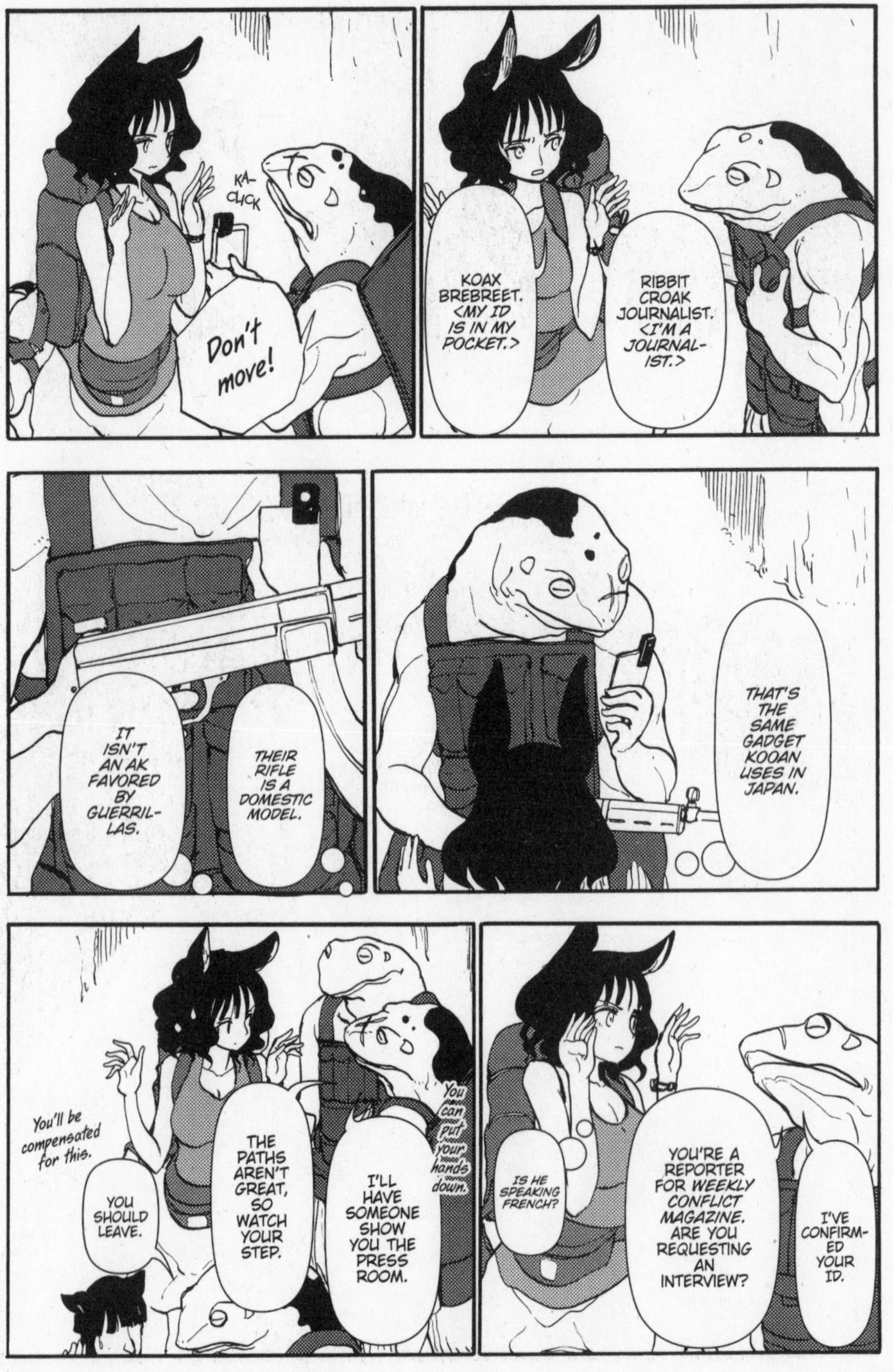
RIBBIT CROAK JOURNALIST. <I'M A JOURNALIST.>
KOAX BREBREET. <MY ID IS IN MY POCKET.>
KA-CLICK
Don't move!
THAT'S THE SAME GADGET KOOAN USES IN JAPAN.
THEIR RIFLE IS A DOMESTIC MODEL.
IT ISN'T AN AK FAVORED BY GUERRILLAS.
I'VE CONFIRMED YOUR ID.
YOU'RE A REPORTER FOR WEEKLY CONFLICT MAGAZINE. ARE YOU REQUESTING AN INTERVIEW?
IS HE SPEAKING FRENCH?
You can put your hands down.
I'LL HAVE SOMEONE SHOW YOU THE PRESS ROOM.
THE PATHS AREN'T GREAT, SO WATCH YOUR STEP.
YOU SHOULD LEAVE.
You'll be compensated for this.

BRIIN

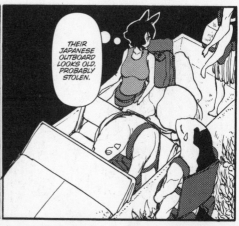

THEIR JAPANESE OUTBOARD LOOKS OLD, PROBABLY STOLEN.

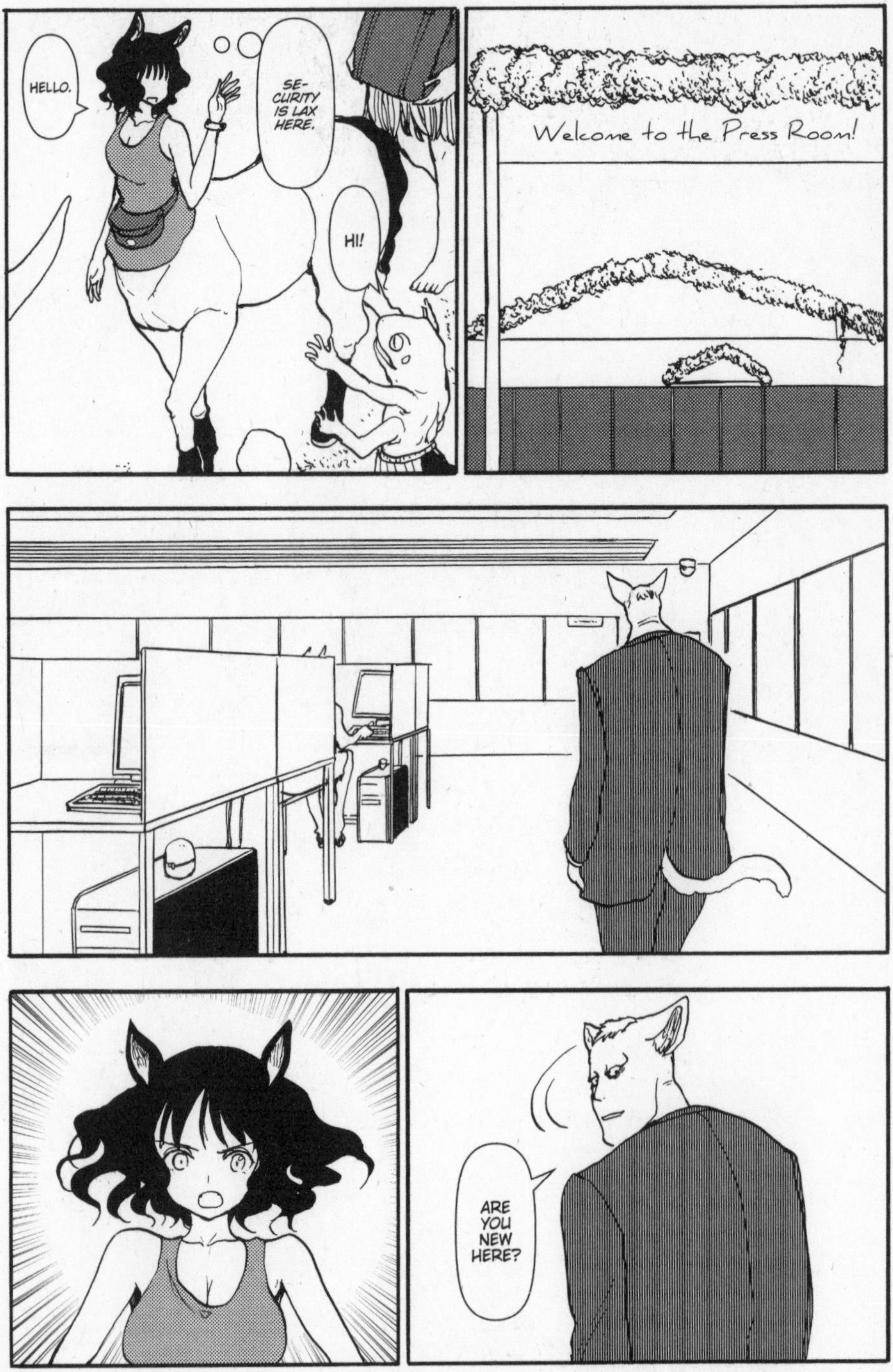
Welcome to the Press Room!
SE-CURITY IS LAX HERE.
HELLO.
HI!
ARE YOU NEW HERE?

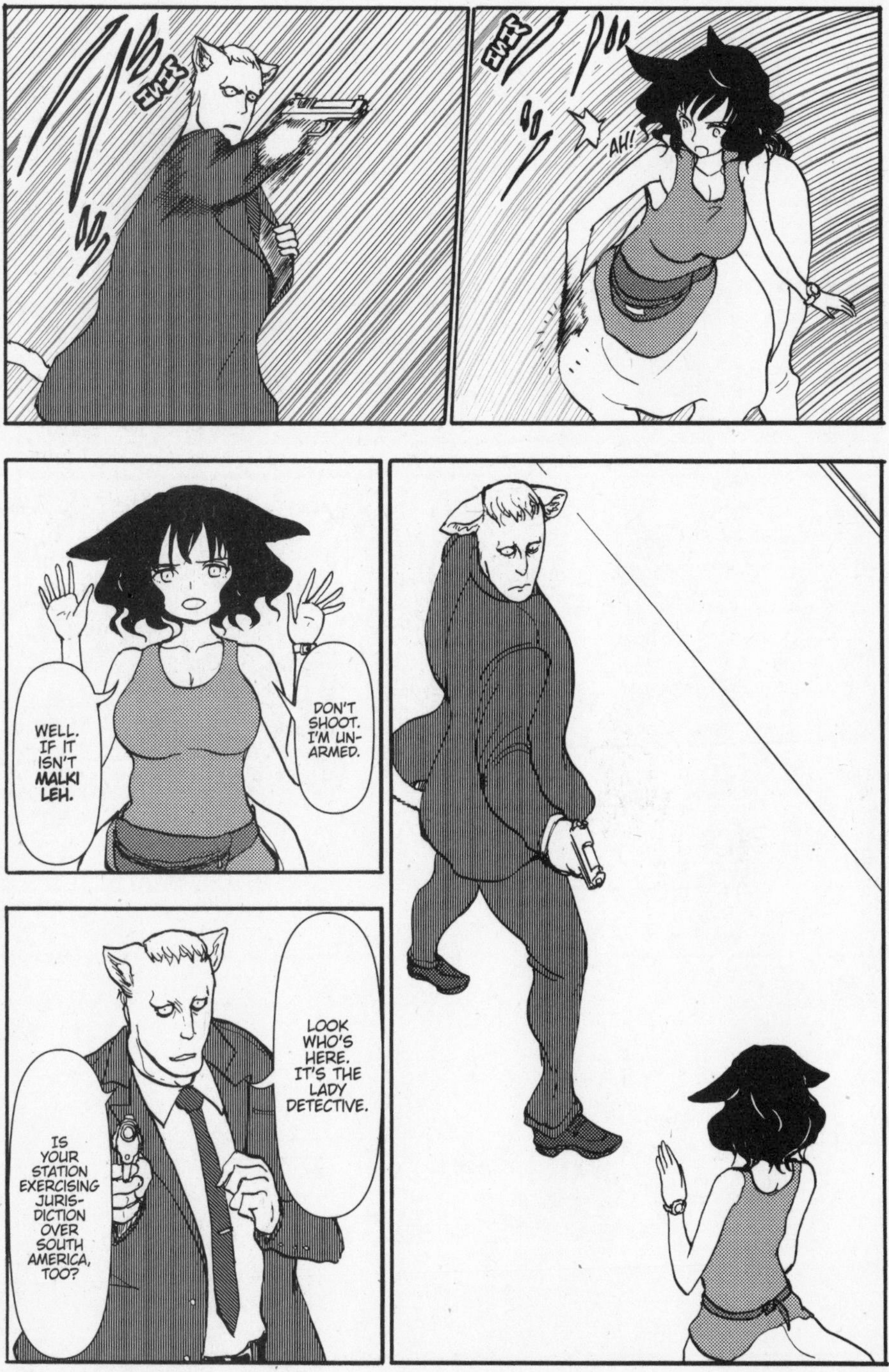
AH!
DON'T SHOOT. I'M UN-ARMED.
WELL. IF IT ISN'T **MALKI LEH.**
LOOK WHO'S HERE. IT'S THE LADY DETECTIVE.
IS YOUR STATION EXERCISING JURIS-DICTION OVER SOUTH AMERICA, TOO?

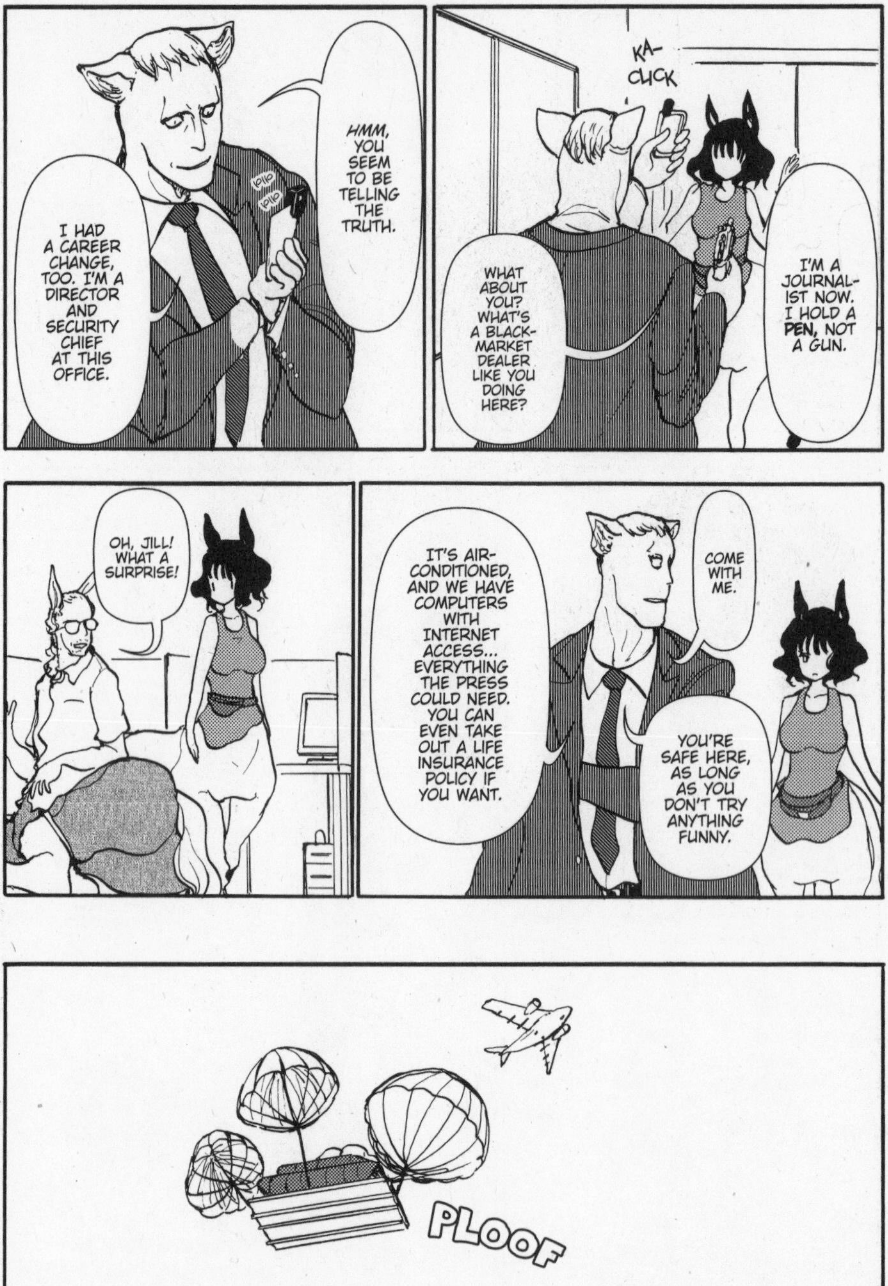
KA-CLICK
WHAT ABOUT YOU? WHAT'S A BLACK-MARKET DEALER LIKE YOU DOING HERE?
I'M A JOURNALIST NOW. I HOLD A PEN, NOT A GUN.
HMM, YOU SEEM TO BE TELLING THE TRUTH.
I HAD A CAREER CHANGE, TOO. I'M A DIRECTOR AND SECURITY CHIEF AT THIS OFFICE.
COME WITH ME.
IT'S AIR-CONDITIONED, AND WE HAVE COMPUTERS WITH INTERNET ACCESS... EVERYTHING THE PRESS COULD NEED. YOU CAN EVEN TAKE OUT A LIFE INSURANCE POLICY IF YOU WANT.
YOU'RE SAFE HERE, AS LONG AS YOU DON'T TRY ANYTHING FUNNY.
OH, JILL! WHAT A SURPRISE!
PLOOF

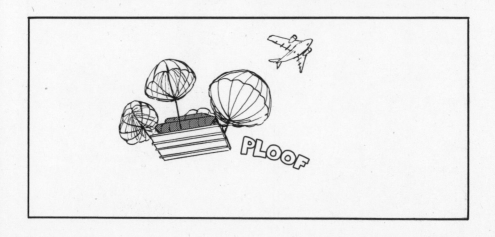

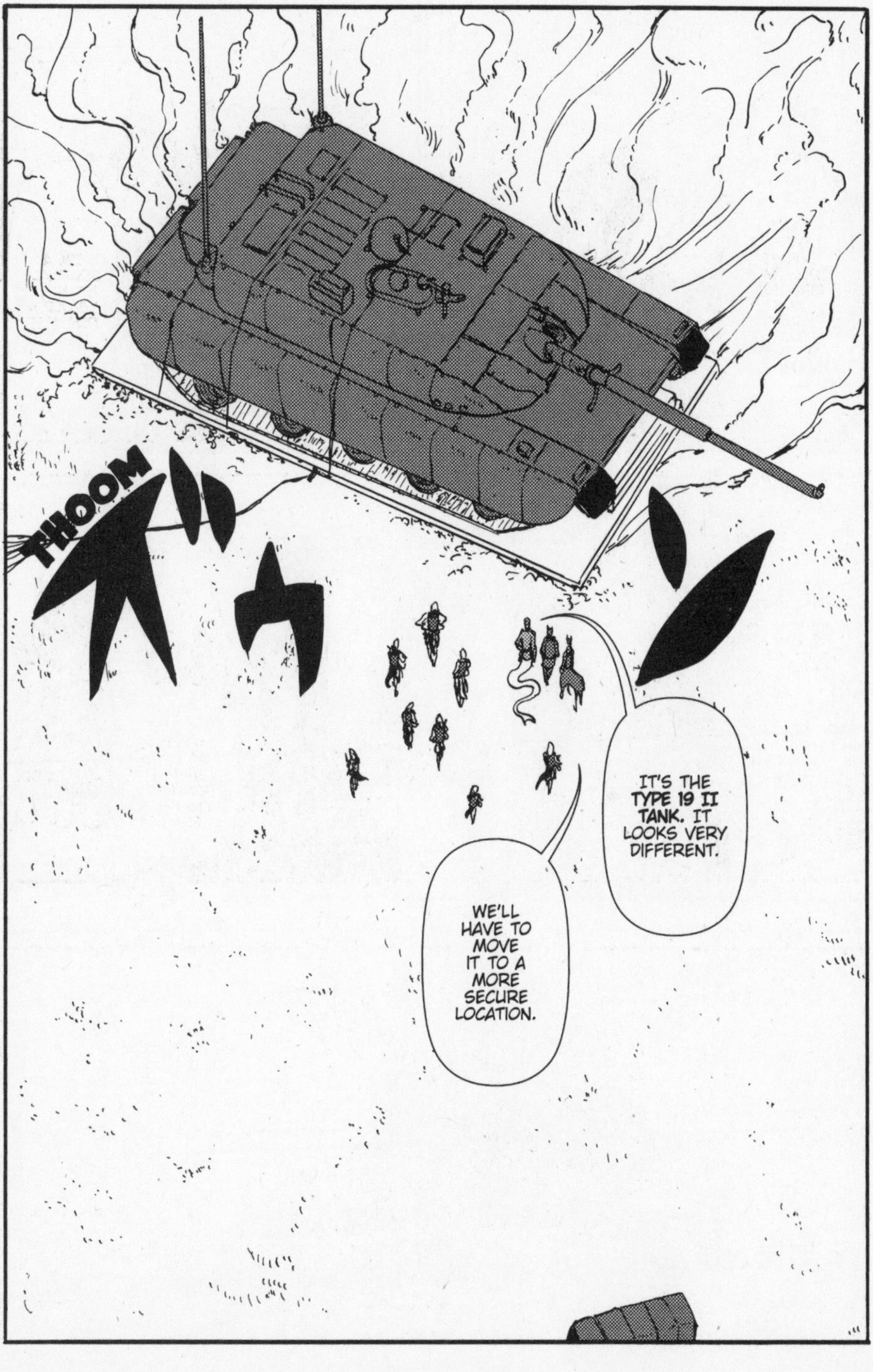
THOOM
IT'S THE TYPE 19 II TANK. IT LOOKS VERY DIFFERENT.
WE'LL HAVE TO MOVE IT TO A MORE SECURE LOCATION.

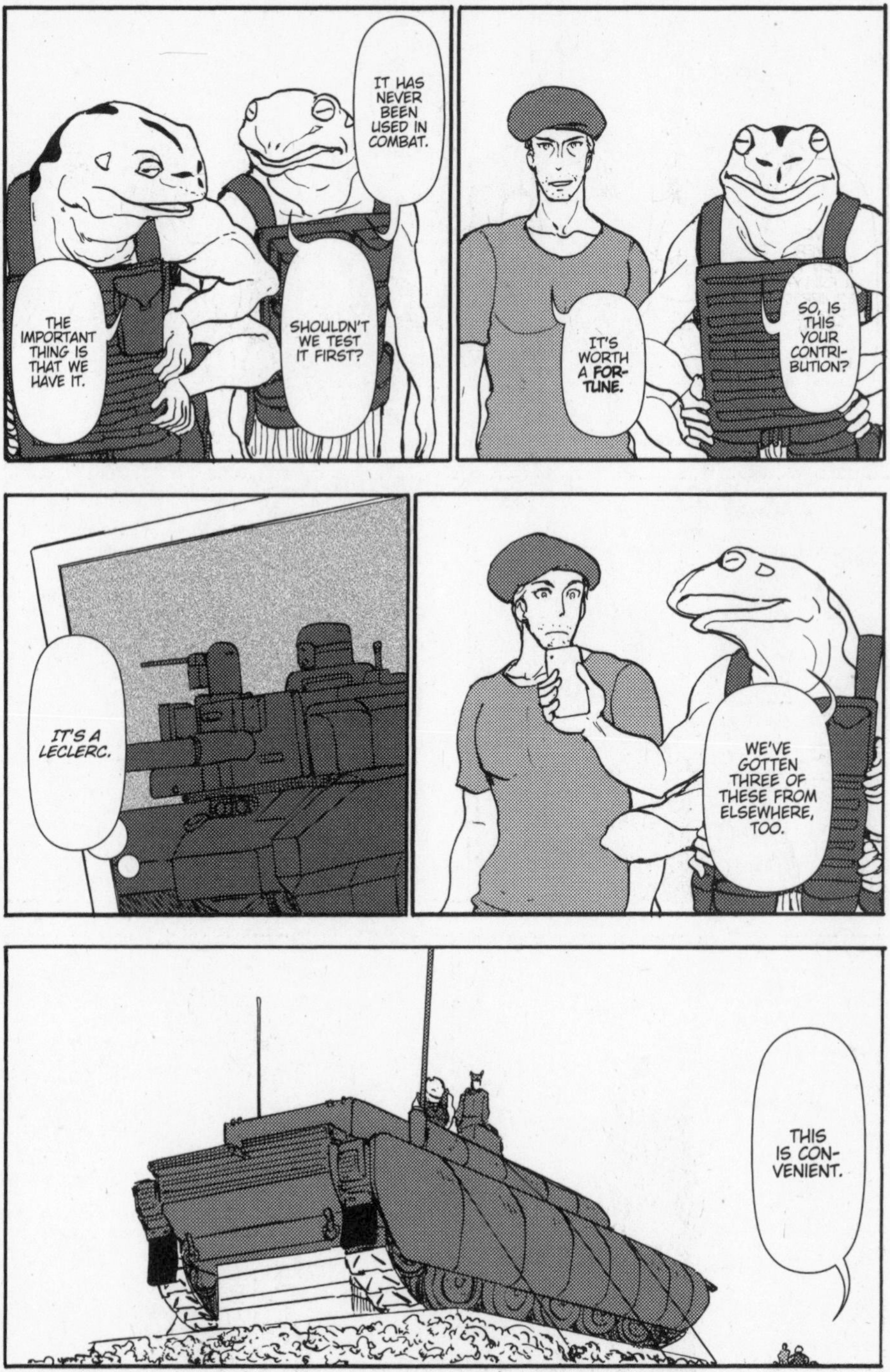
SO, IS THIS YOUR CONTRI-BUTION?
IT'S WORTH A FOR-TUNE.
IT HAS NEVER BEEN USED IN COMBAT.
SHOULDN'T WE TEST IT FIRST?
THE IMPORTANT THING IS THAT WE HAVE IT.
WE'VE GOTTEN THREE OF THESE FROM ELSEWHERE, TOO.
IT'S A LECLERC.
THIS IS CON-VENIENT.

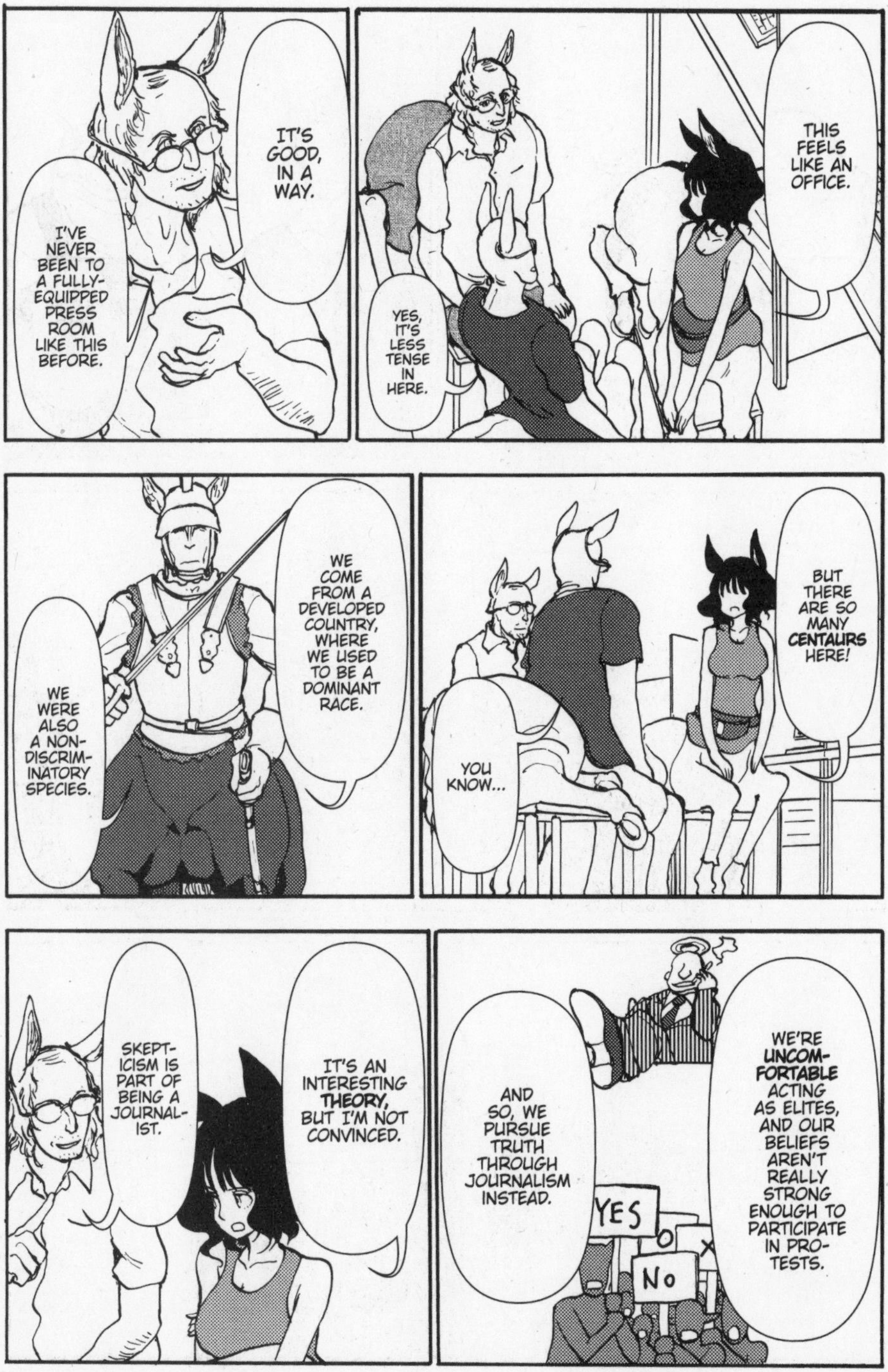
THIS FEELS LIKE AN OFFICE.
YES, IT'S LESS TENSE IN HERE.
IT'S GOOD, IN A WAY.
I'VE NEVER BEEN TO A FULLY-EQUIPPED PRESS ROOM LIKE THIS BEFORE.
BUT THERE ARE SO MANY **CENTAURS** HERE!
YOU KNOW...
WE COME FROM A DEVELOPED COUNTRY, WHERE WE USED TO BE A DOMINANT RACE.
WE WERE ALSO A NON-DISCRIMINATORY SPECIES.
WE'RE **UNCOMFORTABLE** ACTING AS ELITES, AND OUR BELIEFS AREN'T REALLY STRONG ENOUGH TO PARTICIPATE IN PROTESTS.
AND SO, WE PURSUE TRUTH THROUGH JOURNALISM INSTEAD.
YES
No
IT'S AN INTERESTING **THEORY,** BUT I'M NOT CONVINCED.
SKEPTICISM IS PART OF BEING A JOURNALIST.

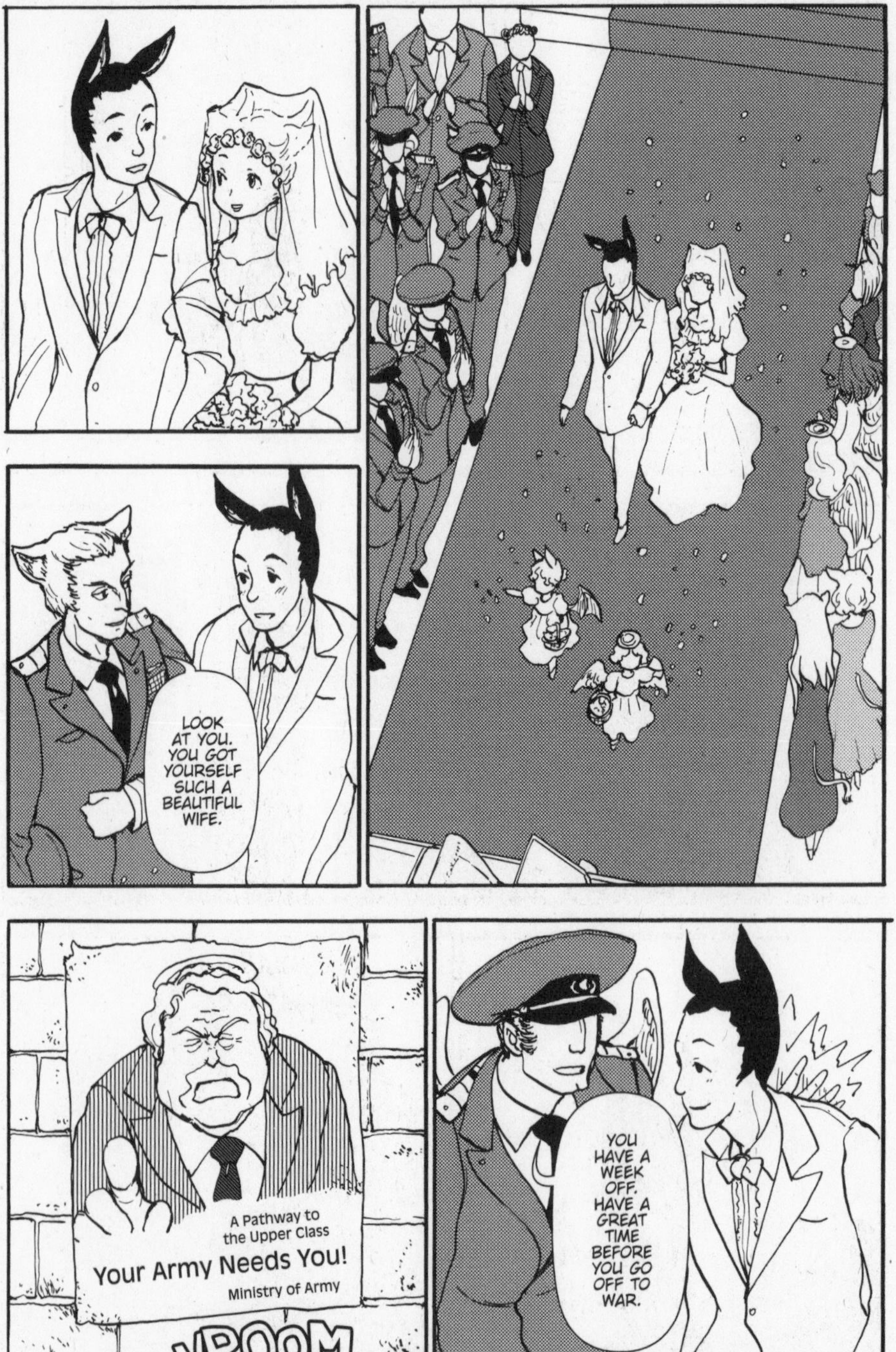
LOOK AT YOU. YOU GOT YOURSELF SUCH A BEAUTIFUL WIFE.
YOU HAVE A WEEK OFF. HAVE A GREAT TIME BEFORE YOU GO OFF TO WAR.
A Pathway to the Upper Class
Your Army Needs You!
Ministry of Army
VROOM

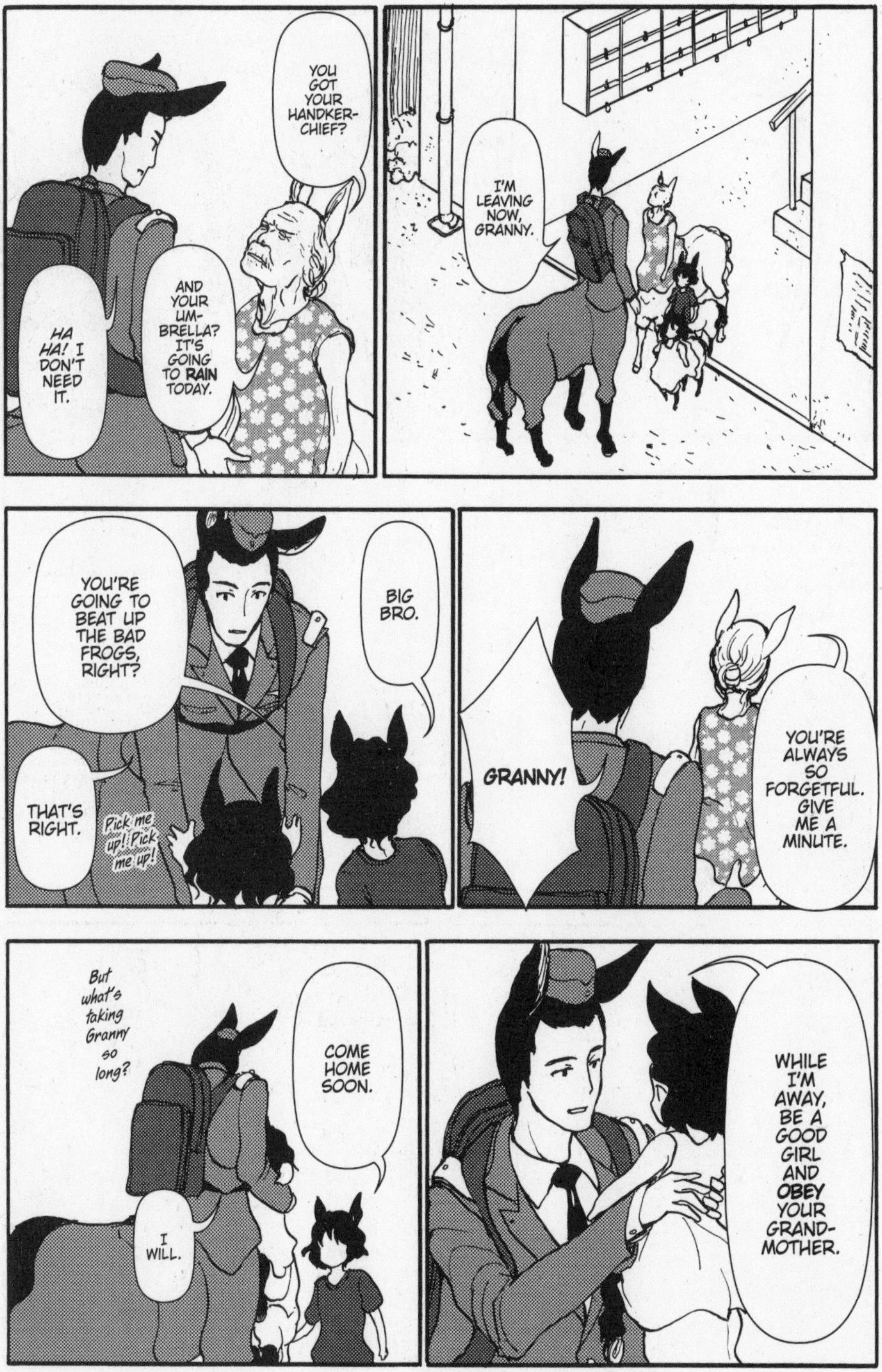
I'M LEAVING NOW, GRANNY.
YOU GOT YOUR HANDKERCHIEF?
AND YOUR UMBRELLA? IT'S GOING TO RAIN TODAY.
HA HA! I DON'T NEED IT.
GRANNY!
YOU'RE ALWAYS SO FORGETFUL. GIVE ME A MINUTE.
BIG BRO.
YOU'RE GOING TO BEAT UP THE BAD FROGS, RIGHT?
THAT'S RIGHT.
Pick me up! Pick me up!
WHILE I'M AWAY, BE A GOOD GIRL AND OBEY YOUR GRANDMOTHER.
COME HOME SOON.
I WILL.
But what's taking Granny so long?

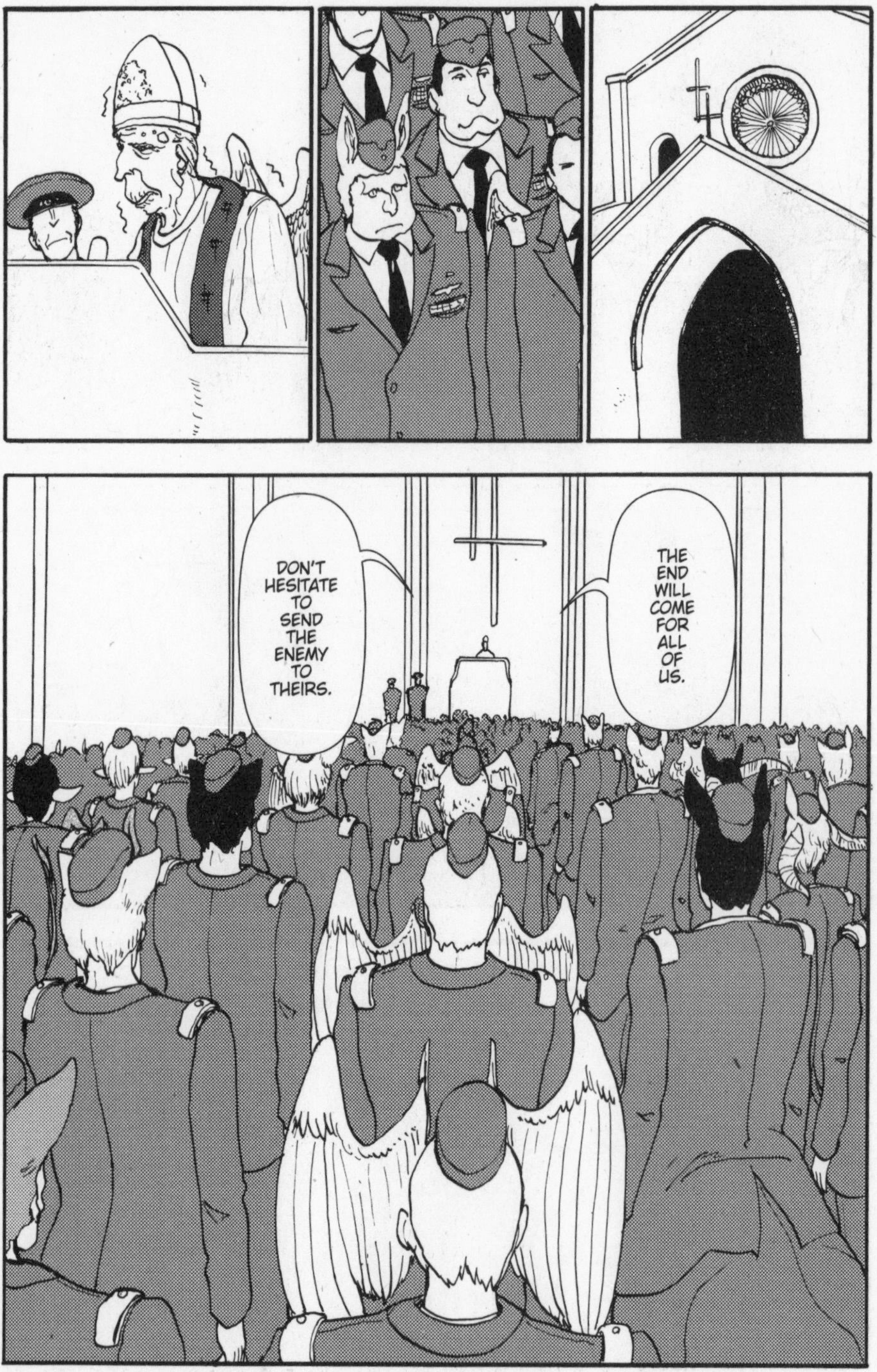
THE END WILL COME FOR ALL OF US.
DON'T HESITATE TO SEND THE ENEMY TO THEIRS.

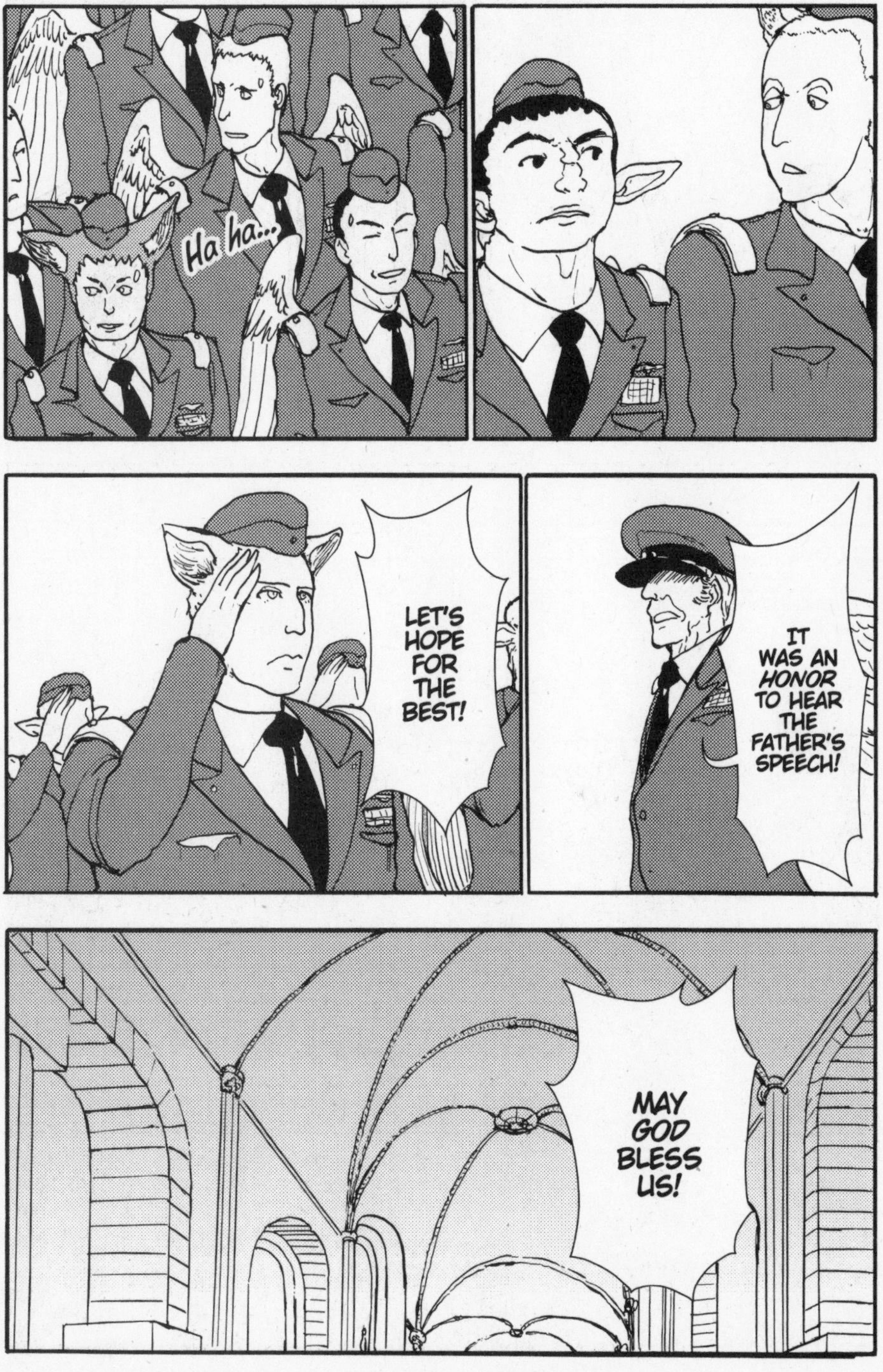
Ha ha...
IT WAS AN *HONOR* TO HEAR THE FATHER'S SPEECH!
LET'S HOPE FOR THE BEST!
MAY GOD BLESS US!

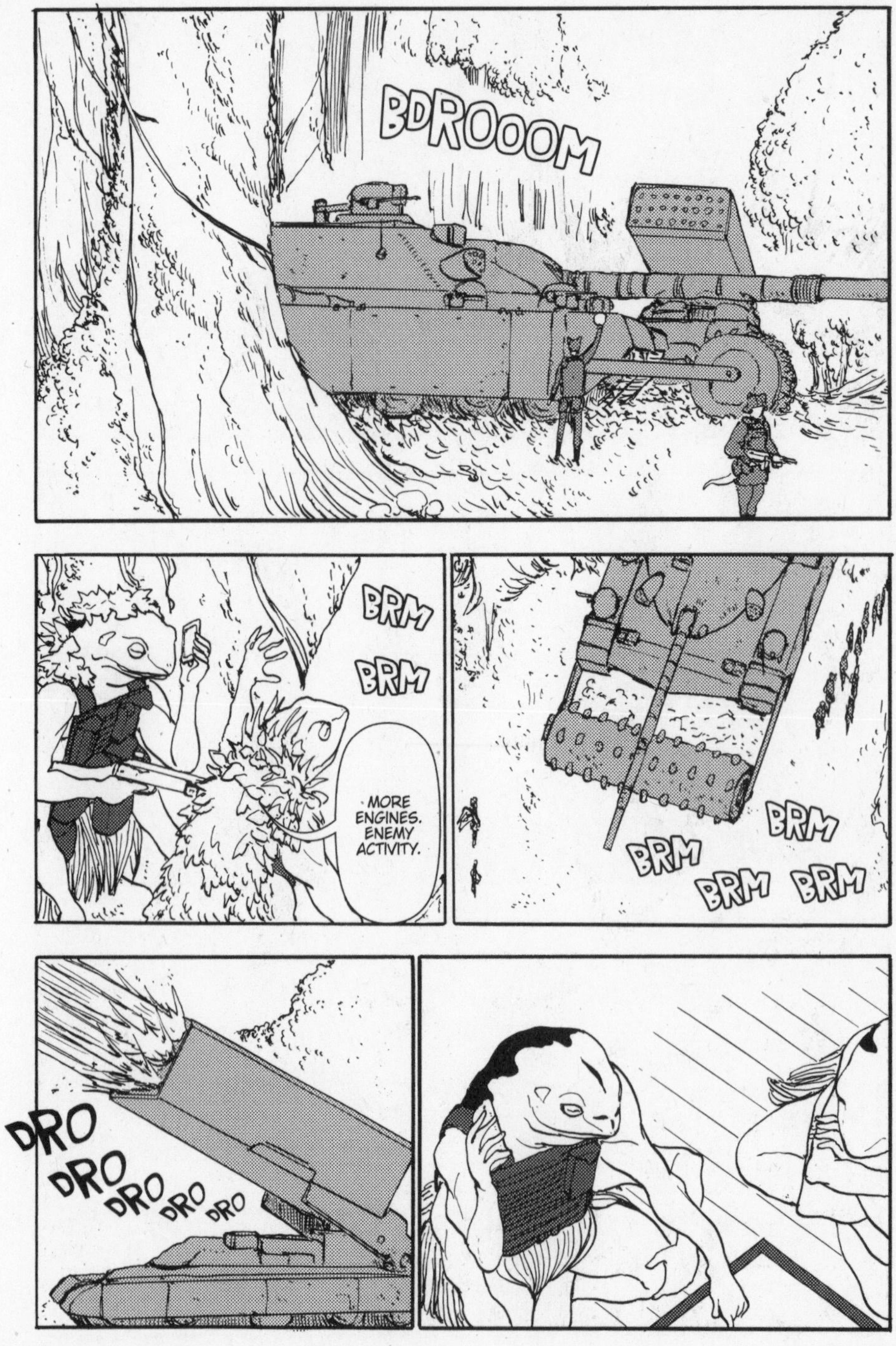
BDROOOM
BRM
BRM
BRM BRM
BRM
BRM
MORE ENGINES. ENEMY ACTIVITY.
DRO
DRO
DRO
DRO
DRO

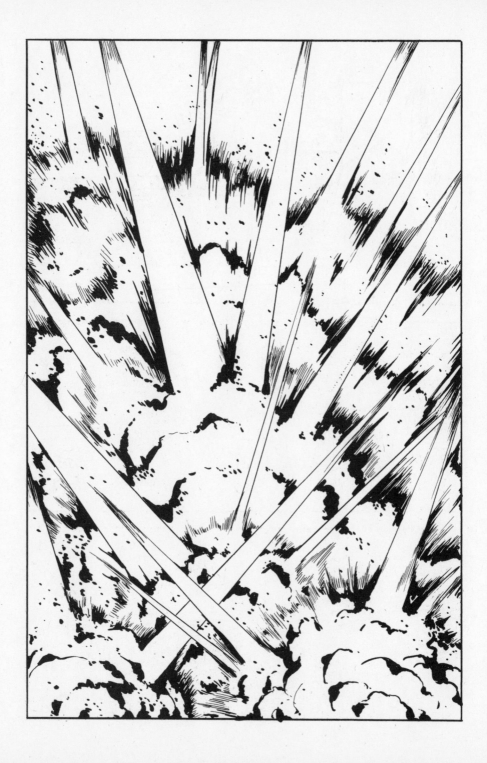

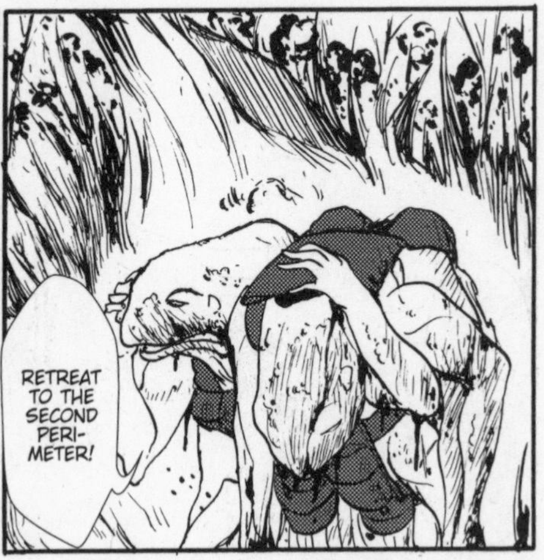
RETREAT TO THE SECOND PERI-METER!

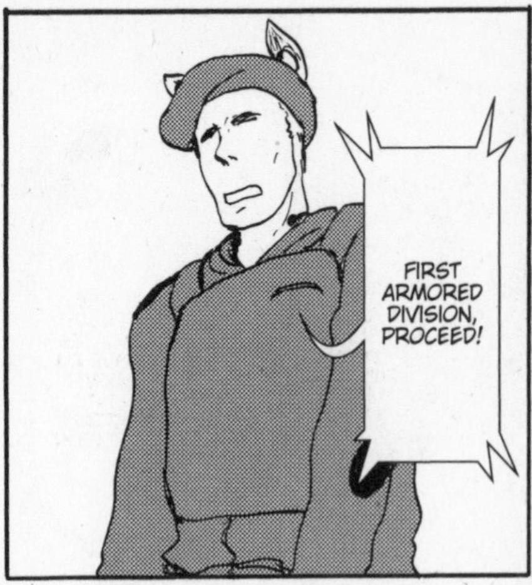
FIRST ARMORED DIVISION, PROCEED!

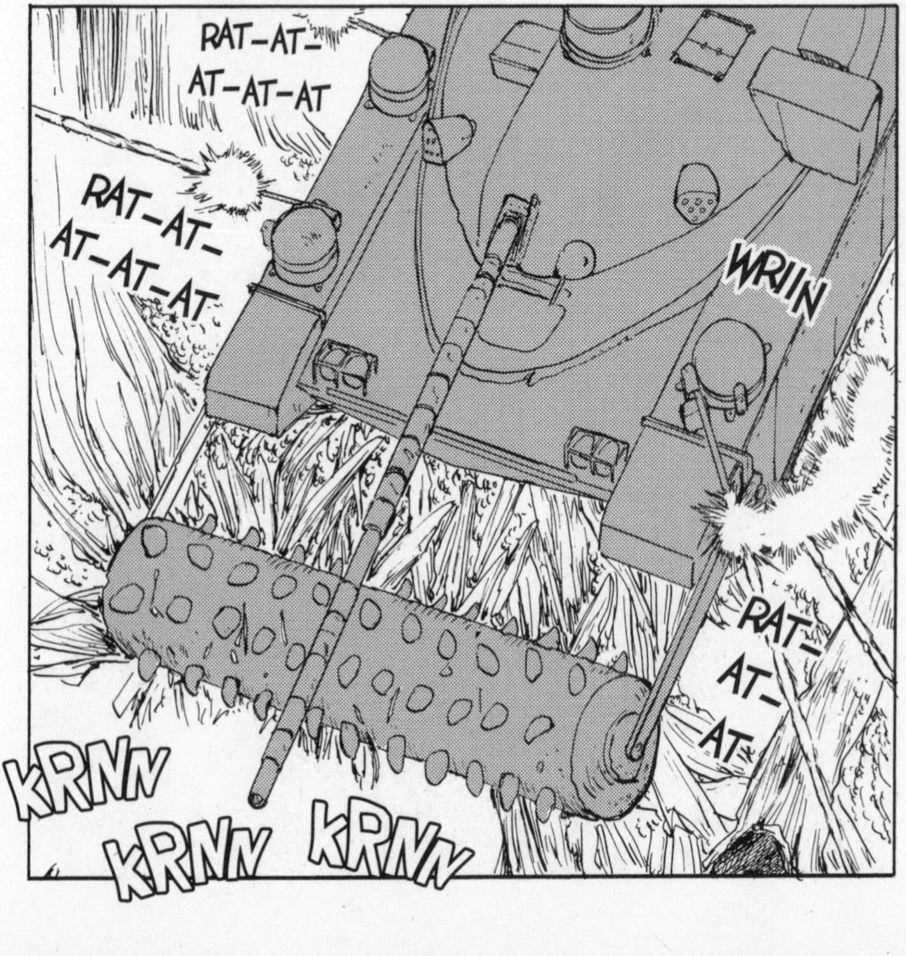
RAT-AT-AT-AT-AT
WRIIN
RAT-AT-AT-AT-AT
RAT-AT-AT
KRNN KRNN KRNN

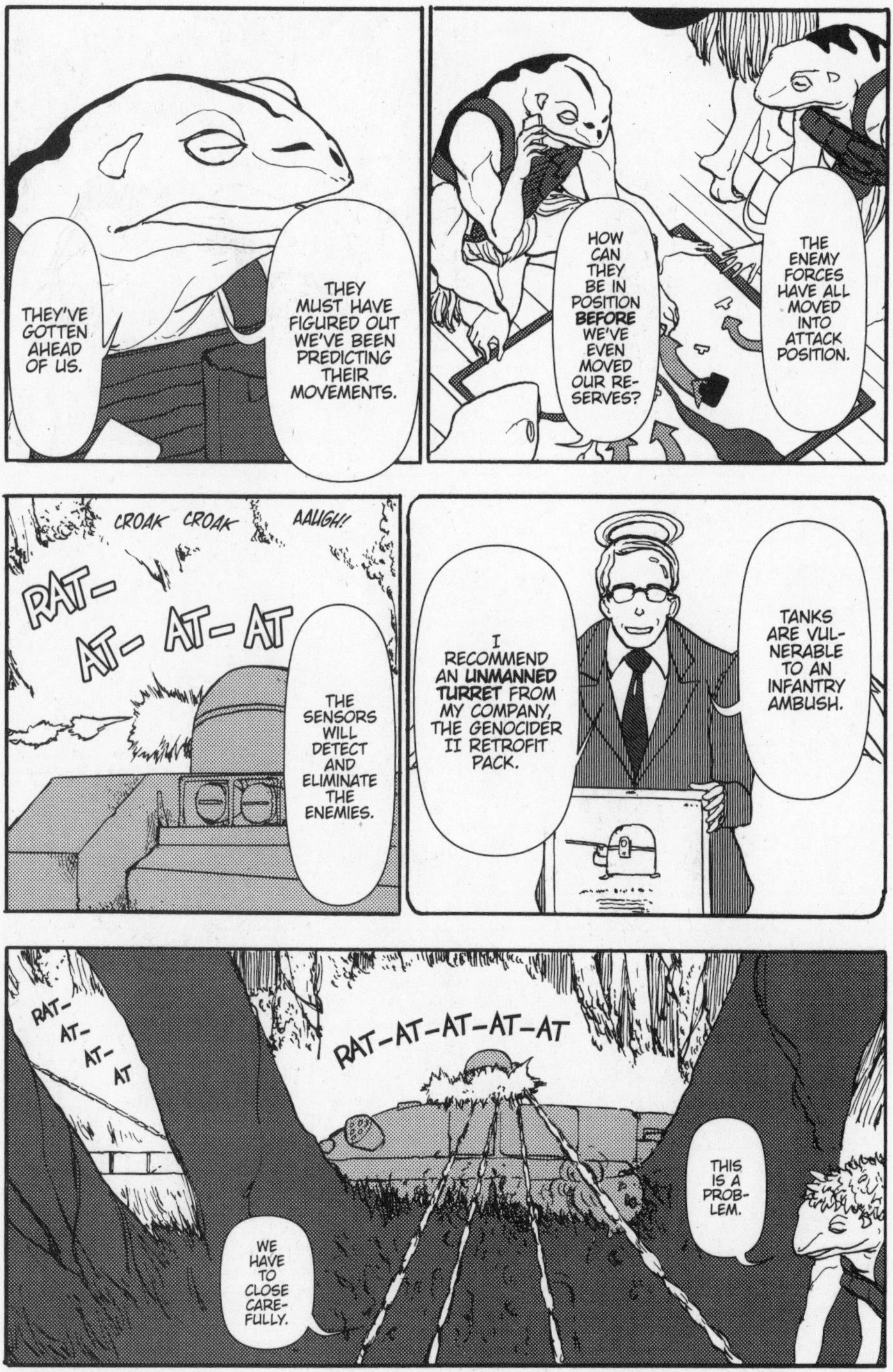
THE ENEMY FORCES HAVE ALL MOVED INTO ATTACK POSITION.
HOW CAN THEY BE IN POSITION **BEFORE** WE'VE EVEN MOVED OUR RESERVES?
THEY MUST HAVE FIGURED OUT WE'VE BEEN PREDICTING THEIR MOVEMENTS.
THEY'VE GOTTEN AHEAD OF US.
TANKS ARE VULNERABLE TO AN INFANTRY AMBUSH.
I RECOMMEND AN **UNMANNED TURRET** FROM MY COMPANY, THE GENOCIDER II RETROFIT PACK.
AAUGH!
CROAK CROAK
RAT-AT-AT-AT
THE SENSORS WILL DETECT AND ELIMINATE THE ENEMIES.
RAT-AT-AT-AT-AT
RAT-AT-AT-AT
THIS IS A PROBLEM.
WE HAVE TO CLOSE CAREFULLY.

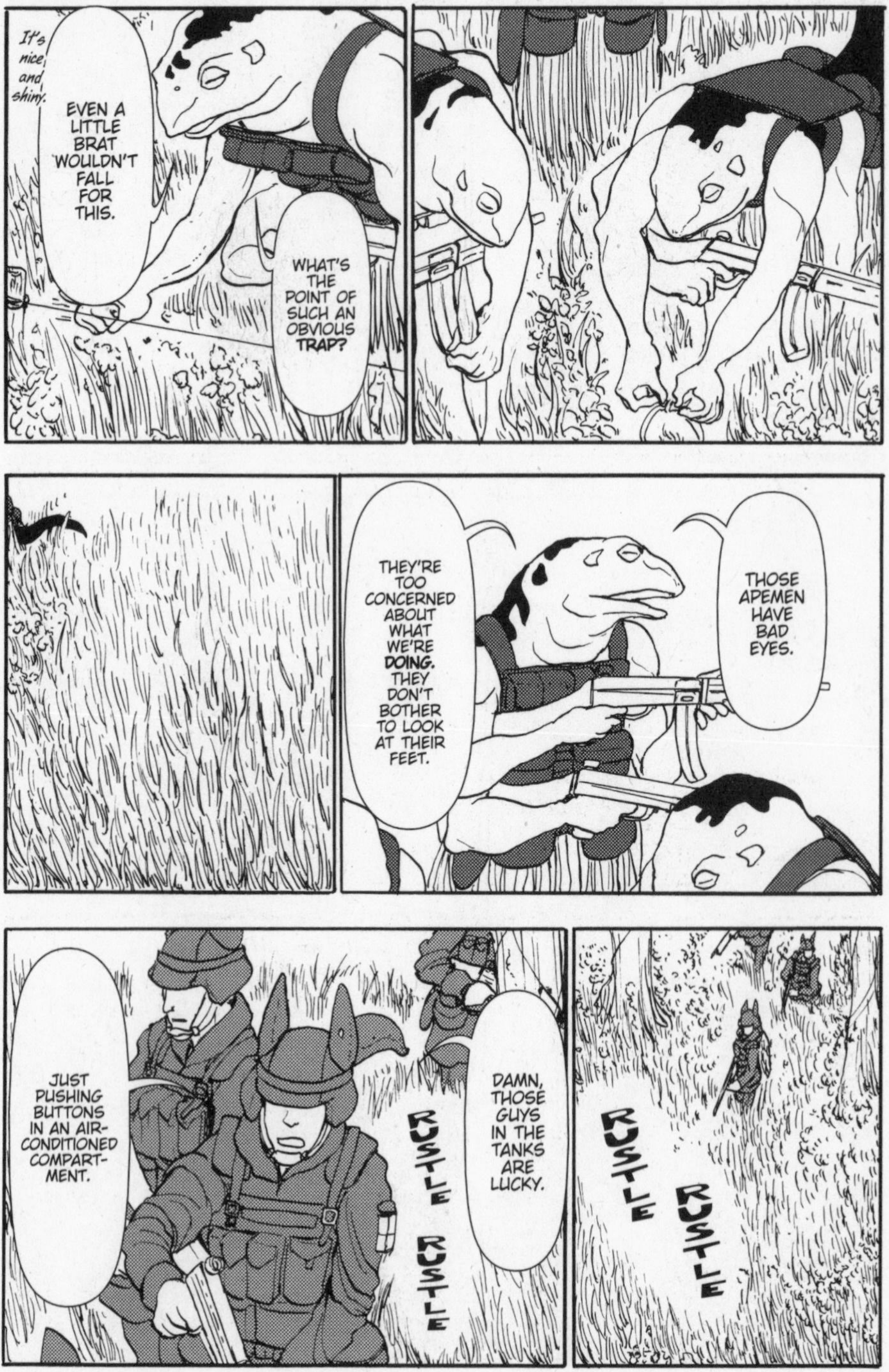
WHAT'S THE POINT OF SUCH AN OBVIOUS **TRAP?**
EVEN A LITTLE BRAT WOULDN'T FALL FOR THIS.
It's nice and shiny.
THOSE APEMEN HAVE BAD EYES.
THEY'RE TOO CONCERNED ABOUT WHAT WE'RE **DOING.** THEY DON'T BOTHER TO LOOK AT THEIR FEET.
RUSTLE
RUSTLE
RUSTLE
DAMN, THOSE GUYS IN THE TANKS ARE LUCKY.
RUSTLE
RUSTLE
JUST PUSHING BUTTONS IN AN AIR-CONDITIONED COMPART-MENT.

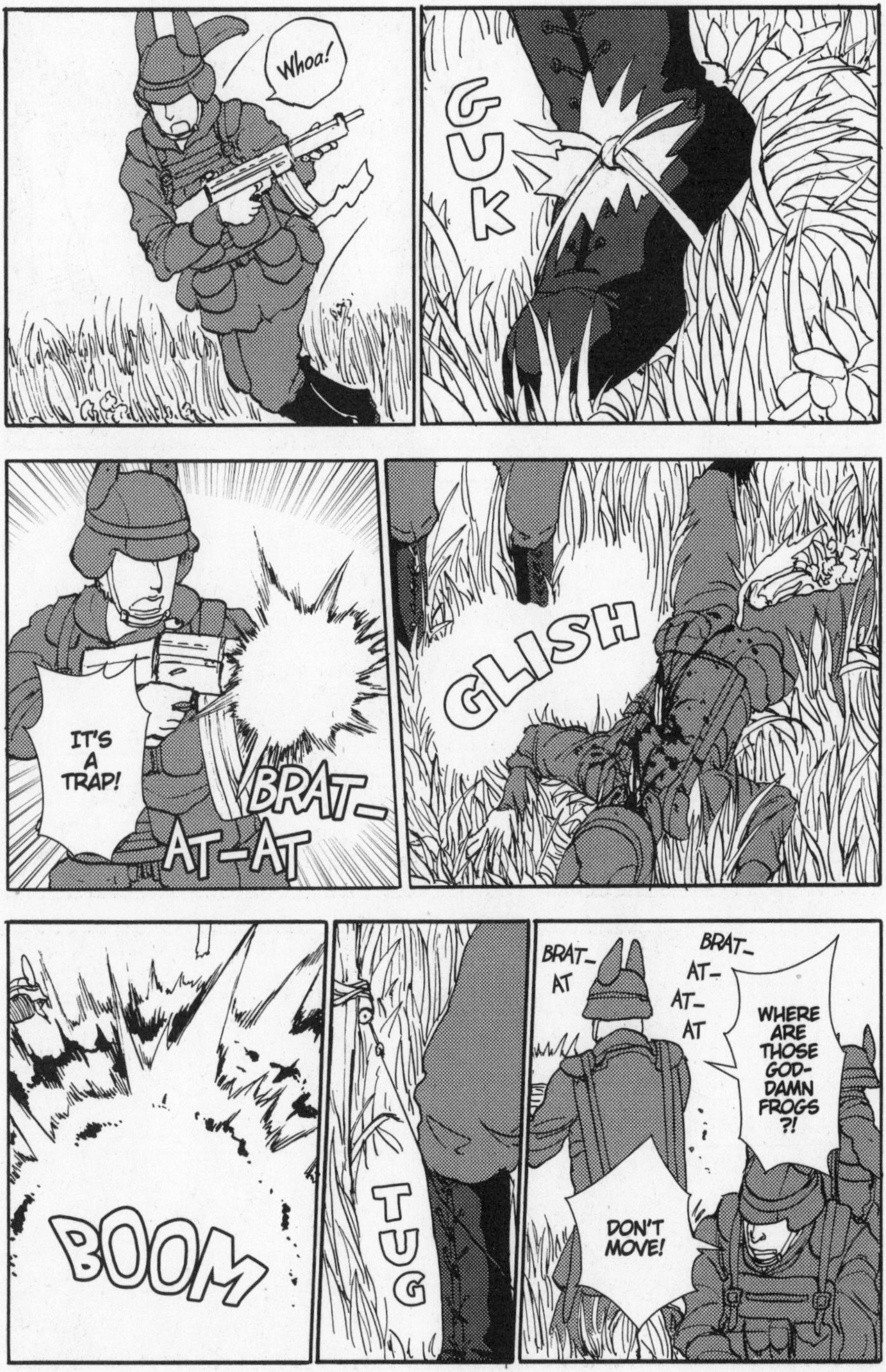
GUK
Whoa!
GLISH
IT'S A TRAP!
BRAT-AT-AT
BRAT-AT-AT-AT
BRAT-AT
WHERE ARE THOSE GOD-DAMN FROGS?!
DON'T MOVE!
TUG
BOOM

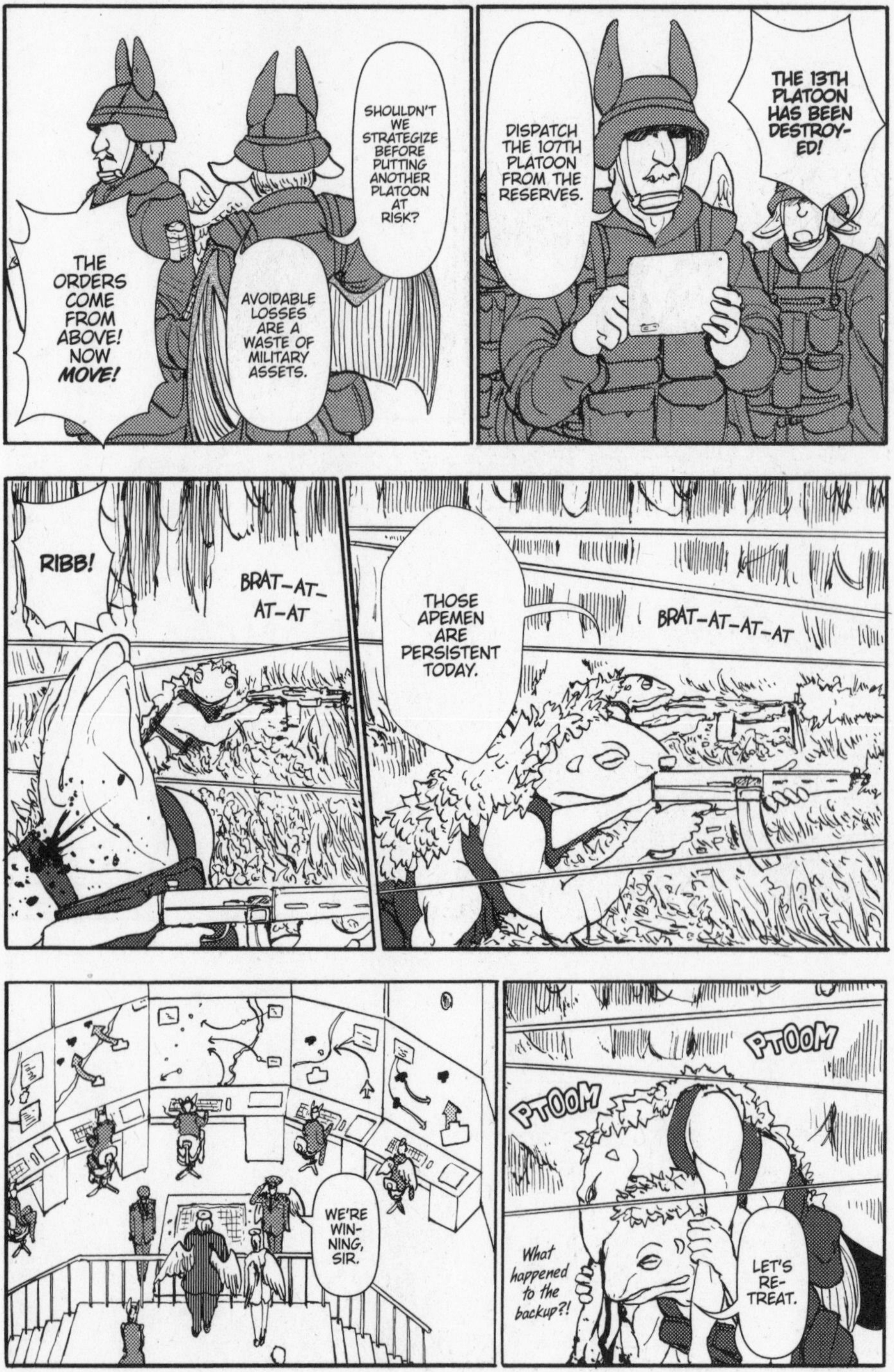
THE 13TH PLATOON HAS BEEN DESTROYED!
DISPATCH THE 107TH PLATOON FROM THE RESERVES.
SHOULDN'T WE STRATEGIZE BEFORE PUTTING ANOTHER PLATOON AT RISK?
AVOIDABLE LOSSES ARE A WASTE OF MILITARY ASSETS.
THE ORDERS COME FROM ABOVE! NOW MOVE!
THOSE APEMEN ARE PERSISTENT TODAY.
BRAT-AT-AT-AT
RIBB!
BRAT-AT-AT-AT
PTOOM
PTOOM
LET'S RETREAT.
What happened to the backup?!
WE'RE WINNING, SIR.

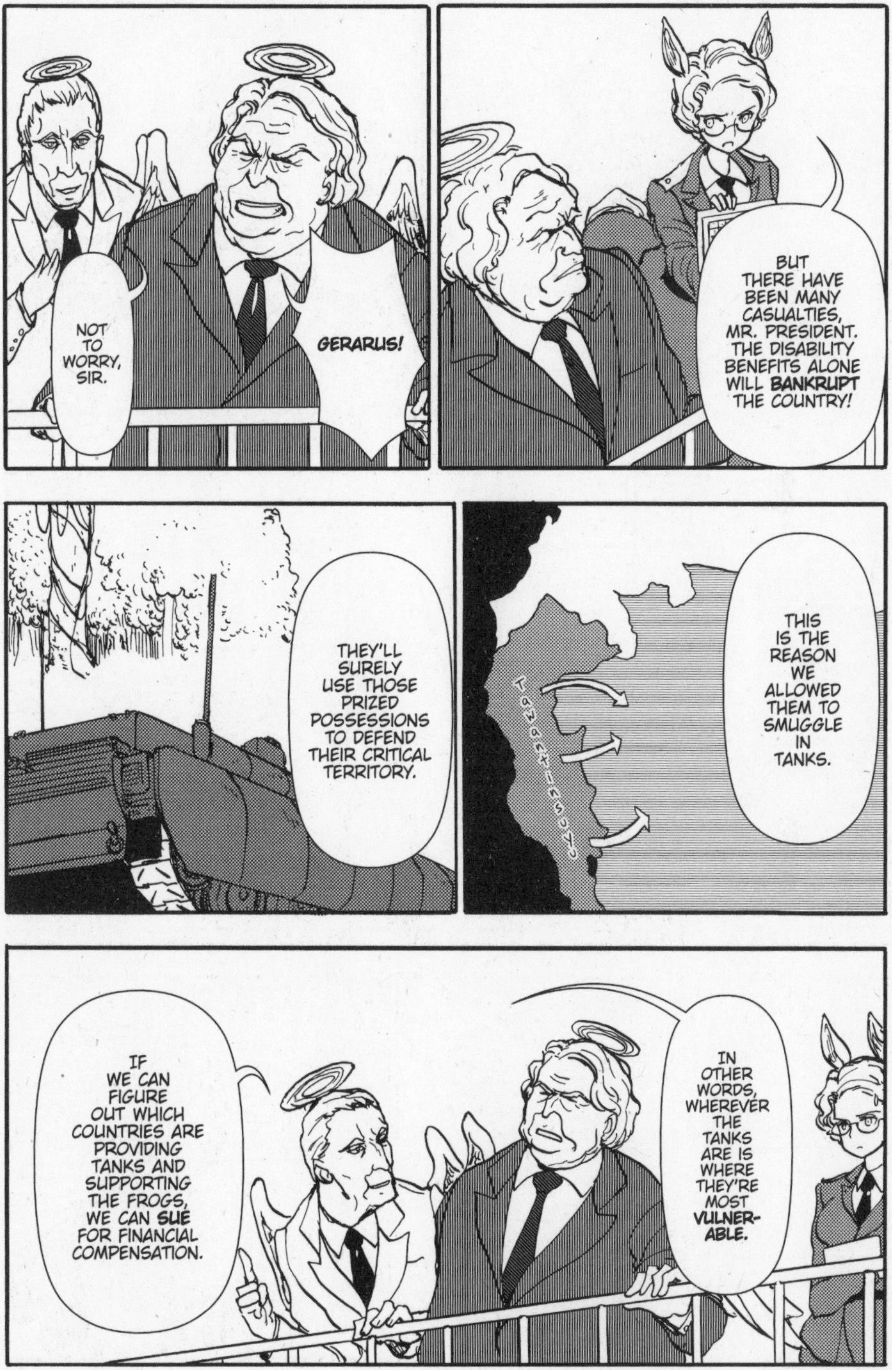
BUT THERE HAVE BEEN MANY CASUALTIES, MR. PRESIDENT. THE DISABILITY BENEFITS ALONE WILL BANKRUPT THE COUNTRY!
GERARUS!
NOT TO WORRY, SIR.
THIS IS THE REASON WE ALLOWED THEM TO SMUGGLE IN TANKS.
Tawantinsuyu
THEY'LL SURELY USE THOSE PRIZED POSSESSIONS TO DEFEND THEIR CRITICAL TERRITORY.
IN OTHER WORDS, WHEREVER THE TANKS ARE IS WHERE THEY'RE MOST VULNER-ABLE.
IF WE CAN FIGURE OUT WHICH COUNTRIES ARE PROVIDING TANKS AND SUPPORTING THE FROGS, WE CAN SUE FOR FINANCIAL COMPENSATION.

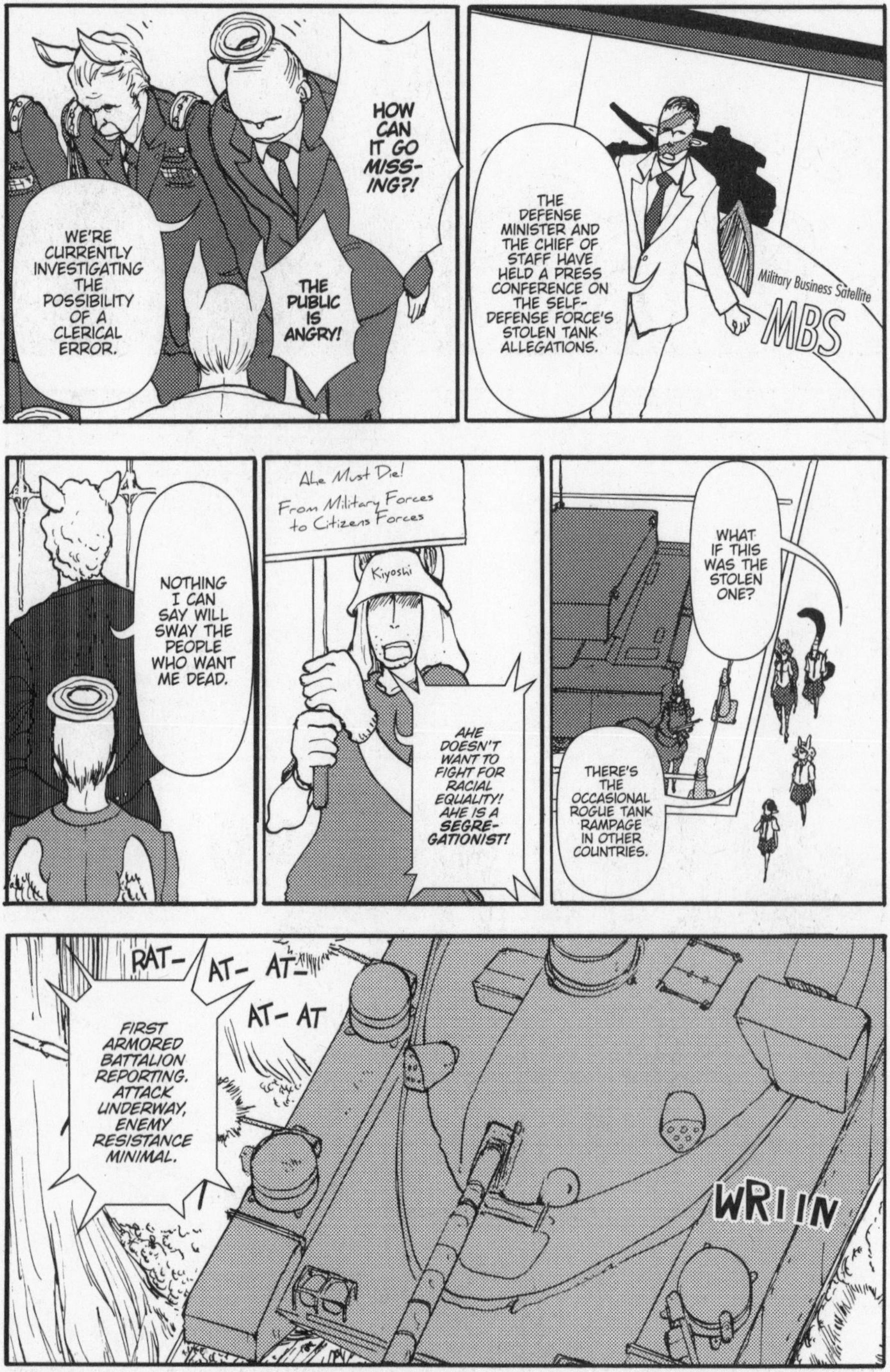
Military Business Satellite
MBS
THE DEFENSE MINISTER AND THE CHIEF OF STAFF HAVE HELD A PRESS CONFERENCE ON THE SELF-DEFENSE FORCE'S STOLEN TANK ALLEGATIONS.
HOW CAN IT GO MISS-ING?!
THE PUBLIC IS ANGRY!
WE'RE CURRENTLY INVESTIGATING THE POSSIBILITY OF A CLERICAL ERROR.
WHAT IF THIS WAS THE STOLEN ONE?
THERE'S THE OCCASIONAL ROGUE TANK RAMPAGE IN OTHER COUNTRIES.
Ahe Must Die!
From Military Forces to Citizens Forces
Kiyoshi
AHE DOESN'T WANT TO FIGHT FOR RACIAL EQUALITY! AHE IS A SEGRE-GATIONIST!
NOTHING I CAN SAY WILL SWAY THE PEOPLE WHO WANT ME DEAD.
RAT- AT- AT- AT- AT
FIRST ARMORED BATTALION REPORTING. ATTACK UNDERWAY, ENEMY RESISTANCE MINIMAL.
WRIIN

BANG
SPLASHH
THIS IS WATERWAY SECURITY. WE'LL PROCEED TO THE RENDEZVOUS POINT UPON LANDING.
THIS IS MORE USEFUL THAN I THOUGHT.
THOSE FROGS ONLY HAVE LIGHT INFANTRY.
KA-BOOM

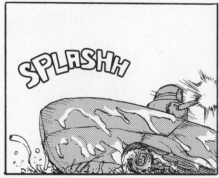

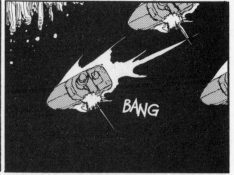

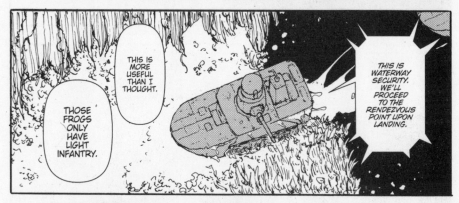

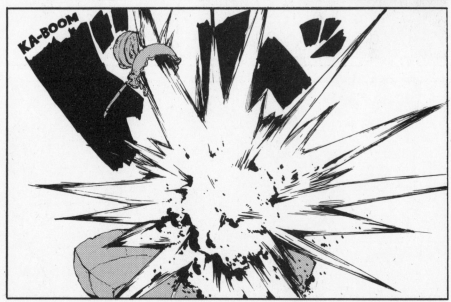

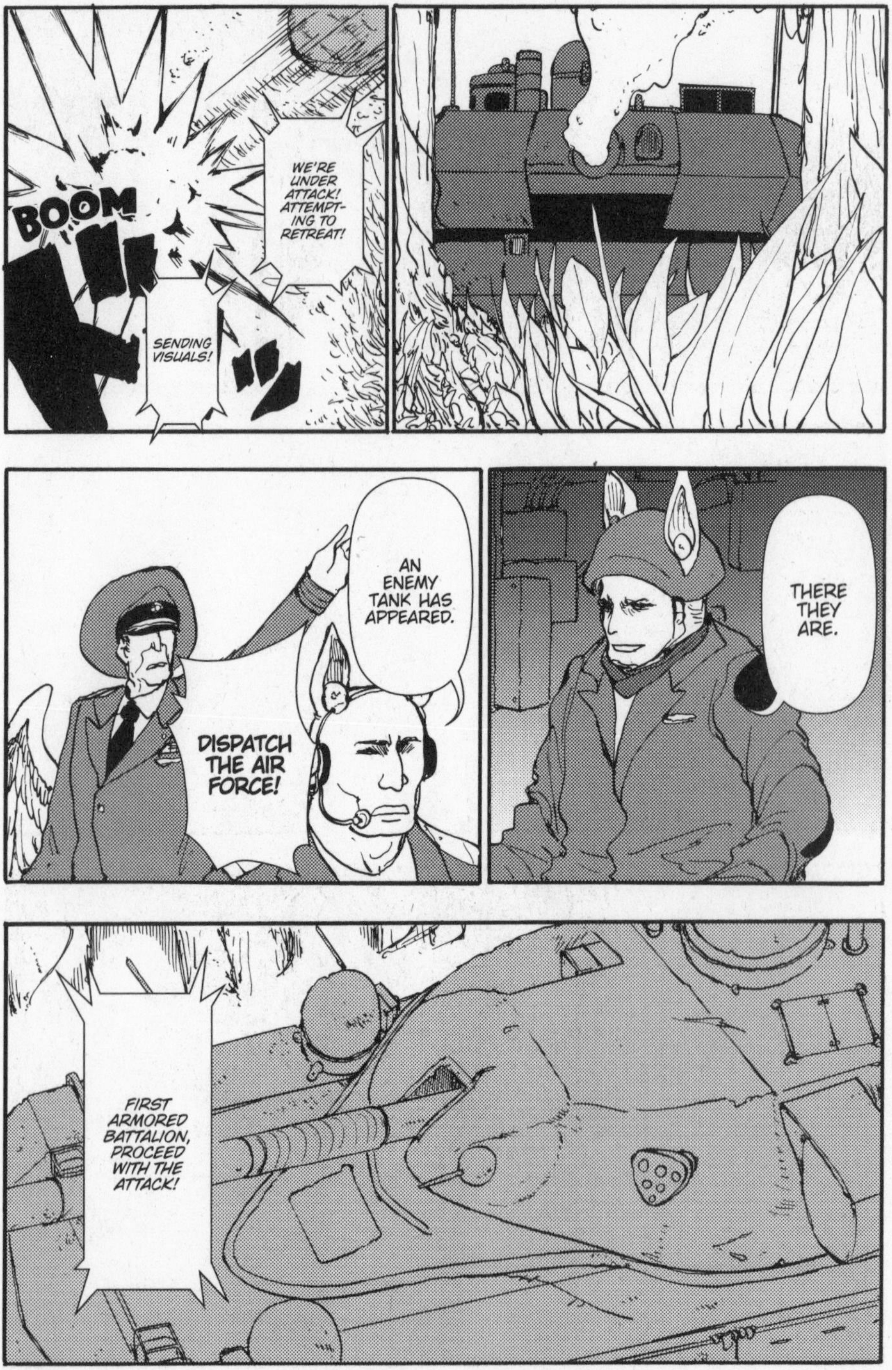
WE'RE UNDER ATTACK! ATTEMPTING TO RETREAT!
BOOM
SENDING VISUALS!
THERE THEY ARE.
AN ENEMY TANK HAS APPEARED.
DISPATCH THE AIR FORCE!
FIRST ARMORED BATTALION, PROCEED WITH THE ATTACK!

WE'RE STUCK HERE UNTIL THE BOAT COMES IN.

SPLISH

CAN'T SWIM IN A RIVER FULL OF ALLIGATORS AND PIRANHAS.

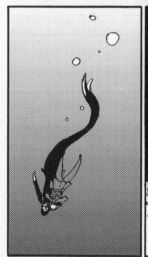

SPLOOSH

HM?

GENERAL?

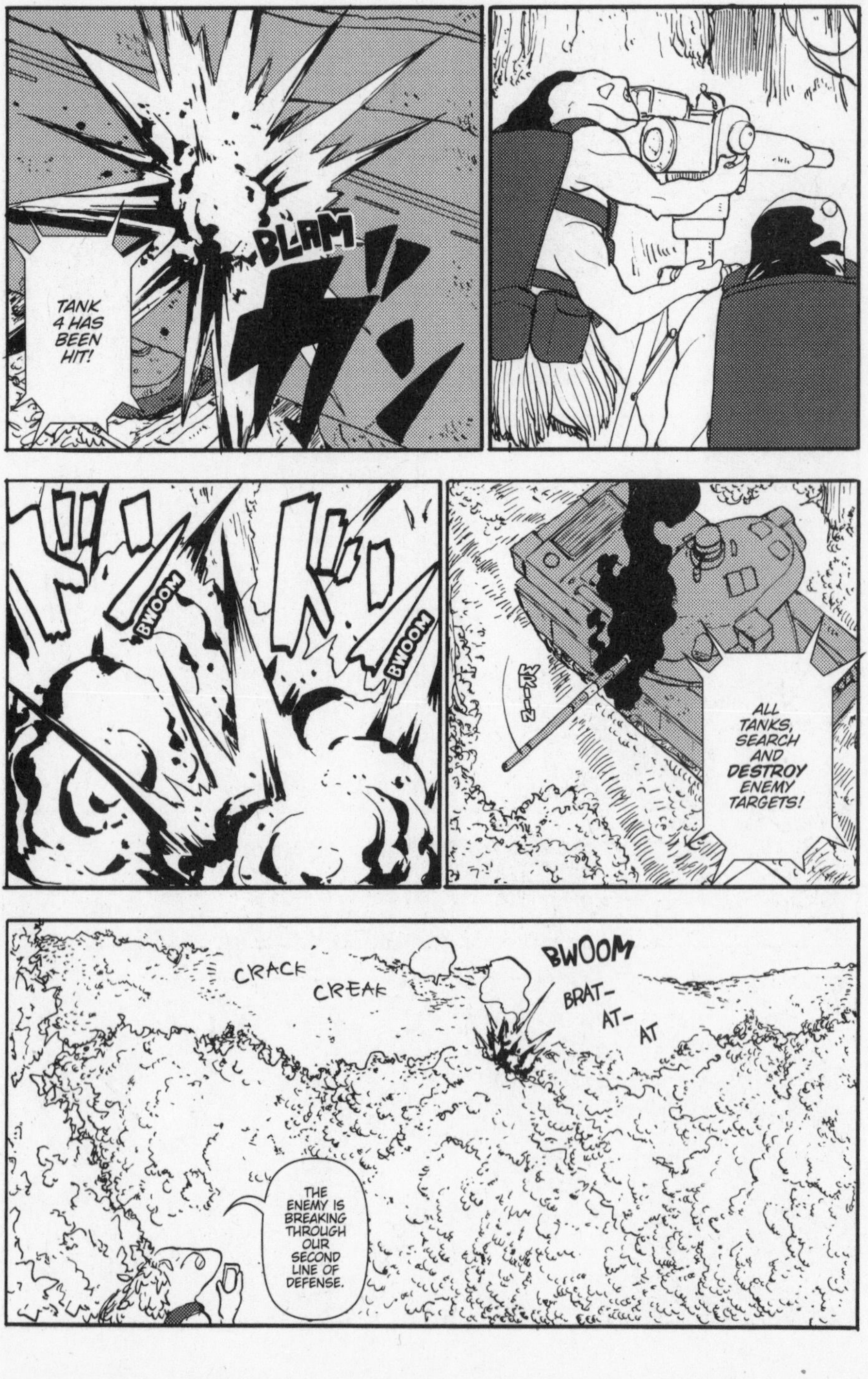
BLAM
TANK 4 HAS BEEN HIT!
ALL TANKS, SEARCH AND **DESTROY** ENEMY TARGETS!
WR-I-N
BWOOM
BWOOM
BWOOM
BRAT-AT-AT
CRACK
CREAK
THE ENEMY IS BREAKING THROUGH OUR SECOND LINE OF DEFENSE.

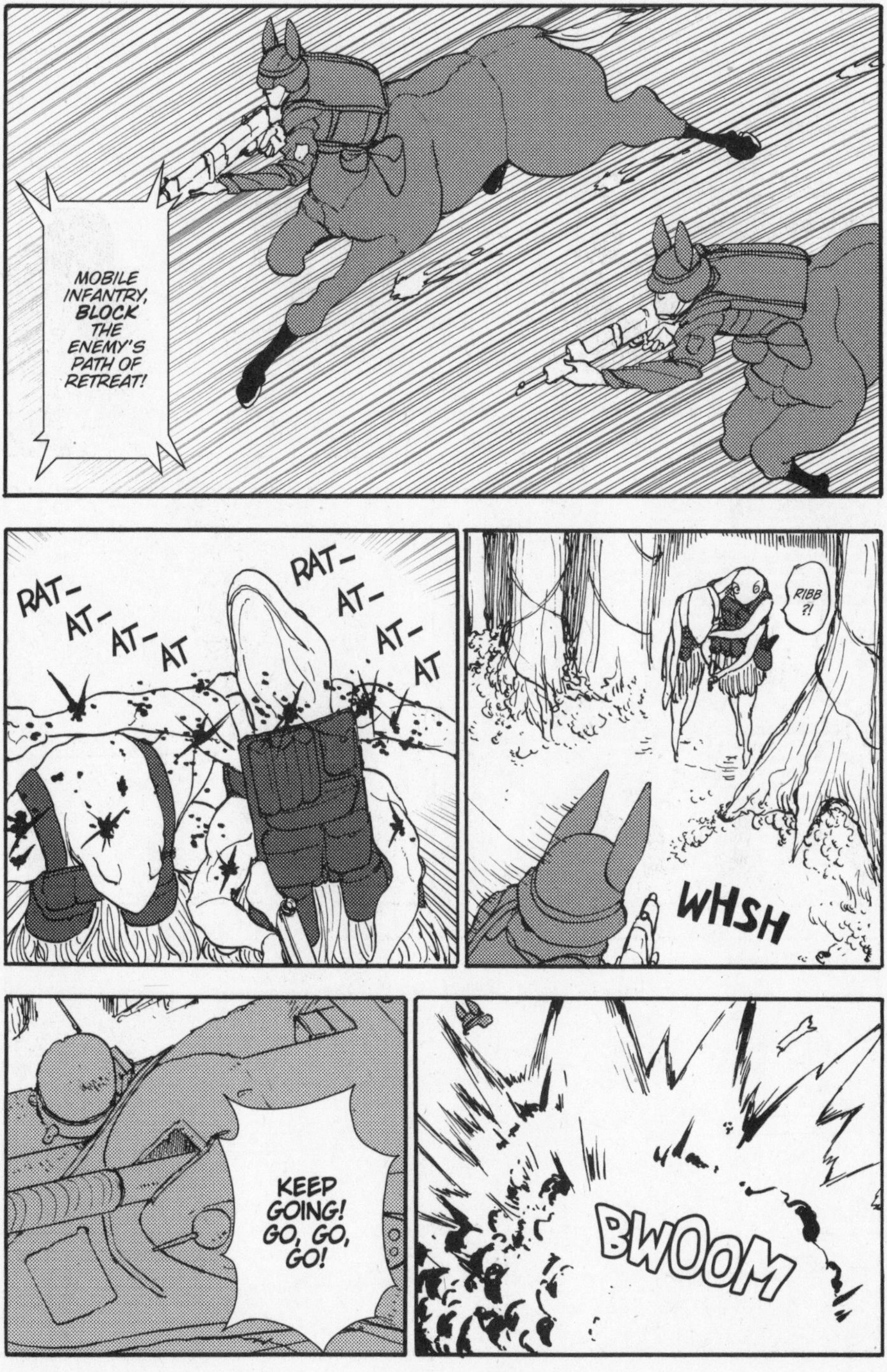
MOBILE INFANTRY, BLOCK THE ENEMY'S PATH OF RETREAT!
RIBB ?!
WHSH
RAT- AT- AT- AT
RAT- AT- AT- AT
BWOOM
KEEP GOING! GO, GO, GO!

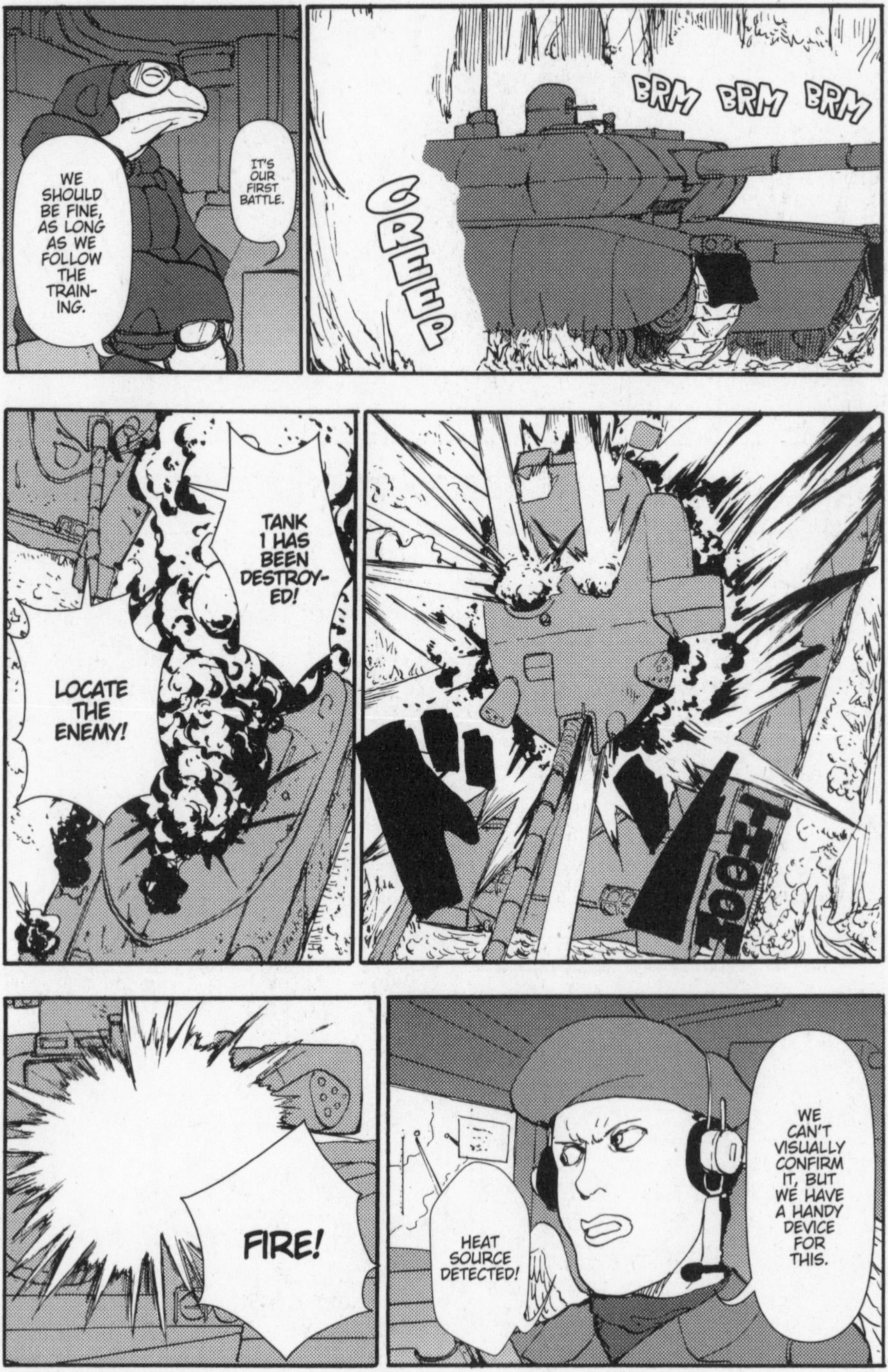
BRM BRM BRM
CREEP
IT'S OUR FIRST BATTLE.
WE SHOULD BE FINE, AS LONG AS WE FOLLOW THE TRAIN-ING.
THOOM
TANK 1 HAS BEEN DESTROY-ED!
LOCATE THE ENEMY!
WE CAN'T VISUALLY CONFIRM IT, BUT WE HAVE A HANDY DEVICE FOR THIS.
HEAT SOURCE DETECTED!
FIRE!

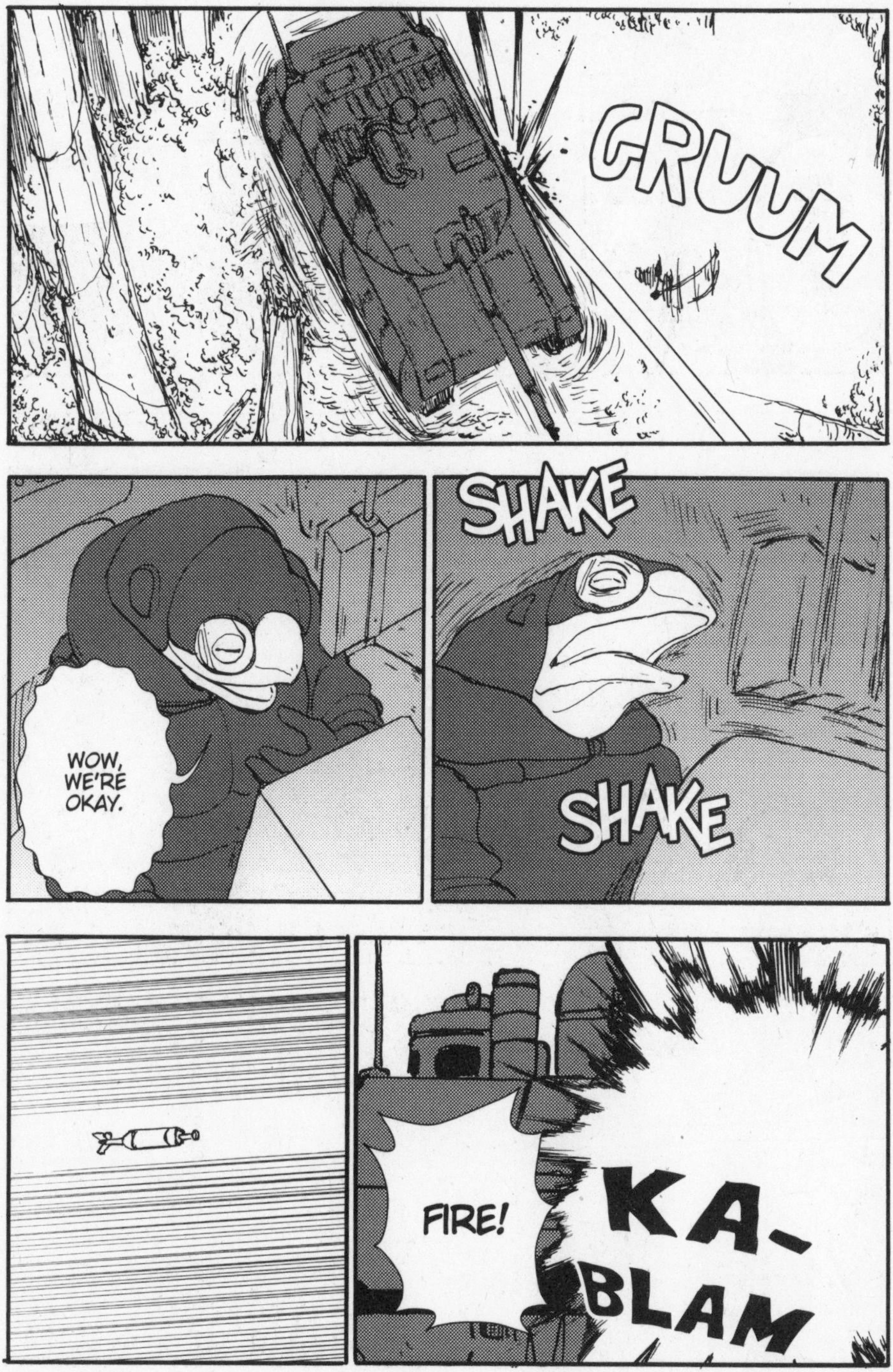
GRUUM
SHAKE
SHAKE
WOW, WE'RE OKAY.
FIRE!
KA-BLAM

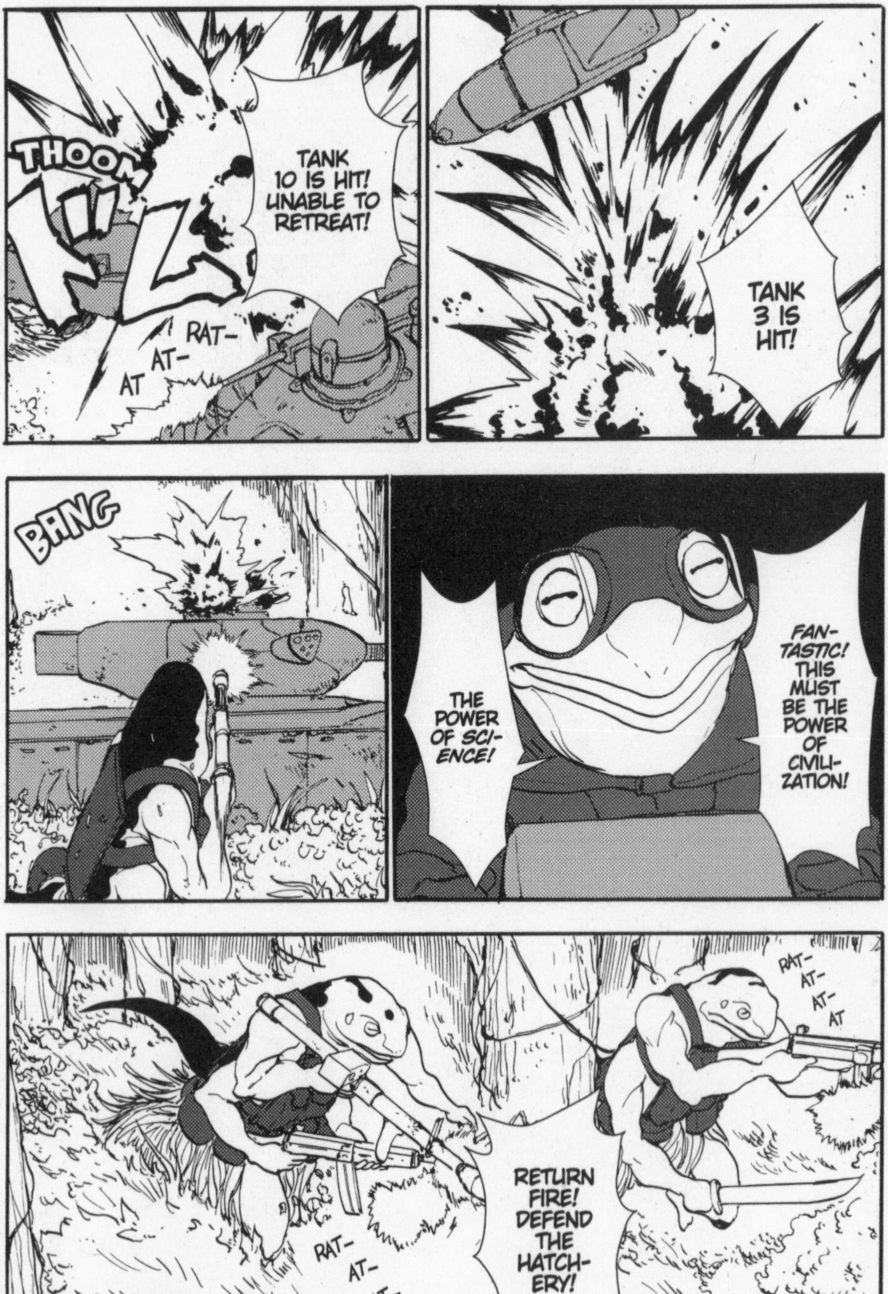
TANK 3 IS HIT!
TANK 10 IS HIT! UNABLE TO RETREAT!
THOOM
RAT- AT- AT
FAN-TASTIC! THIS MUST BE THE POWER OF CIVILI-ZATION!
THE POWER OF SCI-ENCE!
BANG
RAT- AT- AT- AT
RETURN FIRE! DEFEND THE HATCH-ERY!
RAT- AT- AT- AT

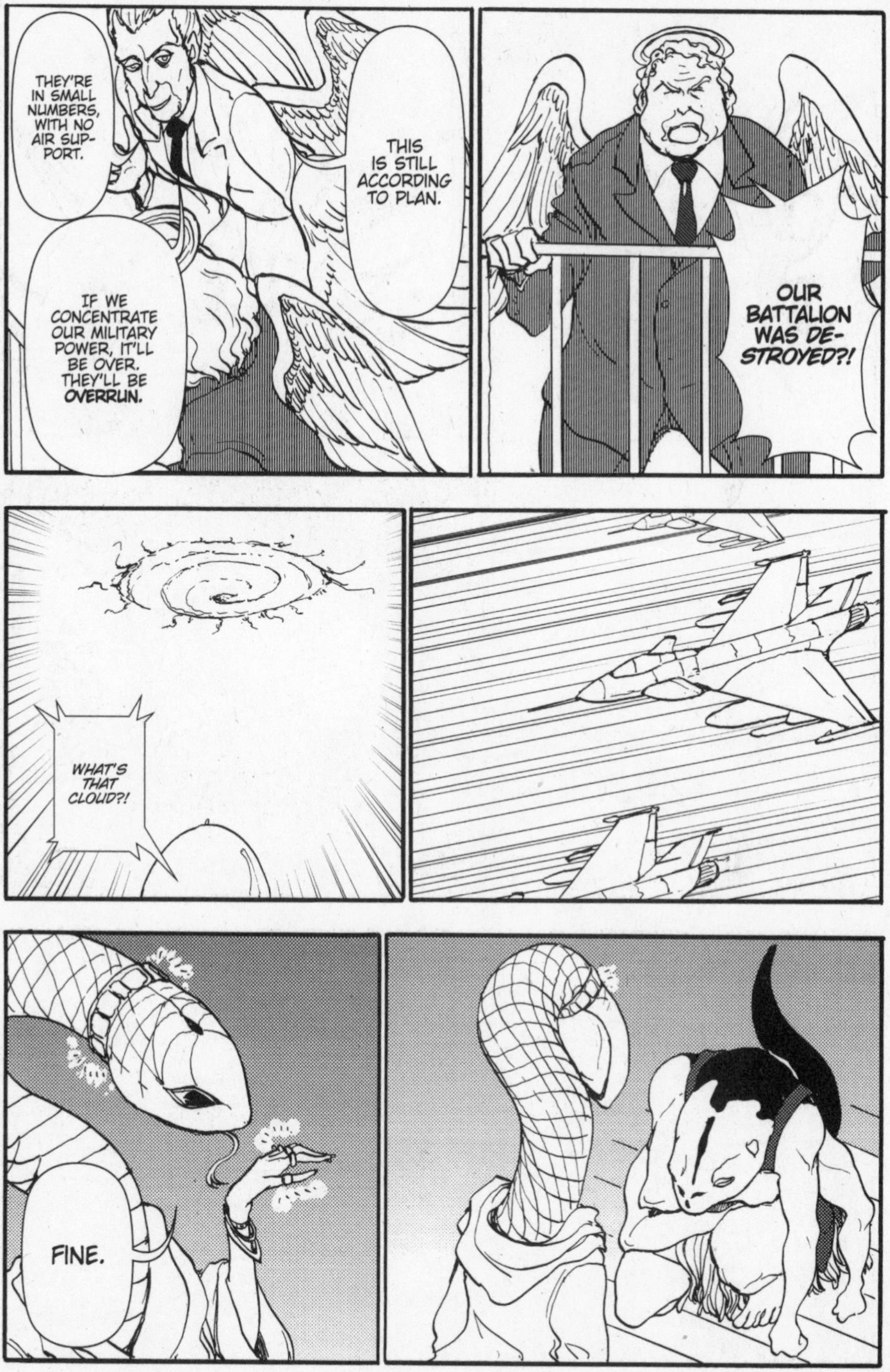
OUR BATTALION WAS DE-STROYED?!
THIS IS STILL ACCORDING TO PLAN.
THEY'RE IN SMALL NUMBERS, WITH NO AIR SUP-PORT.
IF WE CONCENTRATE OUR MILITARY POWER, IT'LL BE OVER. THEY'LL BE **OVERRUN.**
WHAT'S THAT CLOUD?!
FINE.

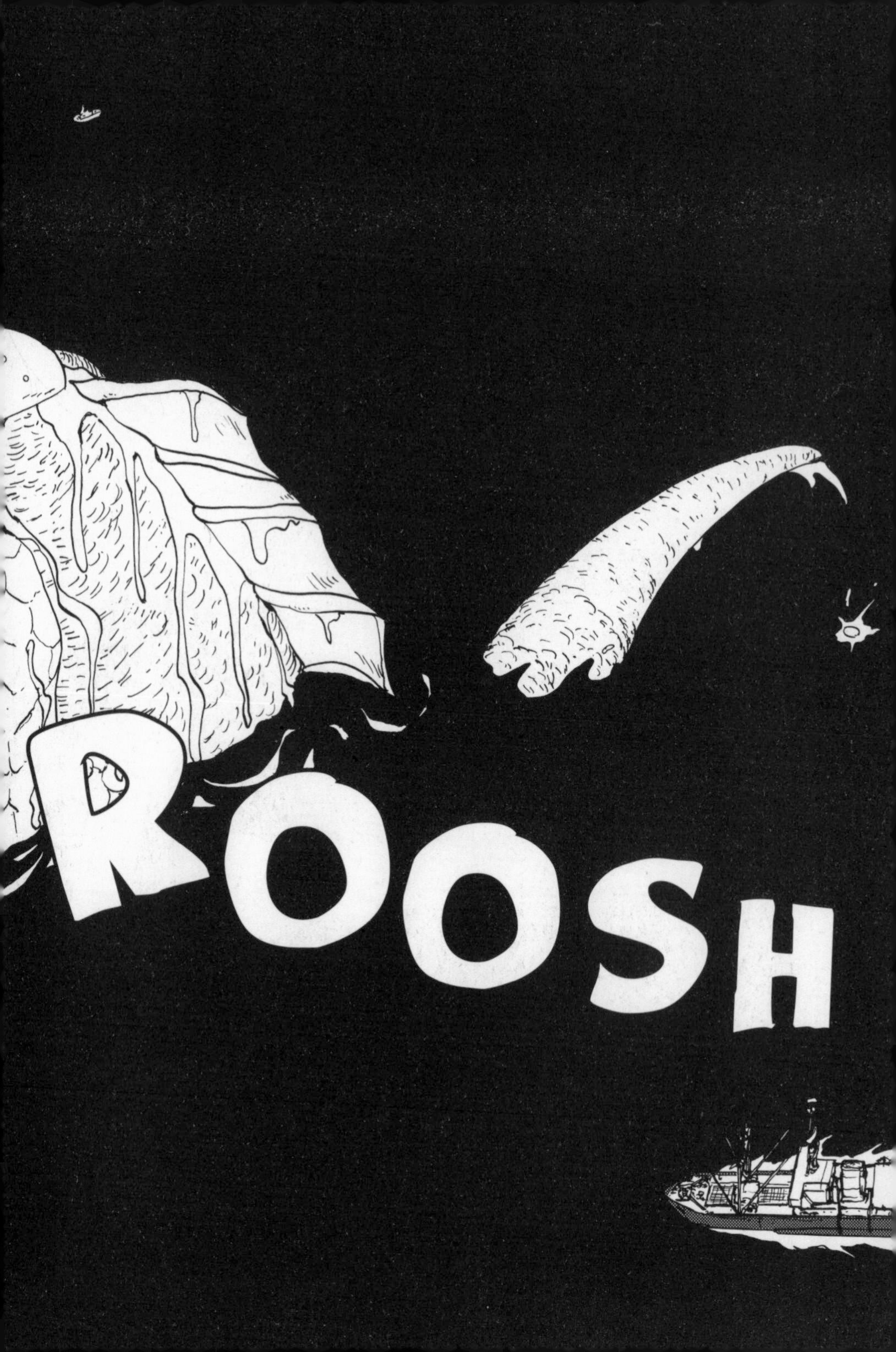
ROOSH

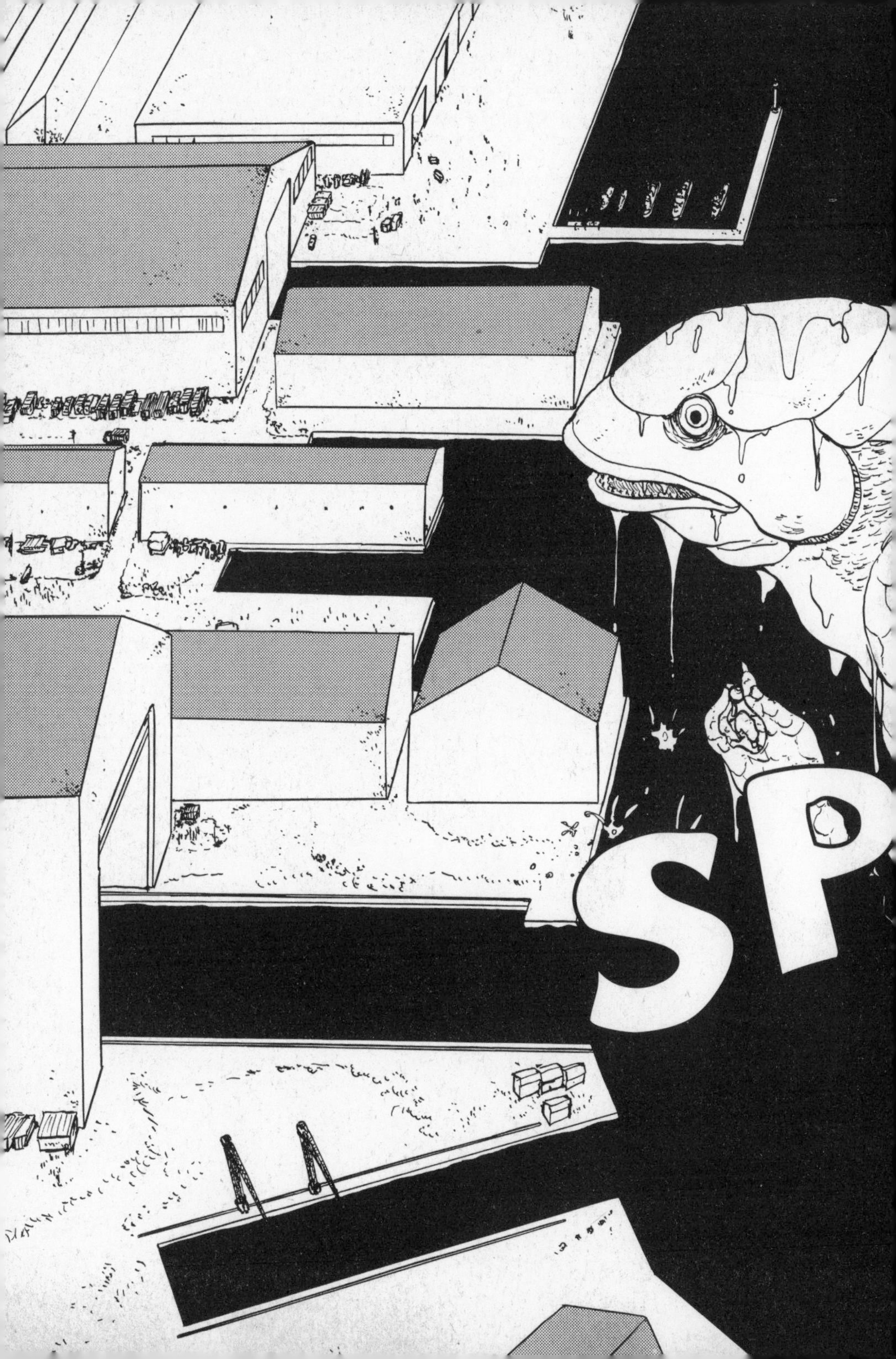
SP

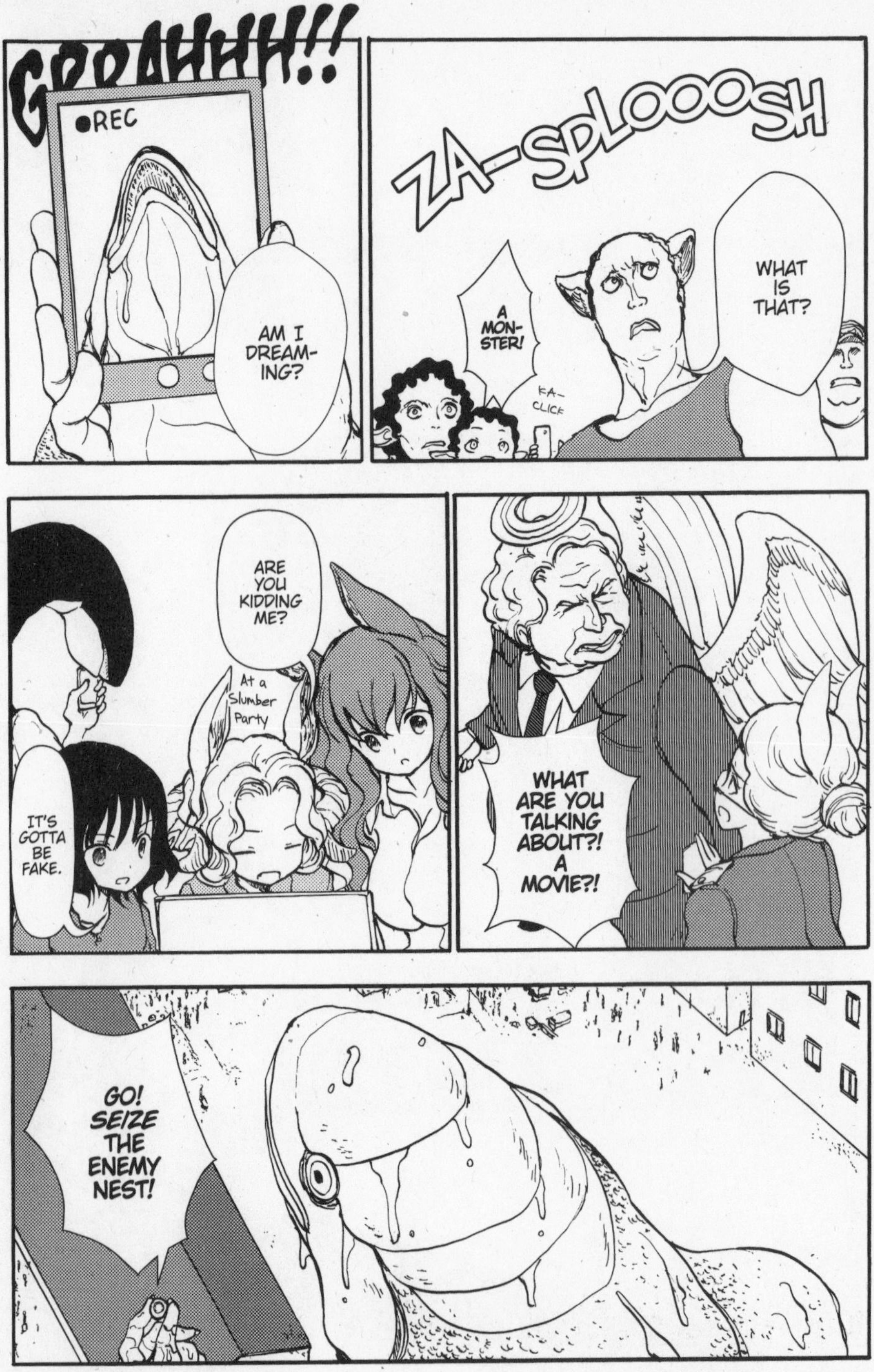
ZA-SPLOOOOSH
WHAT IS THAT?
A MONSTER!
KA-CLICK
GRRAHHH!!
●REC
AM I DREAMING?
WHAT ARE YOU TALKING ABOUT?! A MOVIE?!
ARE YOU KIDDING ME?
At a Slumber Party
IT'S GOTTA BE FAKE.
GO! SEIZE THE ENEMY NEST!

A Centaur's Life

SOLDIERS AROUND THE WORLD:

SAMURAI OF MEDIEVAL JAPAN

SAMURAI ARE SAID TO HAVE ORIGINATED EITHER FROM MILITARY FAMILIES THAT DESCENDED INTO SEVERAL CLANS AND TRACE THEIR LINEAGE BACK TO THE IMPERIAL FAMILY, OR FROM THE WEALTHY, ARMED FARMERS WHO CAME INTO POWER OVER THE REGIONS THEY LIVED IN – THESE THEORIES HAVE SIGNIFICANT PROMINENCE IN THE HISTORICAL COMMUNITY. AS THE DYNASTY'S NORTHWARD EXPANSION ENDED, THE MILITARY CHANGED FROM A LARGE CONQUEST COMPANY COMPOSED OF DRAFTED FARMERS TO RELATIVELY SMALL SECURITY FORCES LED BY EXPERTS IN HIGH MOBILITY. CENTAUR CLANS, SUCH AS MARU, KATA, AND FUJI, COMPRISED SUCH GROUPS.

AS THE SAMURAI CLANS GAINED MORE POWER, HOWEVER, THE ARMY GREW FROM HUNDREDS TO THOUSANDS OF CENTAURS BY THE BEGINNING OF A CONFLICT BETWEEN THE MARU AND KATA CLANS (KNOWN AS THE MATOKATA WAR). SINCE THEY COULDN'T HAVE INCREASED THEIR NUMBERS TRADITIONALLY WITHIN A SINGLE GENERATION, IT'S BELIEVED THAT THEY ABSORBED RULING CLANS OF OTHER REGIONS. LOCAL RULING CLANS FURNISHED THEIR OWN WEAPONS AND ARMOR, AND RODE FARM HORSES TO COMPENSATE FOR THEIR LACK OF MOBILITY AGAINST THE CENTAURS. BECAUSE THEY LACKED THE MARKSMANSHIP THAT COMES ONLY WITH A LIFETIME OF TRAINING, THEY INSTEAD RELIED ON BODY BLOWS, THROWING THEIR WEIGHT AGAINST THEIR ENEMIES TO KNOCKDOWN AND BEHEAD THEM. THESE TACTICS ARE WELL-DOCUMENTED IN THE RECORDS OF THE MATOKATA WAR.

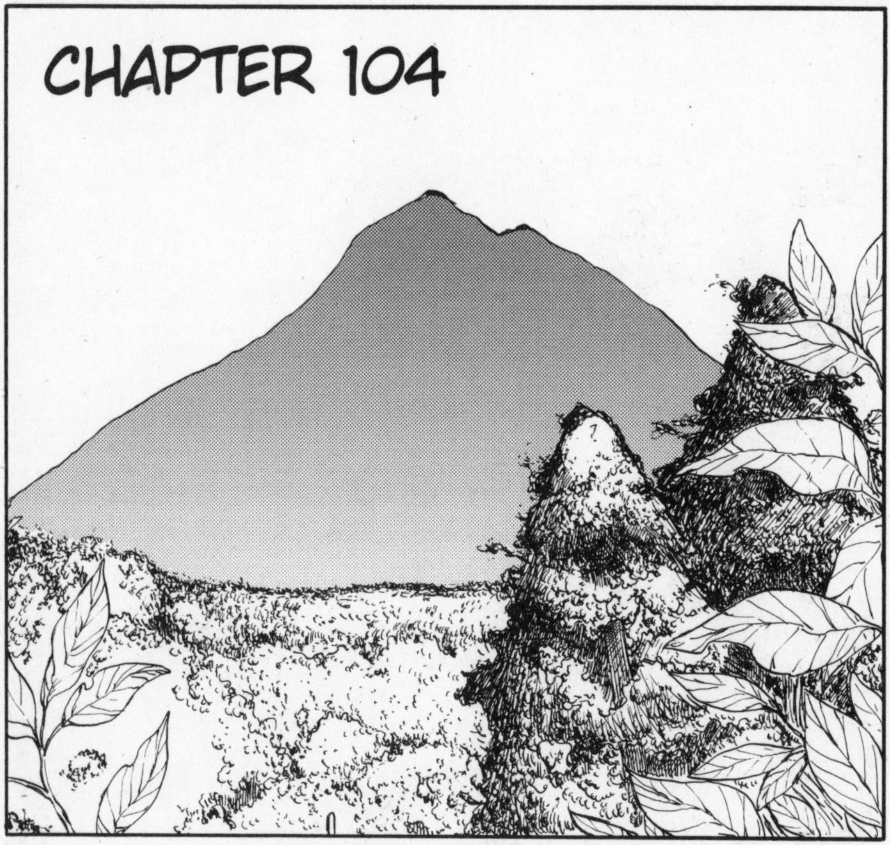
CHAPTER 104
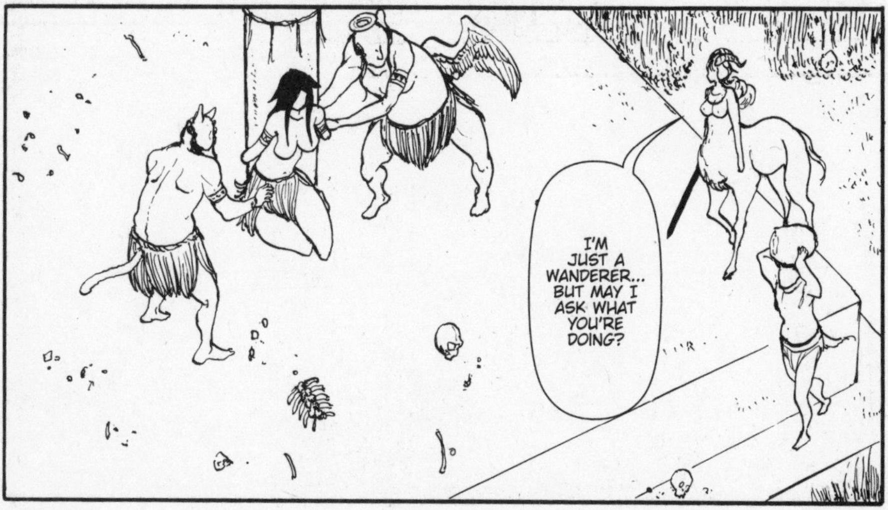
I'M JUST A WANDERER... BUT MAY I ASK WHAT YOU'RE DOING?

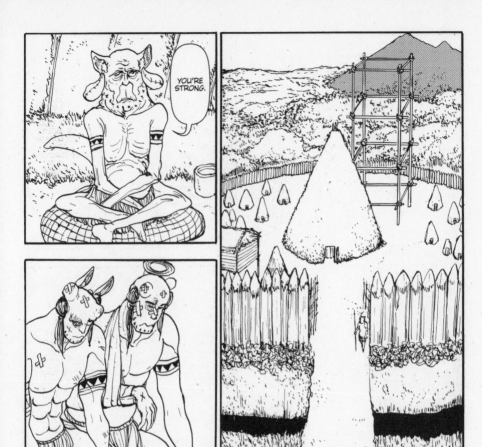

YOU'RE STRONG.
I UNDERSTAND WHAT YOU'RE **CAPABLE** OF.
BUT WE CAN'T STOP OUR SACRIFICIAL RITUAL NOW.

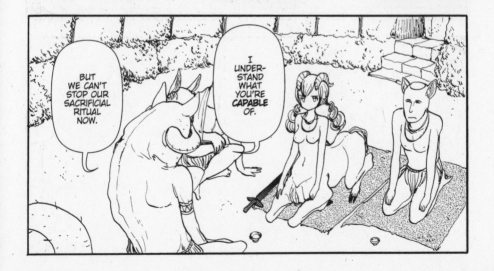

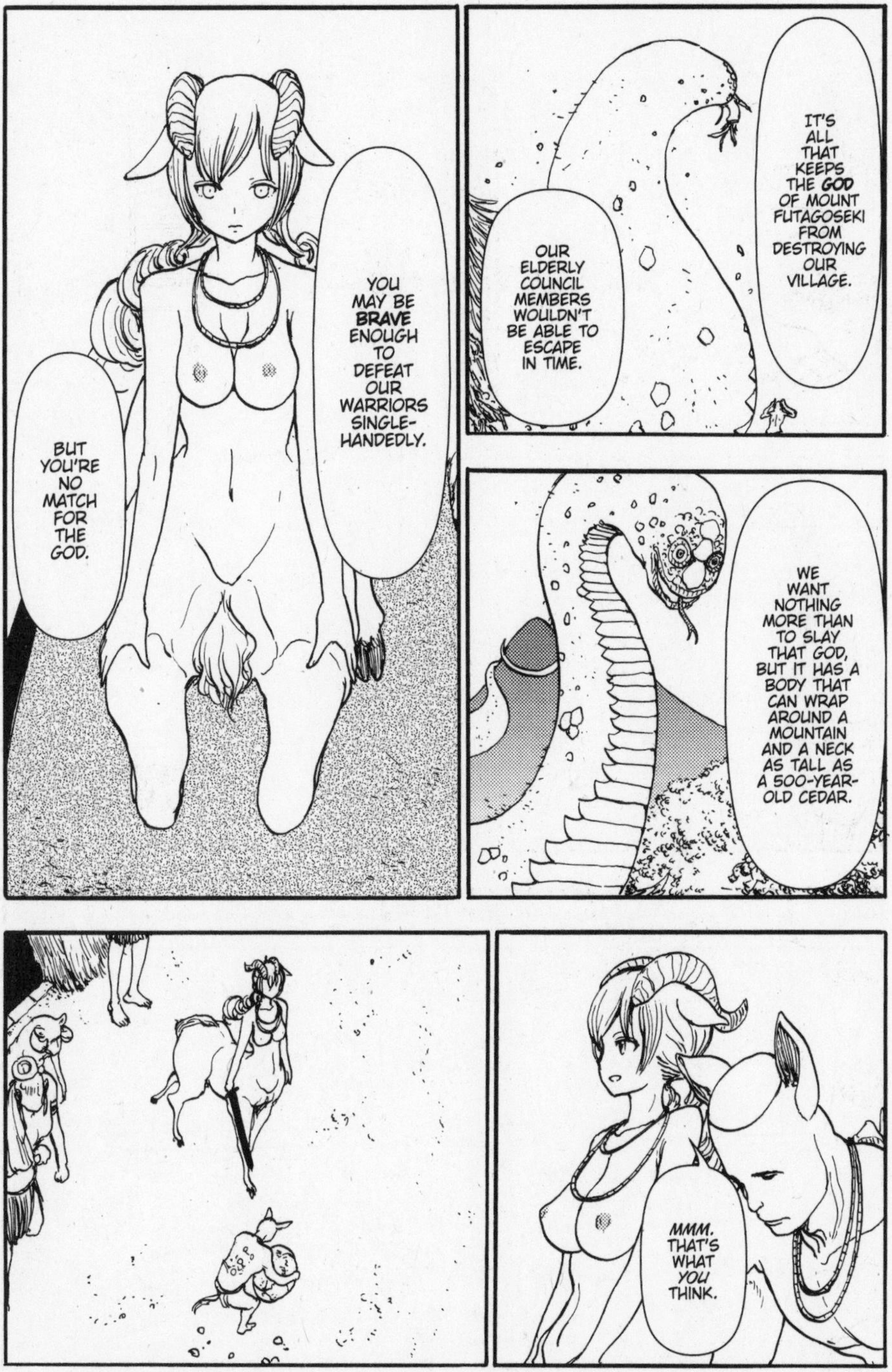
IT'S ALL THAT KEEPS THE **GOD** OF MOUNT FUTAGOSEKI FROM DESTROYING OUR VILLAGE.
OUR ELDERLY COUNCIL MEMBERS WOULDN'T BE ABLE TO ESCAPE IN TIME.
WE WANT NOTHING MORE THAN TO SLAY THAT GOD, BUT IT HAS A BODY THAT CAN WRAP AROUND A MOUNTAIN AND A NECK AS TALL AS A 500-YEAR-OLD CEDAR.
YOU MAY BE **BRAVE** ENOUGH TO DEFEAT OUR WARRIORS SINGLE-HANDEDLY.
BUT YOU'RE NO MATCH FOR THE GOD.
MMM. THAT'S WHAT *YOU* THINK.

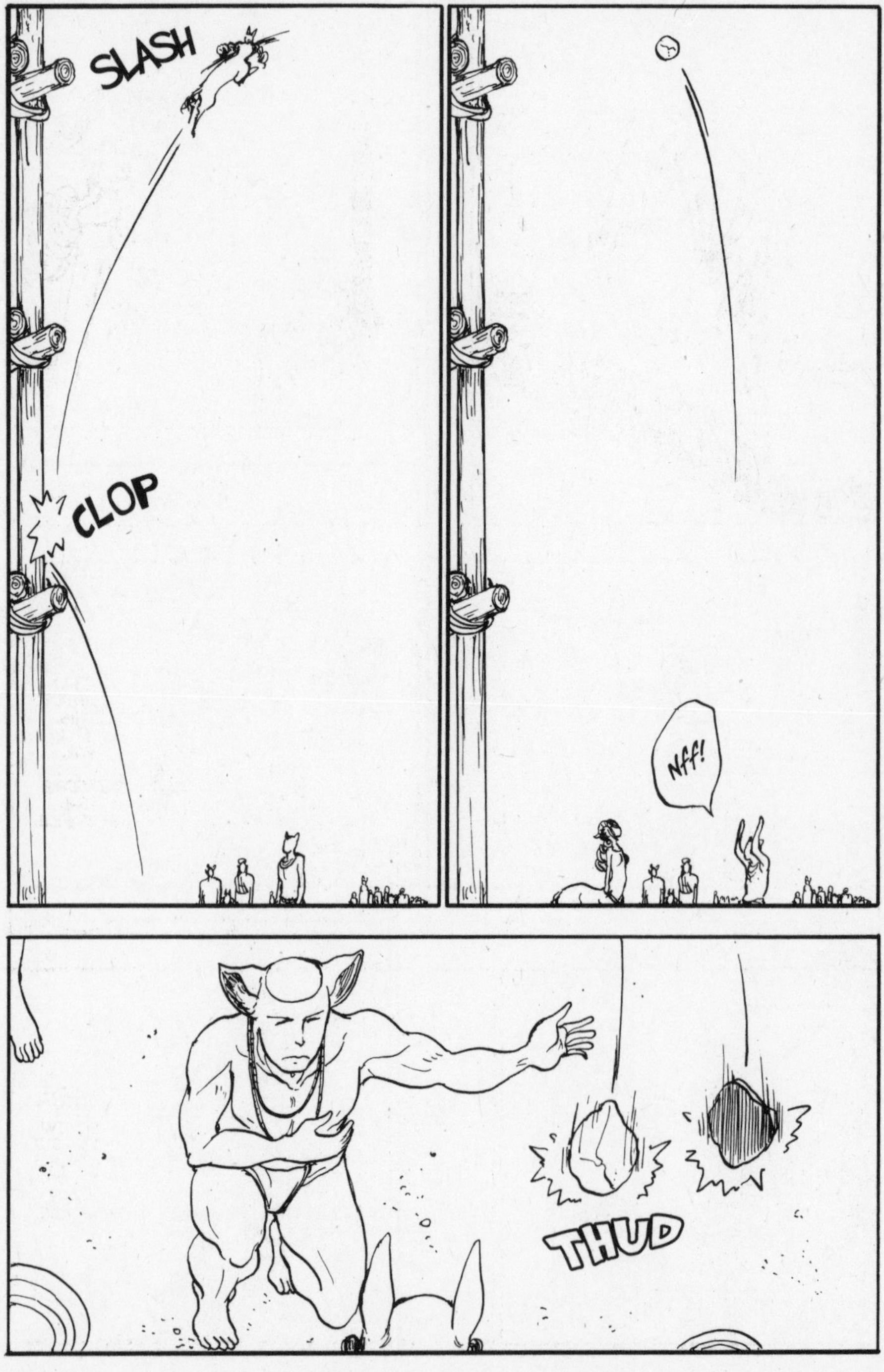
SLASH
CLOP
Nff!
THUD

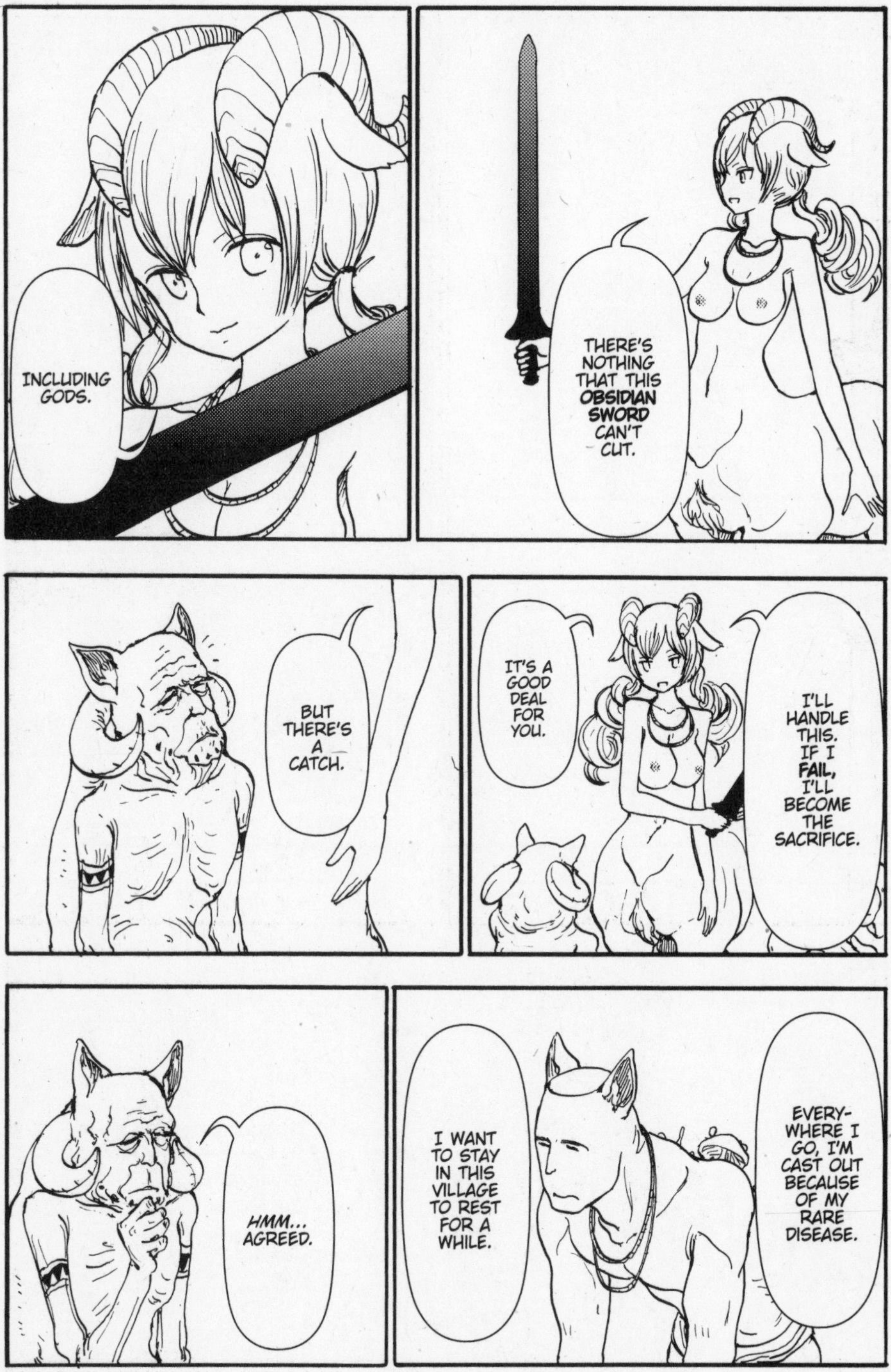
THERE'S NOTHING THAT THIS OBSIDIAN SWORD CAN'T CUT.
INCLUDING GODS.
I'LL HANDLE THIS. IF I FAIL, I'LL BECOME THE SACRIFICE.
IT'S A GOOD DEAL FOR YOU.
BUT THERE'S A CATCH.
EVERY-WHERE I GO, I'M CAST OUT BECAUSE OF MY RARE DISEASE.
I WANT TO STAY IN THIS VILLAGE TO REST FOR A WHILE.
HMM... AGREED.

POOFF
GUWAA!

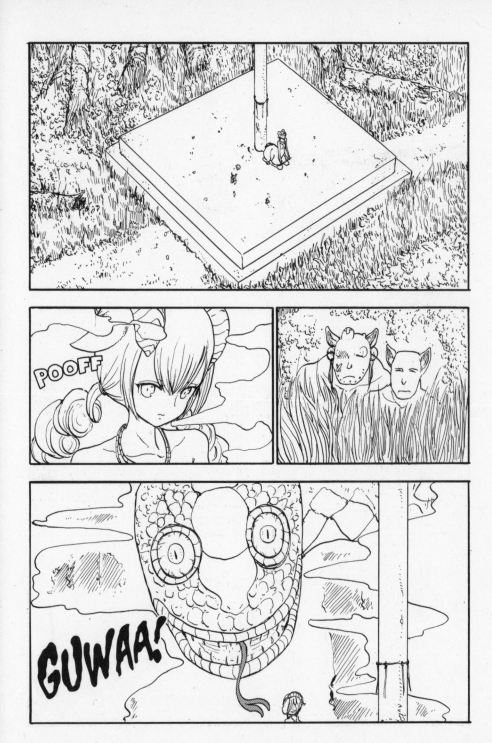

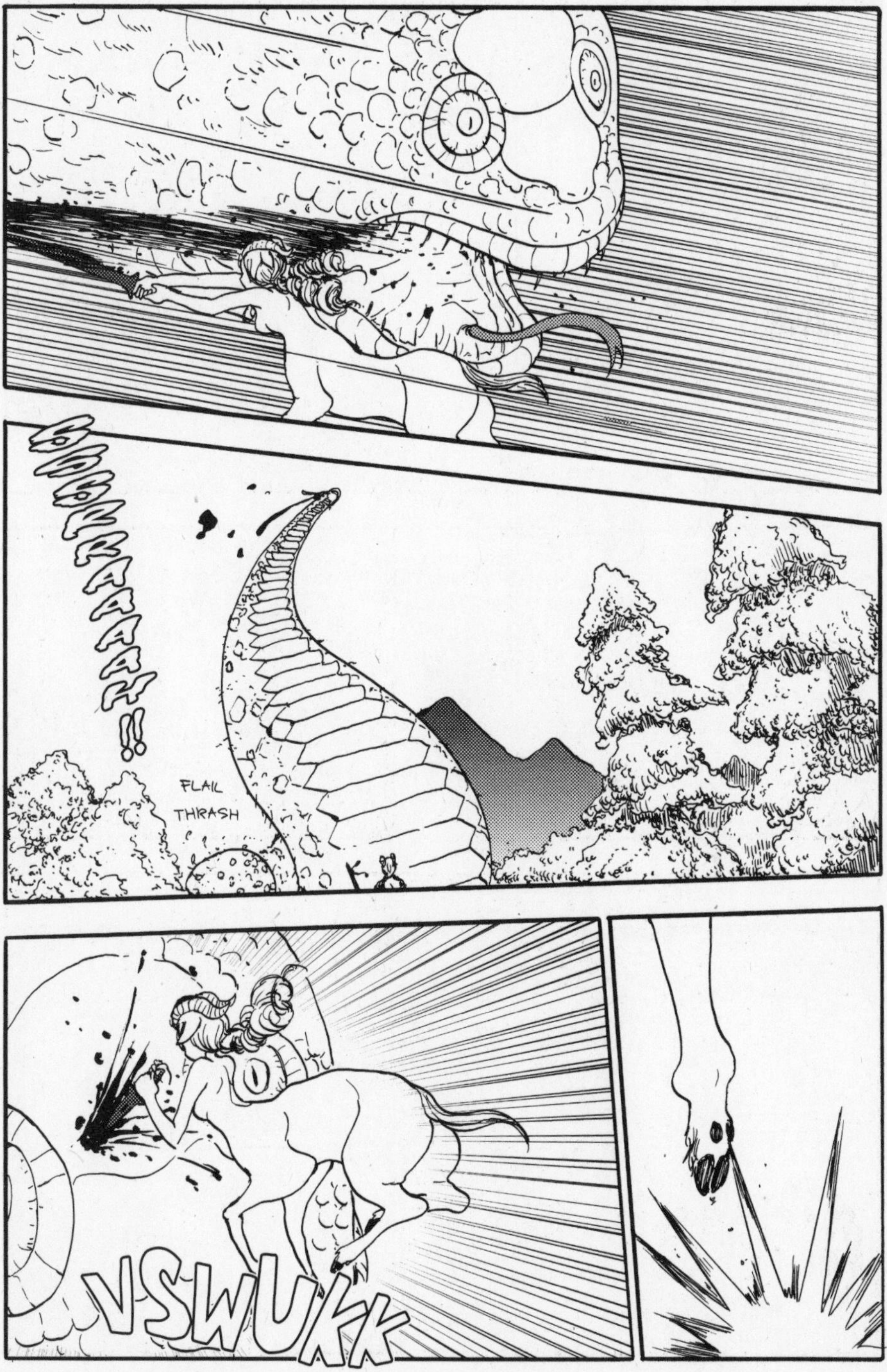
FLAIL
THRASH
VSWUKK

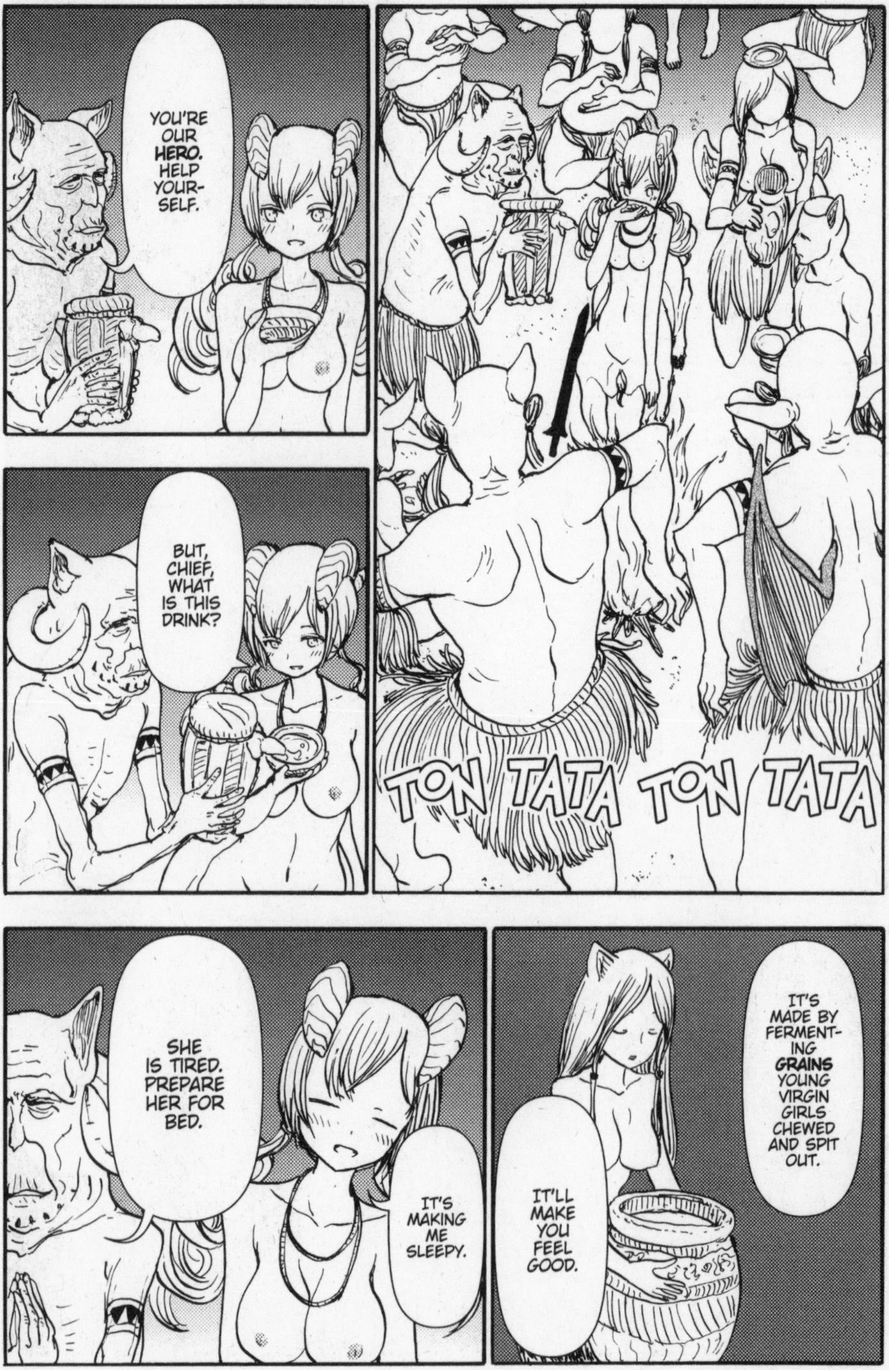
TON TATA TON TATA
YOU'RE OUR **HERO.** HELP YOURSELF.
BUT, CHIEF, WHAT IS THIS DRINK?
IT'S MADE BY FERMENTING **GRAINS** YOUNG VIRGIN GIRLS CHEWED AND SPIT OUT.
IT'LL MAKE YOU FEEL GOOD.
IT'S MAKING ME SLEEPY.
SHE IS TIRED. PREPARE HER FOR BED.

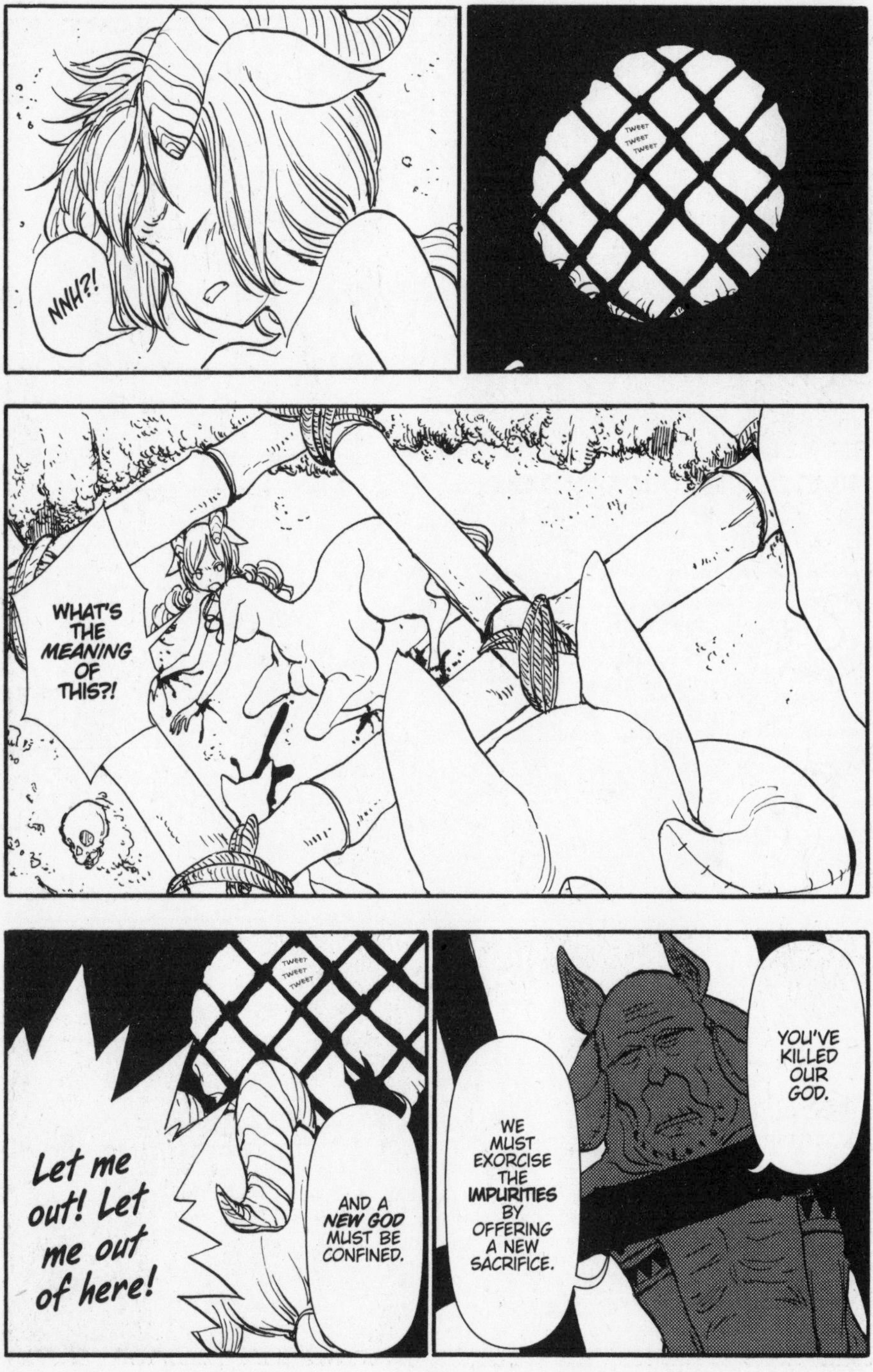
TWEET TWEET TWEET
NNH?!
WHAT'S THE MEANING OF THIS?!
YOU'VE KILLED OUR GOD.
WE MUST EXORCISE THE IMPURITIES BY OFFERING A NEW SACRIFICE.
TWEET TWEET TWEET
AND A NEW GOD MUST BE CONFINED.
Let me out! Let me out of here!

IT'S A NATURAL CAVERN.

SO, THE MYTH *IS* TRUE.

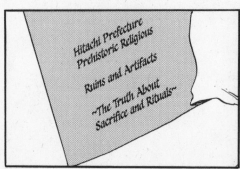

Hitachi Prefecture
Prehistoric Religious

Ruins and Artifacts

~The Truth About
Sacrifice and Rituals~

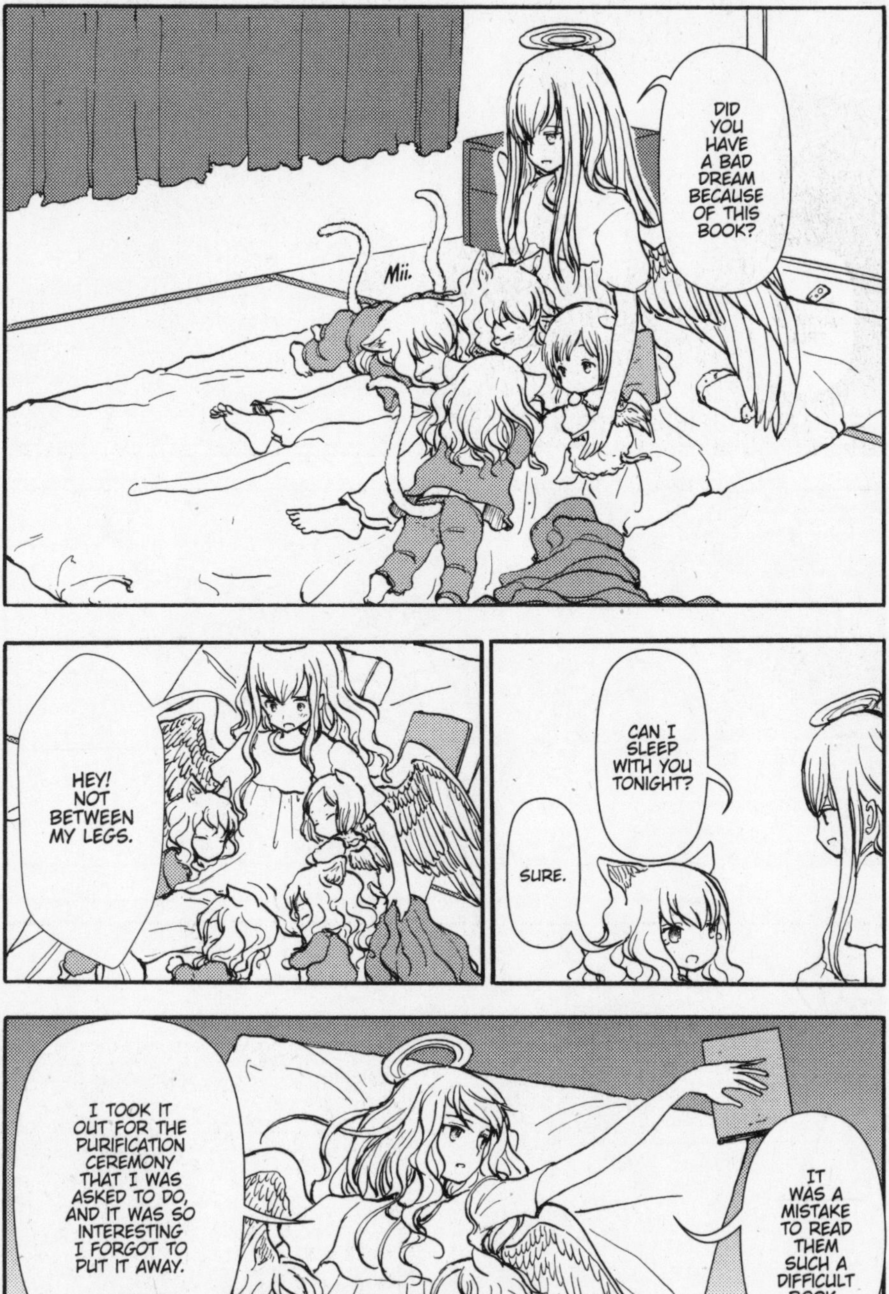
DID YOU HAVE A BAD DREAM BECAUSE OF THIS BOOK?
Mii.
CAN I SLEEP WITH YOU TONIGHT?
SURE.
HEY! NOT BETWEEN MY LEGS.
IT WAS A MISTAKE TO READ THEM SUCH A DIFFICULT BOOK.
I TOOK IT OUT FOR THE PURIFICATION CEREMONY THAT I WAS ASKED TO DO, AND IT WAS SO INTERESTING I FORGOT TO PUT IT AWAY.

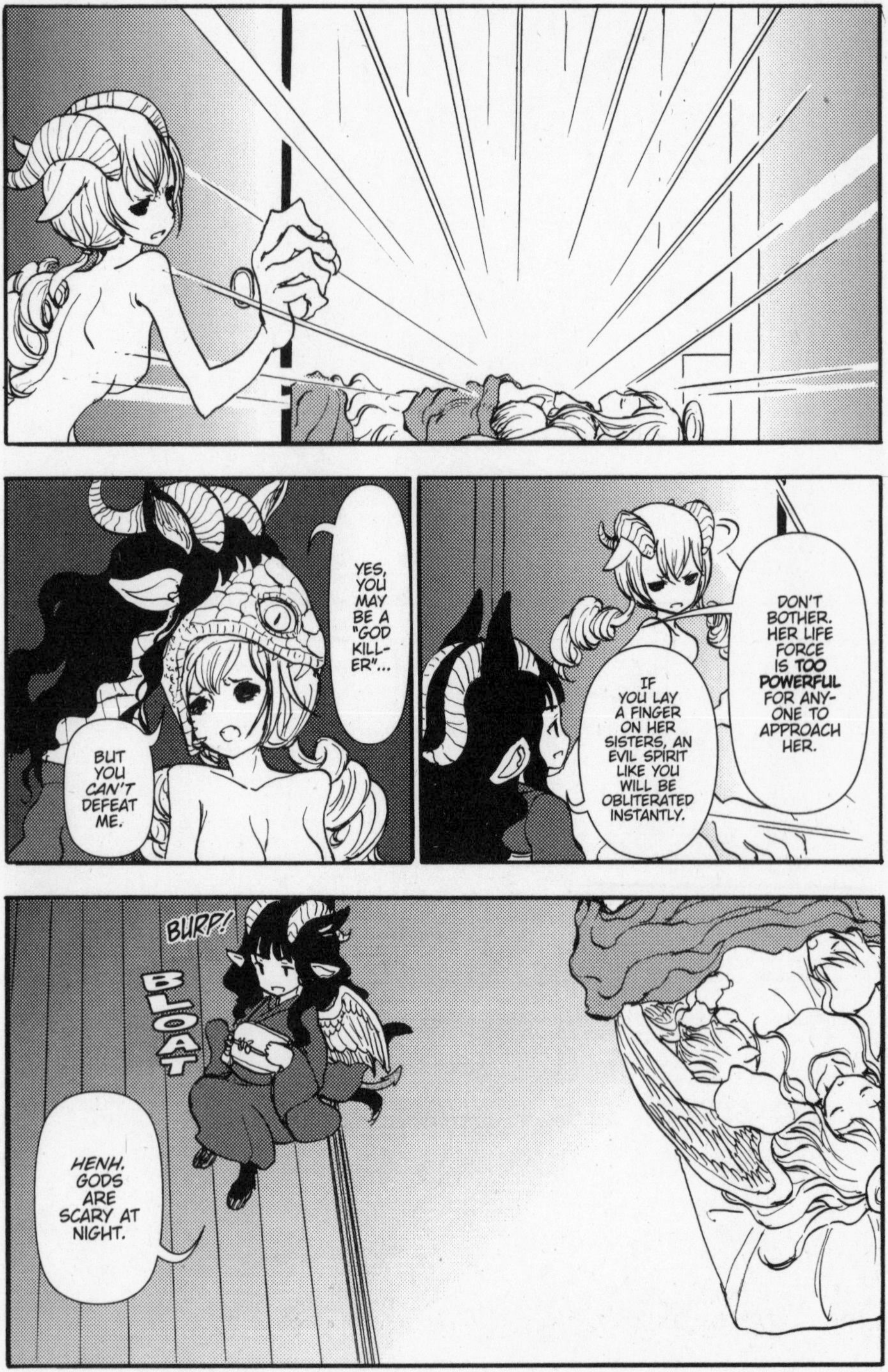
DON'T BOTHER. HER LIFE FORCE IS **TOO POWERFUL** FOR ANYONE TO APPROACH HER.
IF YOU LAY A FINGER ON HER SISTERS, AN EVIL SPIRIT LIKE YOU WILL BE OBLITERATED INSTANTLY.
YES, YOU MAY BE A "GOD KILLER"...
BUT YOU CAN'T DEFEAT ME.
BURP!
BLOAT
HENH. GODS ARE SCARY AT NIGHT.

A Centaur's Life

SOLDIERS AROUND THE WORLD:
NORMAN KNIGHTS

WHEN THINKING OF EUROPEAN KNIGHTS, ONE USUALLY ENVISIONS A MAN IN PLATE ARMOR ASTRIDE A HORSE. HOWEVER, THE NUMBER OF HORSES USED SOLELY FOR RIDING WAS LIMITED, AND THEY WERE LARGELY CONSIDERED A STATUS SYMBOL FOR ARISTOCRATS; MOST OF THE KNIGHTS ON THE FRONT LINES WERE ON HORSEBACK. PLATE ARMOR APPEARED LATE IN THE HISTORY OF ARMOR, AND WAS RENDERED OBSOLETE BY THE DEVELOPMENT OF FIREARMS.

THE ILLUSTRATION ABOVE DEPICTS A TYPICAL 11TH CENTURY NORMAN KNIGHT. THE NORMANS WERE OF VIKING ORIGIN, AND IN THE 8TH CENTURY THEY BEGAN TO INVADE, CONQUER, AND ESTABLISH DYNASTIES ALL OVER EUROPE. THESE INCLUDED THE RURIK DYNASTY IN RUSSIA, THE KINGDOM OF SICILY IN SICILY, THE DUCHY OF NORMANDY IN NORTHERN FRANCE, AND LATER THE ANGEVIN EMPIRE IN FRANCE AND ENGLAND. THE COUNT OF ANJOU WAS IN THE ODD POSITION OF BEING THE AGNATIC DESCENDANT OF FRENCH NOBILITY AS WELL AS THE KING OF ENGLAND.

THE SUCCESS OF THE NORMAN CONQUEST WAS MADE POSSIBLE BY THEIR POWERFUL CAVALRY CHARGES. THEIR ARMOR AND WOOD-FRAMED SADDLES, ACQUIRED FROM THE AVARS IN THE INVASION OF CENTRAL EUROPE, HELD THE CAVALRYMAN'S BODY STEADY AND HELPED HIM KEEP HIS FOOTING. COUCHING A LANCE UNDER HIS ARM ENABLED THE CAVALRYMAN TO UTILIZE THE MOMENTUM OF THE HORSE IN HIS STRIKE, THE DEADLIEST TACTIC OF THE EUROPEAN KNIGHTS.

I can't get you...!

PITTER PATTER

CLOP CLOP CLOP

WOOF WOOF

HERE I COME!

Hee hee!

NNH... TAG!

OH DARN, YOU CAUGHT ME.

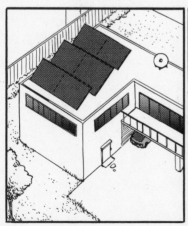

Almost got you~!

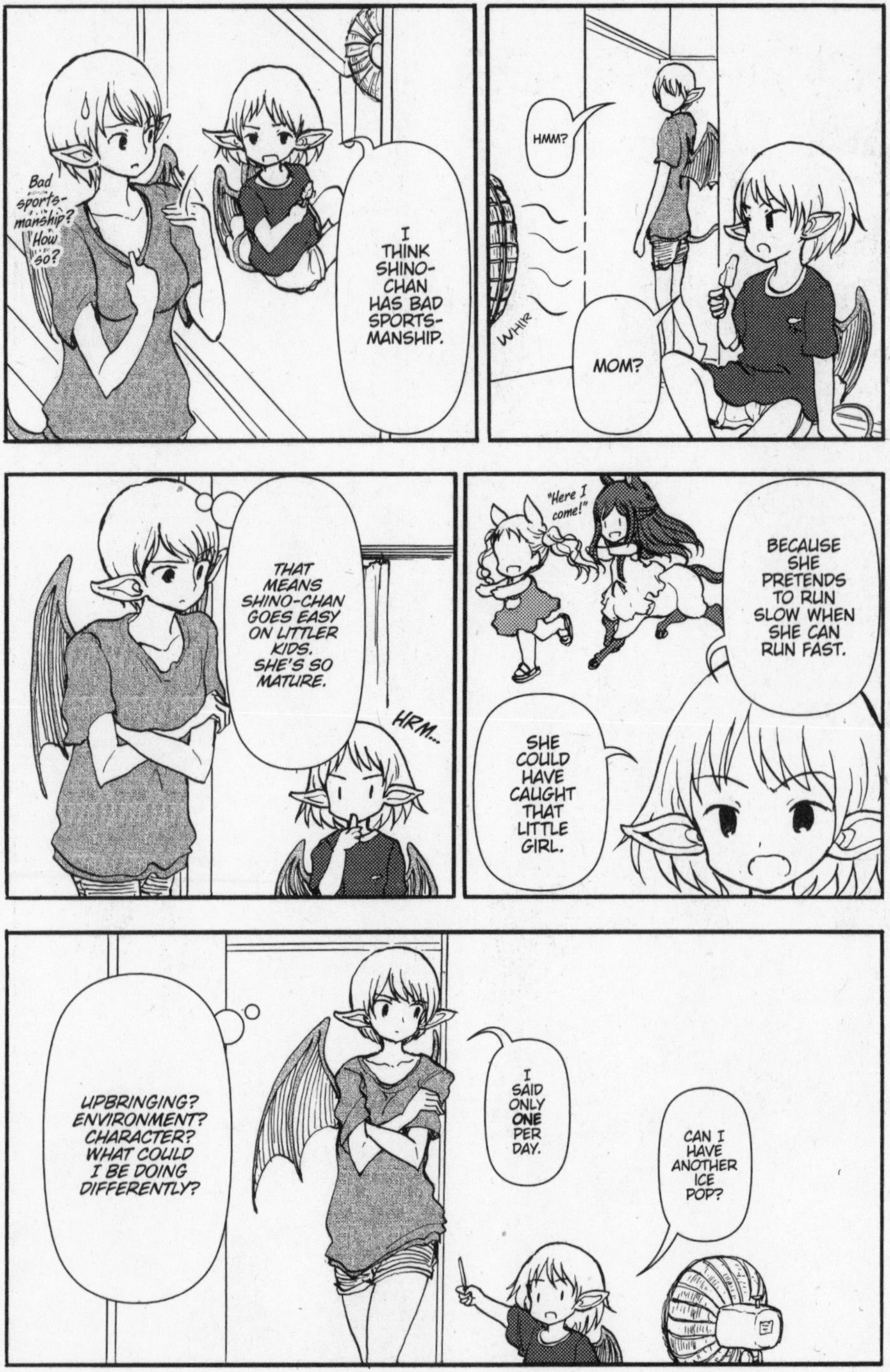
MOM?
HMM?
WHIR
I THINK SHINO-CHAN HAS BAD SPORTSMANSHIP.
Bad sportsmanship? How so?
BECAUSE SHE PRETENDS TO RUN SLOW WHEN SHE CAN RUN FAST.
"Here I come!"
SHE COULD HAVE CAUGHT THAT LITTLE GIRL.
THAT MEANS SHINO-CHAN GOES EASY ON LITTLER KIDS. SHE'S SO MATURE.
HRM...
CAN I HAVE ANOTHER ICE POP?
I SAID ONLY ONE PER DAY.
UPBRINGING? ENVIRONMENT? CHARACTER? WHAT COULD I BE DOING DIFFERENTLY?

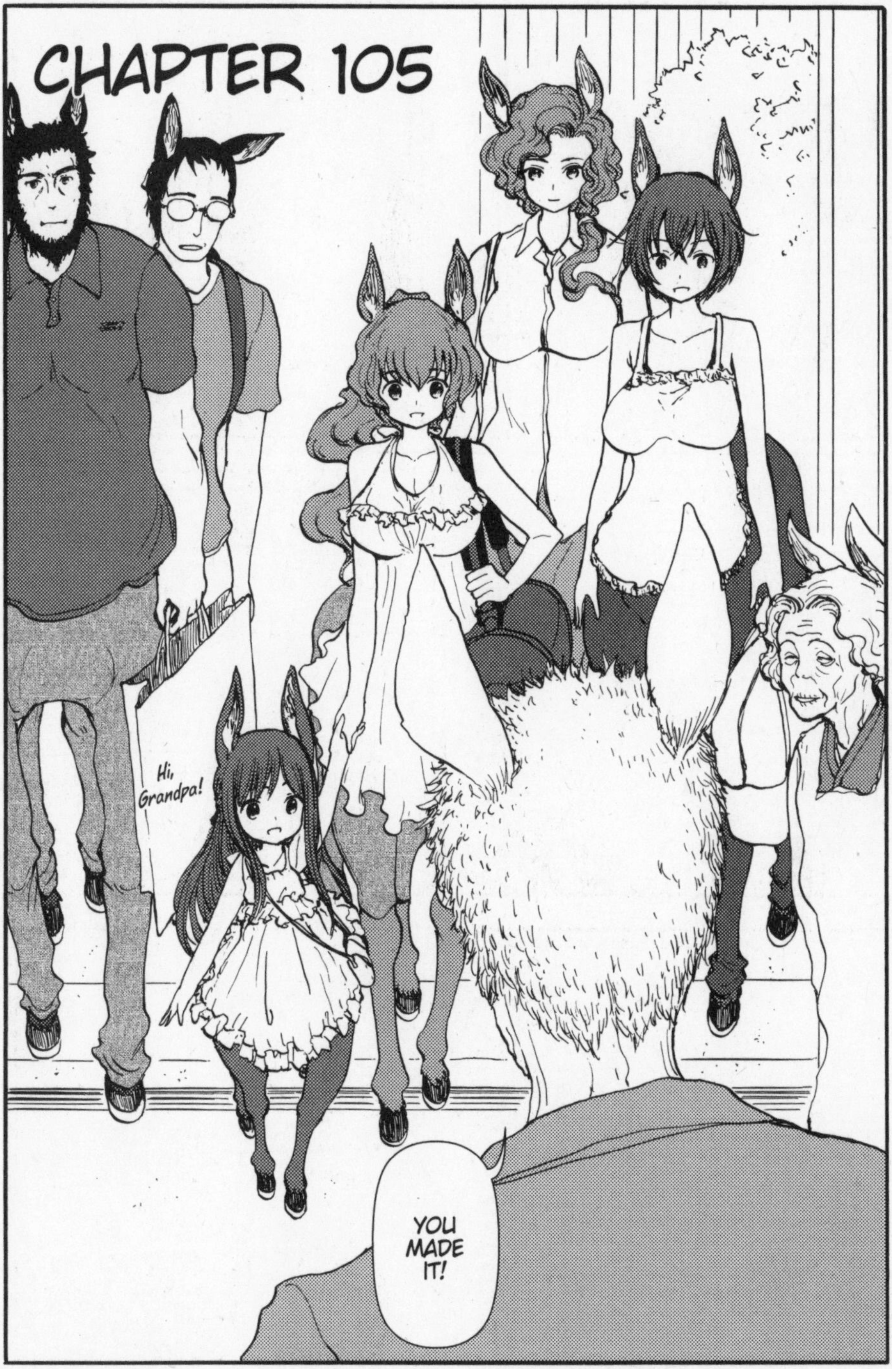
CHAPTER 105
Hi, Grandpa!
YOU MADE IT!

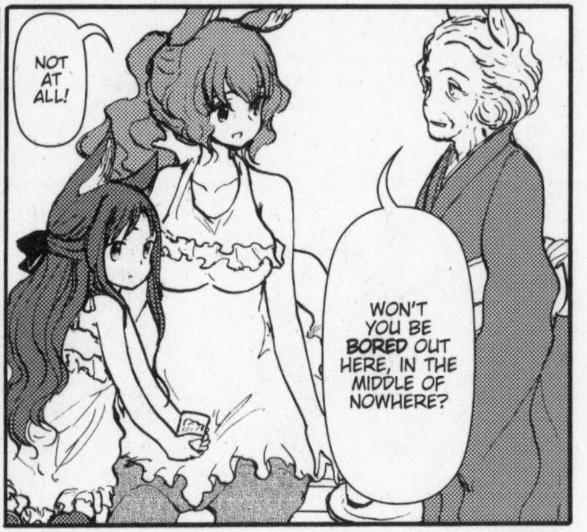
WON'T YOU BE BORED OUT HERE, IN THE MIDDLE OF NOWHERE?
NOT AT ALL!

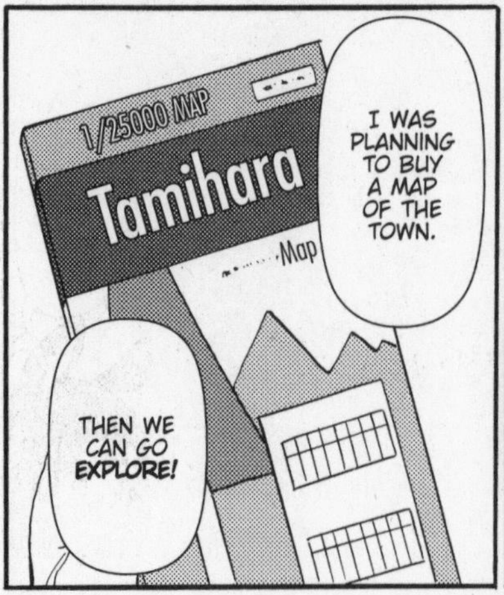
I WAS PLANNING TO BUY A MAP OF THE TOWN.
1/25000 MAP
Tamihara
Map
THEN WE CAN GO EXPLORE!

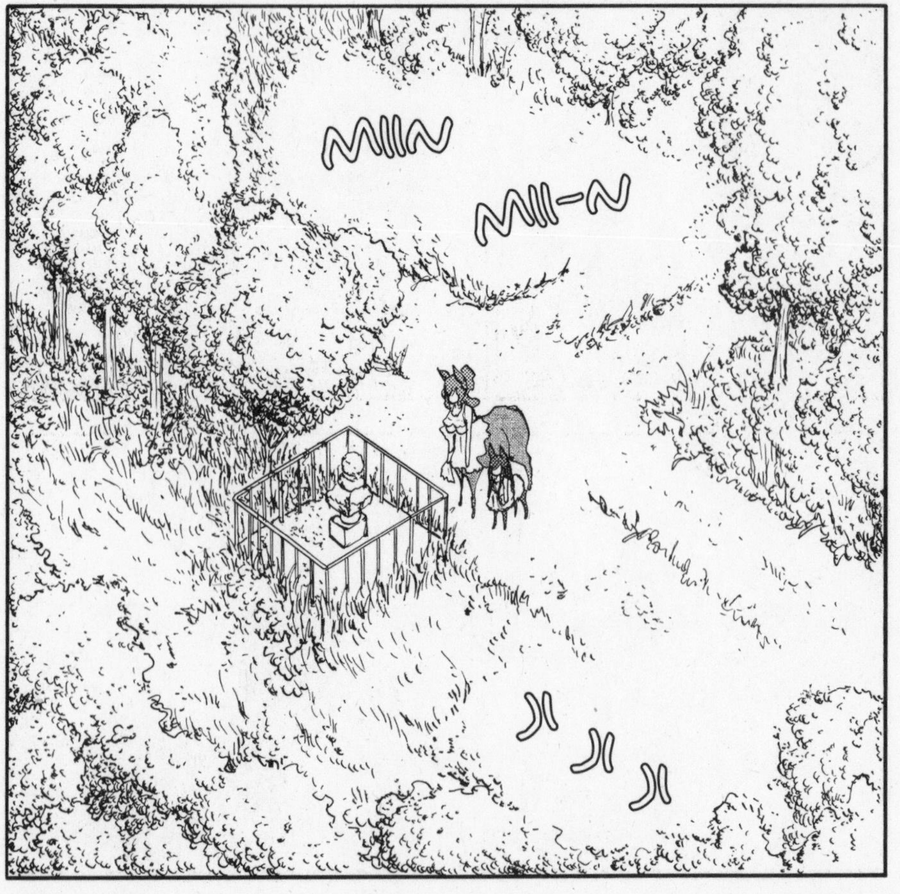
MIIN
MII-N

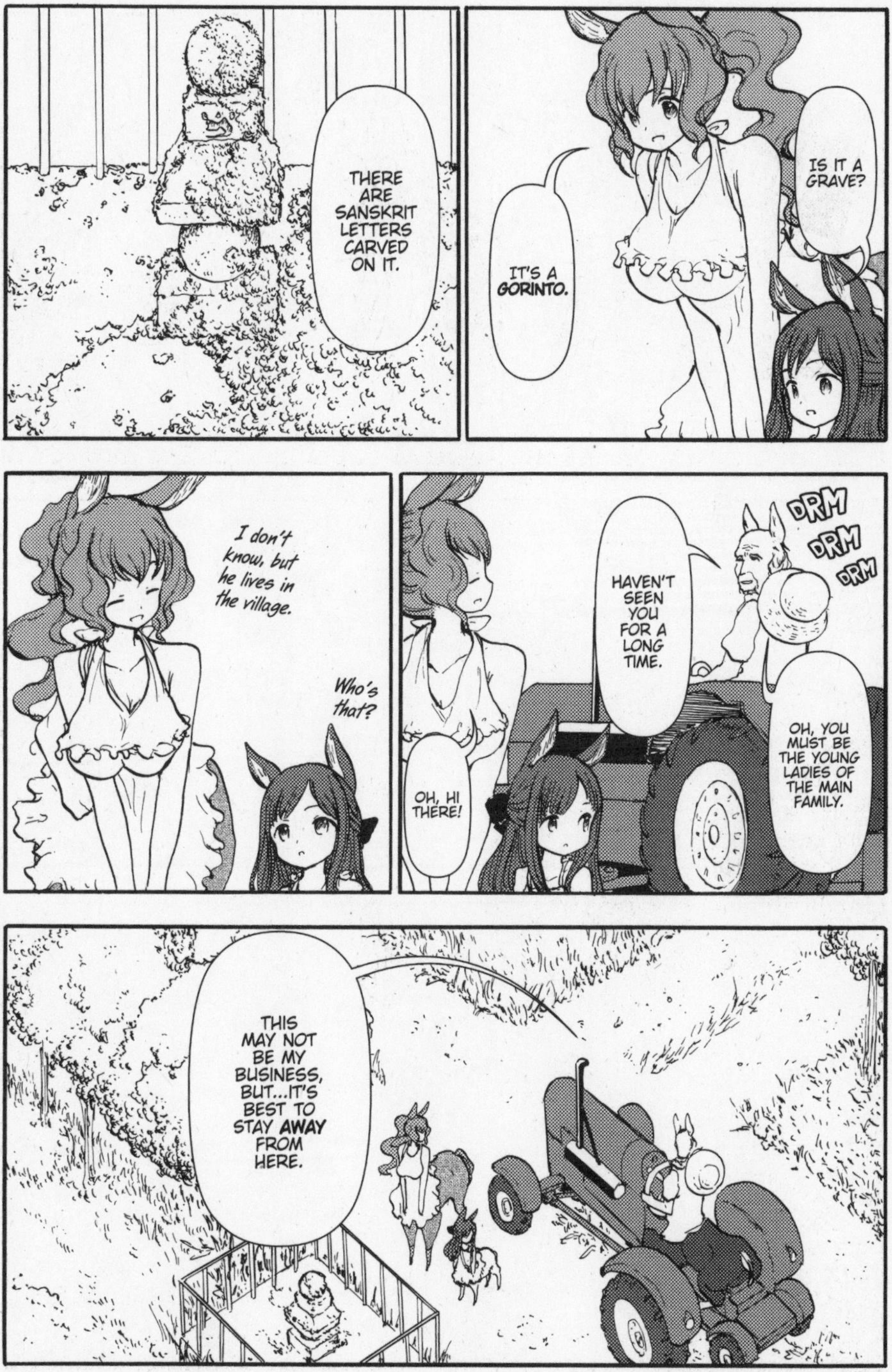
IS IT A GRAVE?
IT'S A **GORINTO.**
THERE ARE SANSKRIT LETTERS CARVED ON IT.
DRM DRM DRM
HAVEN'T SEEN YOU FOR A LONG TIME.
OH, YOU MUST BE THE YOUNG LADIES OF THE MAIN FAMILY.
OH, HI THERE!
Who's that?
I don't know, but he lives in the village.
THIS MAY NOT BE MY BUSINESS, BUT...IT'S BEST TO STAY **AWAY** FROM HERE.

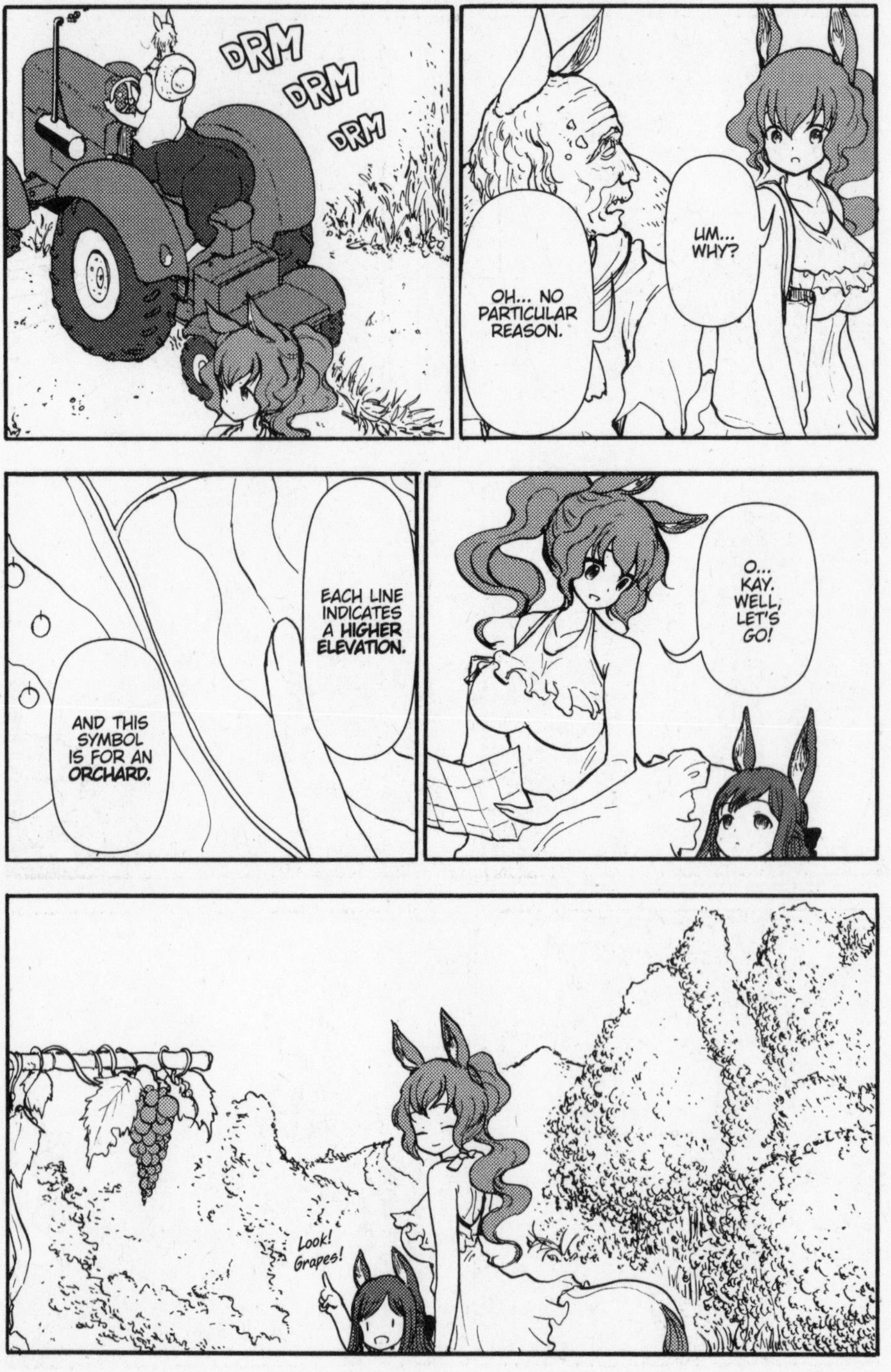
UM... WHY?
OH... NO PARTICULAR REASON.
DRM
DRM
DRM
O... KAY. WELL, LET'S GO!
EACH LINE INDICATES A HIGHER ELEVATION.
AND THIS SYMBOL IS FOR AN ORCHARD.
Look! Grapes!

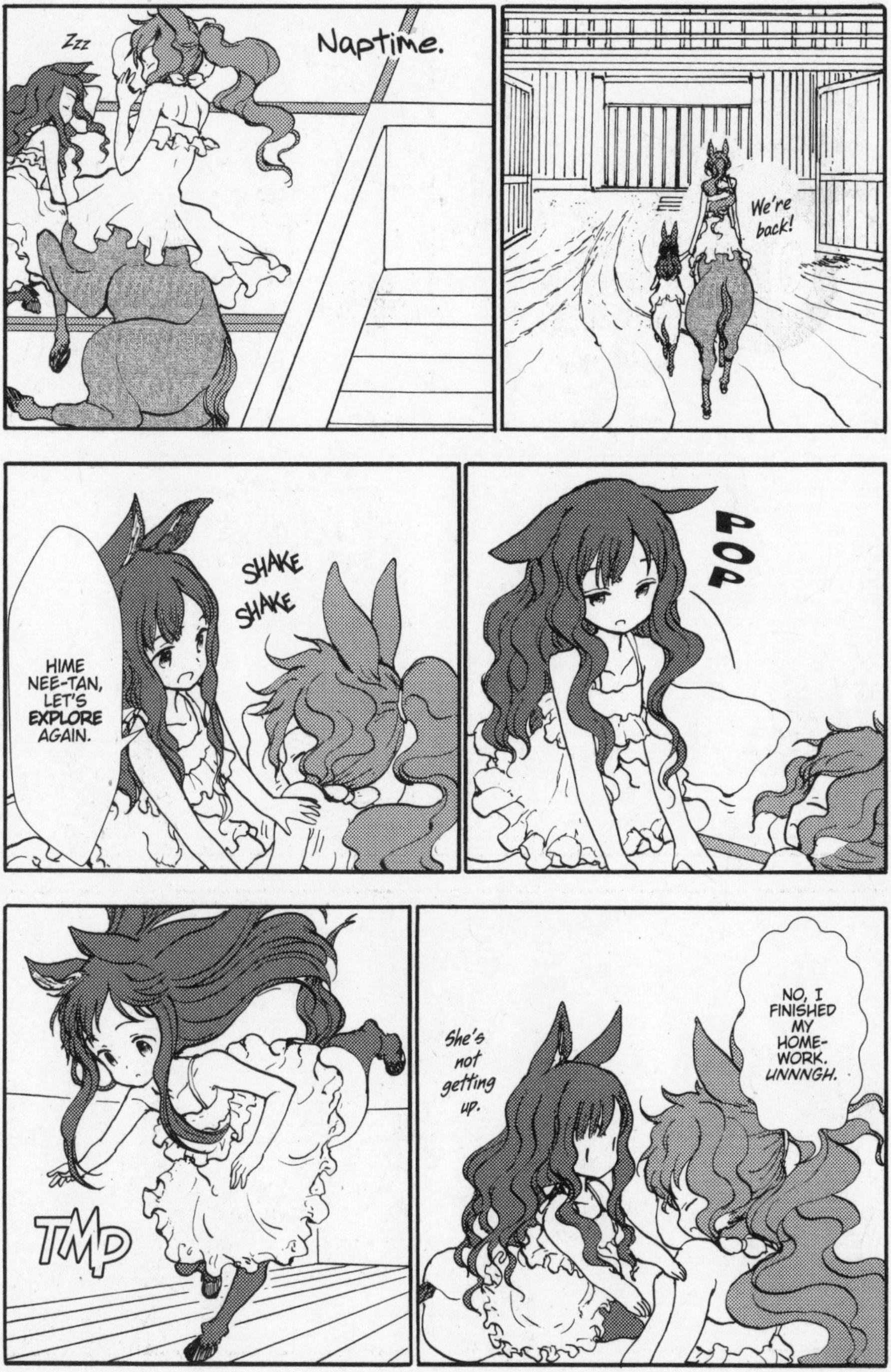
We're back!
Zzz
Naptime.
POP
SHAKE SHAKE
HIME NEE-TAN, LET'S EXPLORE AGAIN.
NO, I FINISHED MY HOMEWORK. UNNNGH.
She's not getting up.
TMP

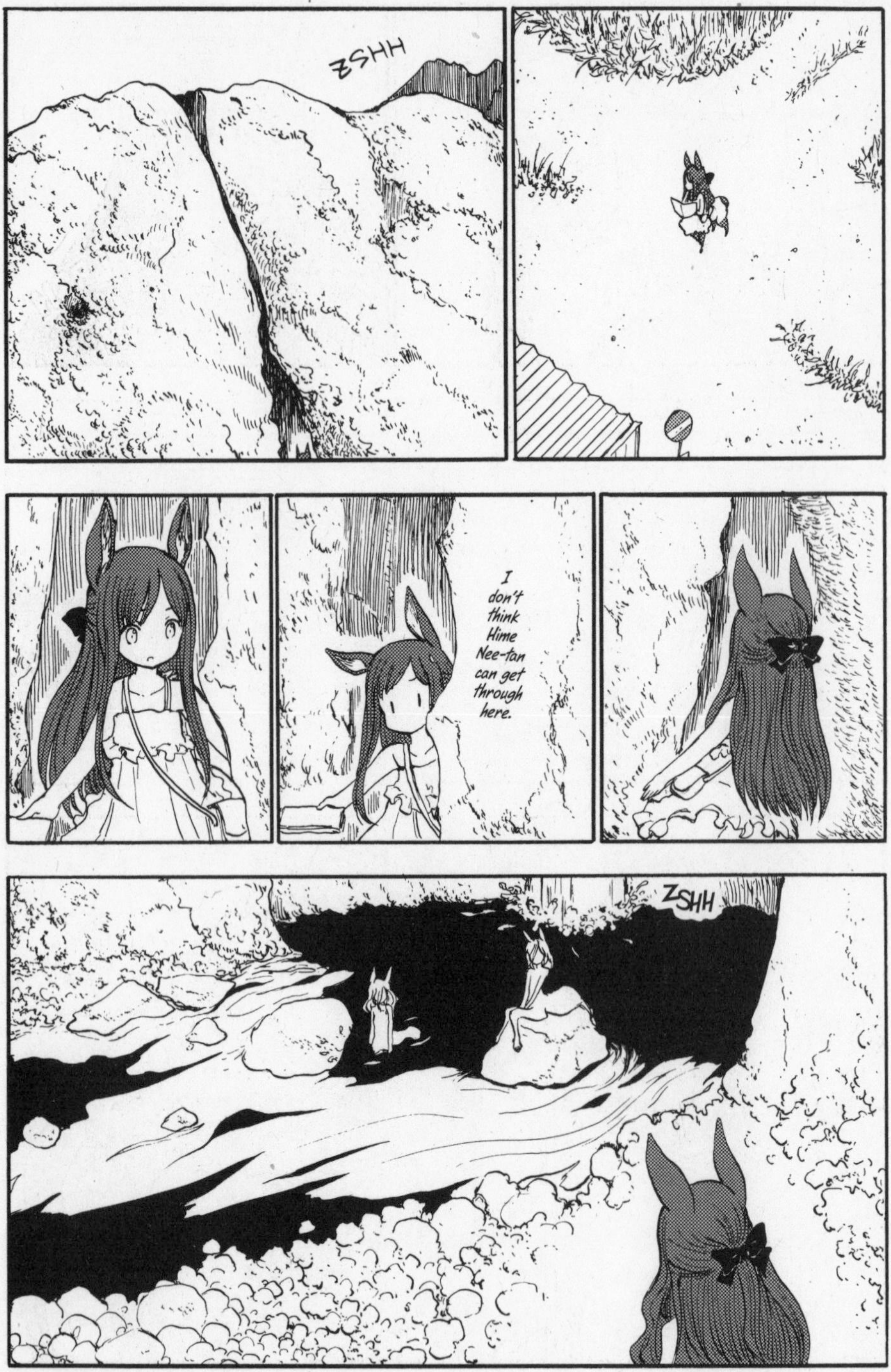
ZSHH
I don't think Hime Nee-tan can get through here.
ZSHH

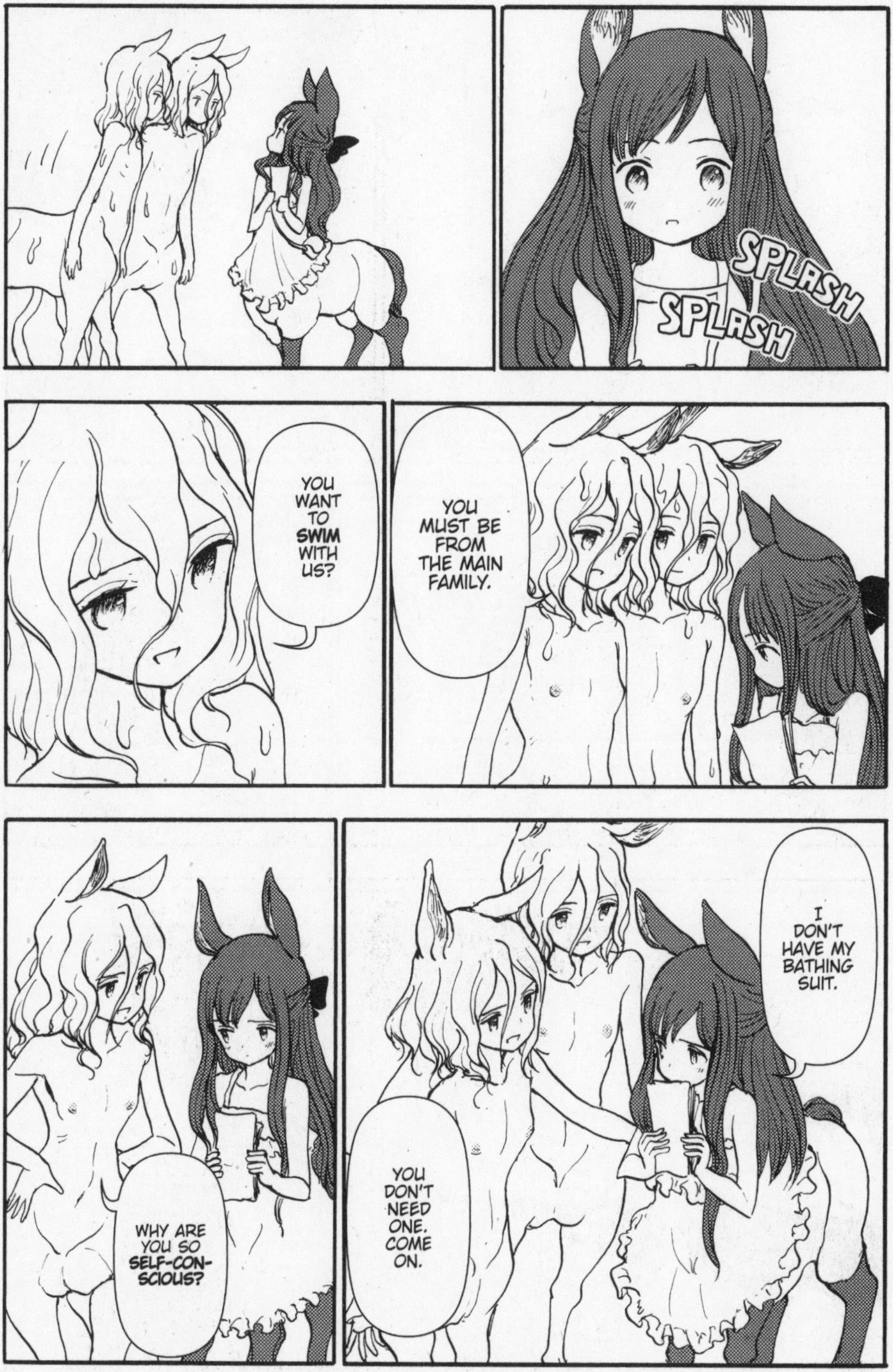
SPLASH
SPLASH
YOU MUST BE FROM THE MAIN FAMILY.
YOU WANT TO SWIM WITH US?
I DON'T HAVE MY BATHING SUIT.
YOU DON'T NEED ONE. COME ON.
WHY ARE YOU SO SELF-CONSCIOUS?

THE WATER'S **GREAT.** FEELS GOOD!

SPLISH SPLISH

Huh?

Hmm.

SPLISH

SPLISH

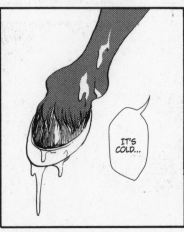

IT'S COLD...

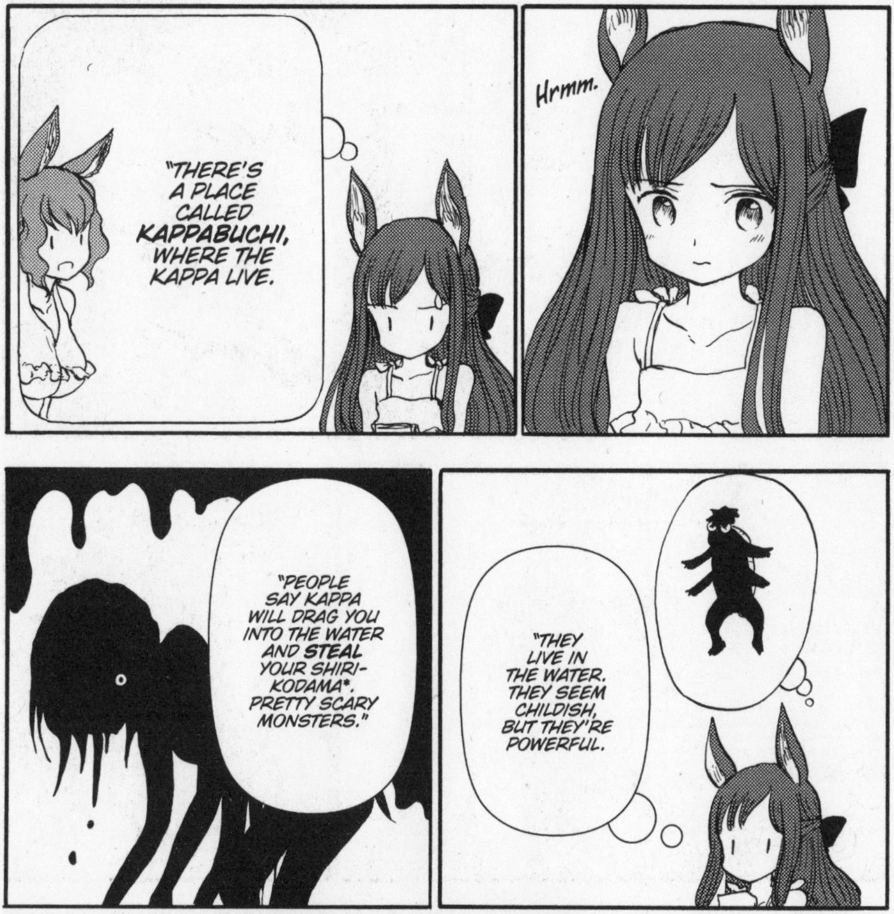
Hrmm.
"THERE'S A PLACE CALLED **KAPPABUCHI,** WHERE THE KAPPA LIVE.
"THEY LIVE IN THE WATER. THEY SEEM CHILDISH, BUT THEY'RE POWERFUL.
"PEOPLE SAY KAPPA WILL DRAG YOU INTO THE WATER AND **STEAL** YOUR SHIRI-KODAMA*. PRETTY SCARY MONSTERS."

*A mythical ball in the anus, said to store the soul.

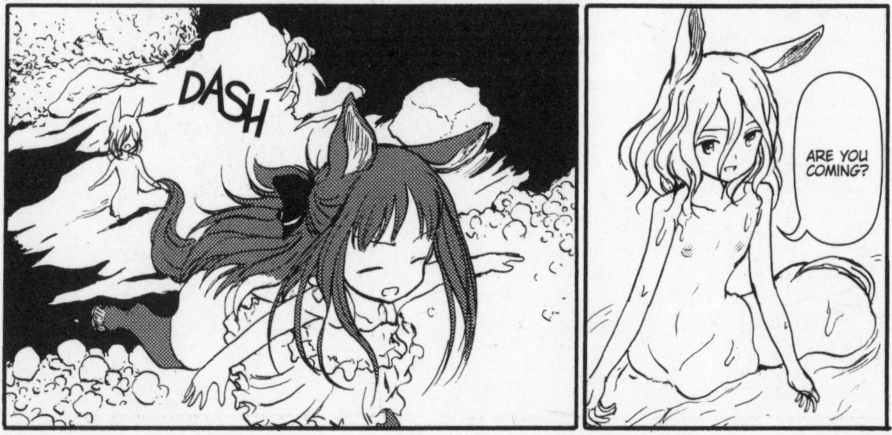
ARE YOU COMING?
DASH

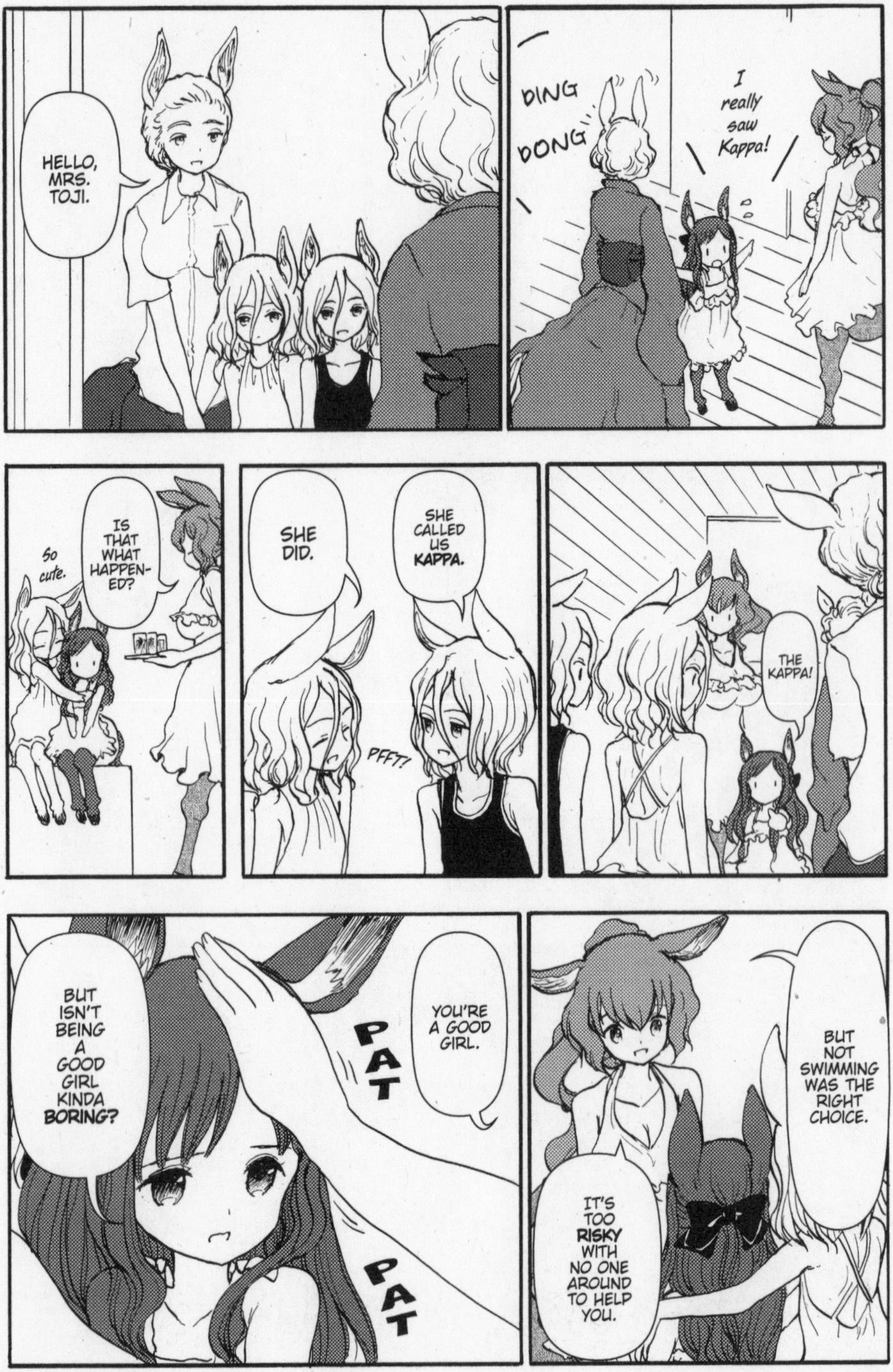
DING
DONG
I really saw Kappa!
HELLO, MRS. TOJI.
THE KAPPA!
SHE CALLED US KAPPA.
SHE DID.
PFFT!
IS THAT WHAT HAPPENED?
So cute.
BUT NOT SWIMMING WAS THE RIGHT CHOICE.
IT'S TOO RISKY WITH NO ONE AROUND TO HELP YOU.
YOU'RE A GOOD GIRL.
PAT
PAT
BUT ISN'T BEING A GOOD GIRL KINDA BORING?

A Centaur's Life

SOLDIERS AROUND THE WORLD:

NAZI GERMAN TANKERS

DESPITE ITS DISCRIMINATORY ETHNIC
EUGENICS PHILOSOPHY, NAZI GERMANY
WAS COMMITTED TO EQUALITY
BETWEEN THE RACES WITHIN THE
GERMAN ETHNICITY. THIS EQUALITY
CONTRASTED WITH NEIGHBORING
COUNTRIES, WHERE DISCRIMINATION
BASED ON BODY FORM STILL TENDED
TO BE A PROBLEM.

THE GERMAN MILITARY DESIGNED
THEIR EQUIPMENT, TANKS, AND OTHER
VEHICLES TO ACCOMMODATE THE
BODIES OF THE DIVERSE RACES OF
THE GERMAN PEOPLE, INCLUDING
CENTAURS. NATURALLY, THIS MEANT
THAT THE VEHICLES WERE MUCH
LARGER; THE INTERIOR COMPARTMENTS
WERE LARGE ENOUGH TO SUPPORT
A RADIO, A RADIO COMMUNICATIONS
SPECIALIST, AND A COMMANDER.
THE SIZE OF THE VEHICLES ALSO
NECESSITATED THE DEVELOPMENT
OF MORE POWERFUL ENGINES.
THE TANKS WERE EQUIPPED WITH
ENORMOUS GUNS THAT USED MASSIVE
AMMUNITION, AND COULD ONLY BE
OPERATED BY LARGE CENTAURS.
WITH THE TECHNICAL STRENGTH THEY
GAINED THROUGH RACIAL EQUALITY
AMONG GERMANS, THE THIRD REICH
WAS VERY SUCCESSFUL IN THE
BEGINNING OF A WORLD WAR AGAINST
THE MORE POWERFUL ALLIED FORCES.
NAZI GERMANY AND ITS POLICIES
OF ETHNIC DISCRIMINATION WERE
ULTIMATELY DEFEATED, HOWEVER, BY
NATIONS THAT LACKED THEIR RACIAL
TOLERANCE.

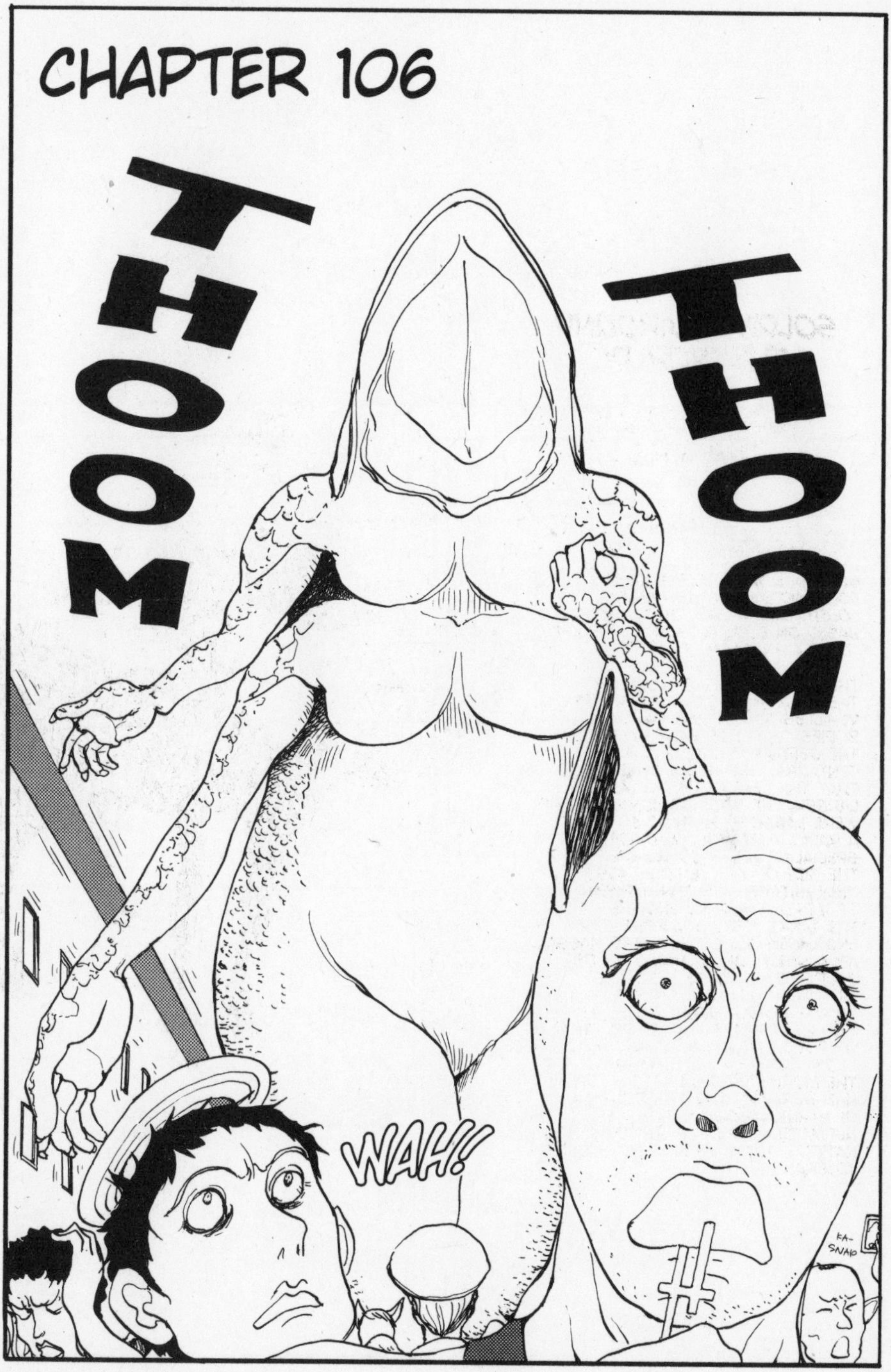
CHAPTER 106
THOOM
THOOM
WAH!
KA-SNAP

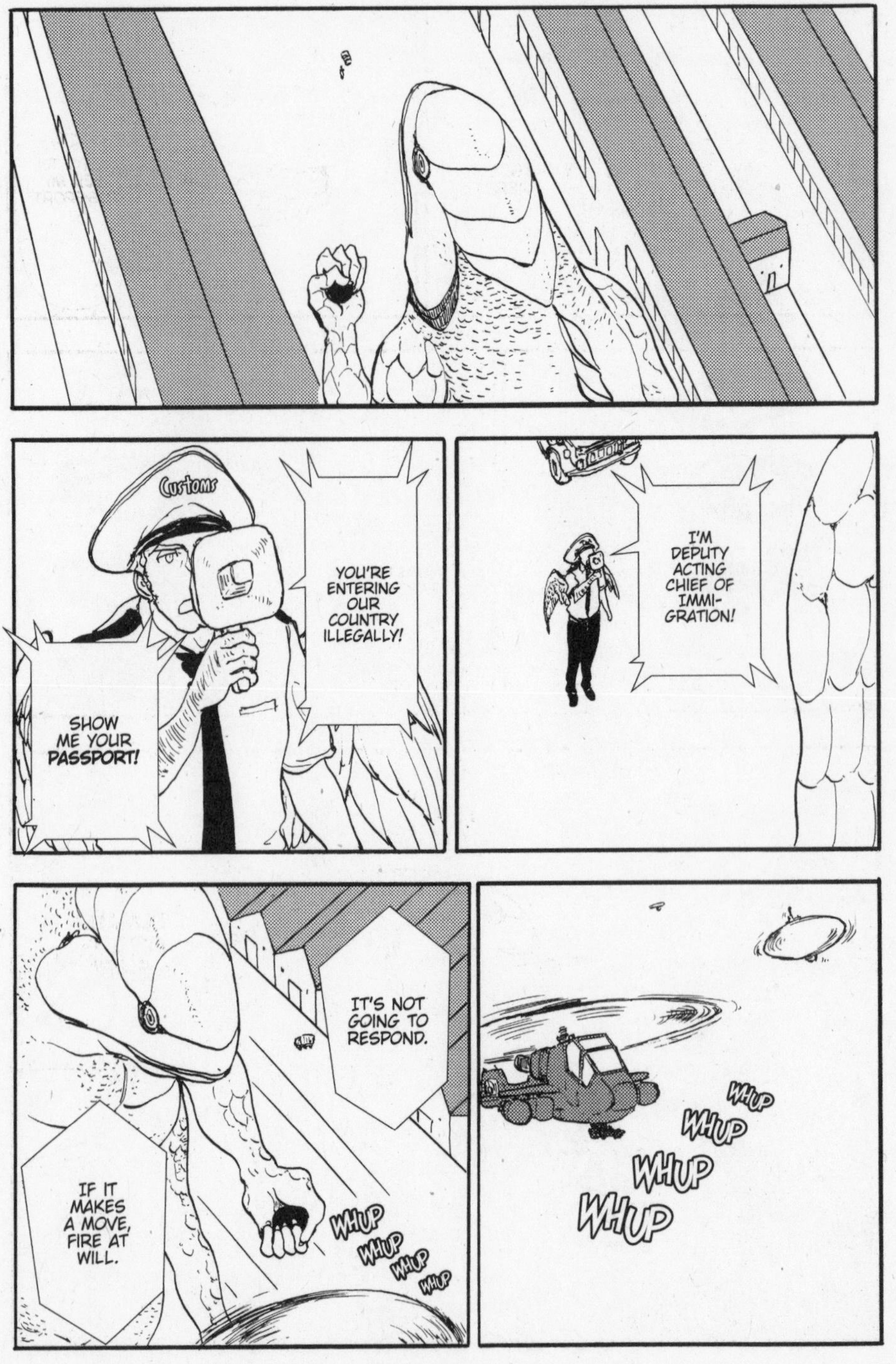
I'M DEPUTY ACTING CHIEF OF IMMIGRATION!
Customs
YOU'RE ENTERING OUR COUNTRY ILLEGALLY!
SHOW ME YOUR PASSPORT!
WHUP
WHUP
WHUP
WHUP
IT'S NOT GOING TO RESPOND.
IF IT MAKES A MOVE, FIRE AT WILL.
WHUP
WHUP
WHUP
WHUP

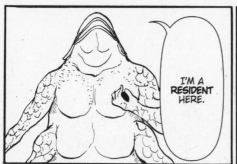

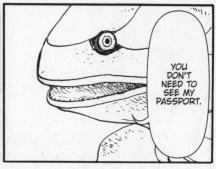

YOU DON'T NEED TO SEE MY PASSPORT.
I'M A RESIDENT HERE.
NOBODY TOLD ME THIS THING COULD TALK!
Customs
THEN LET'S SEE SOME ID, OR PROOF OF RESIDENCE!
IT WAS YOUR GOVERNMENT THAT REFUSED TO RECOGNIZE ME AS A "PERSON."
I DEMAND CITIZEN-SHIP!
CIVIL RIGHTS! UNIVERSAL HEALTH-CARE!

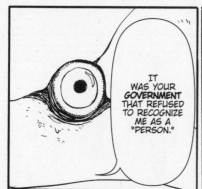

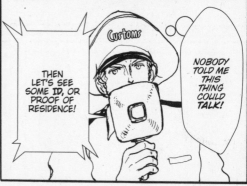

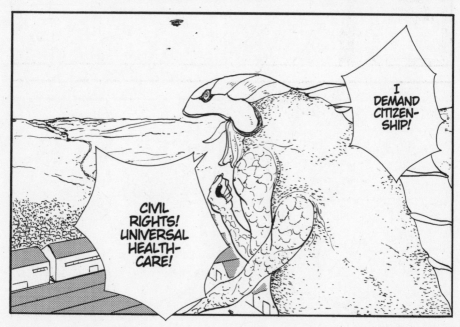

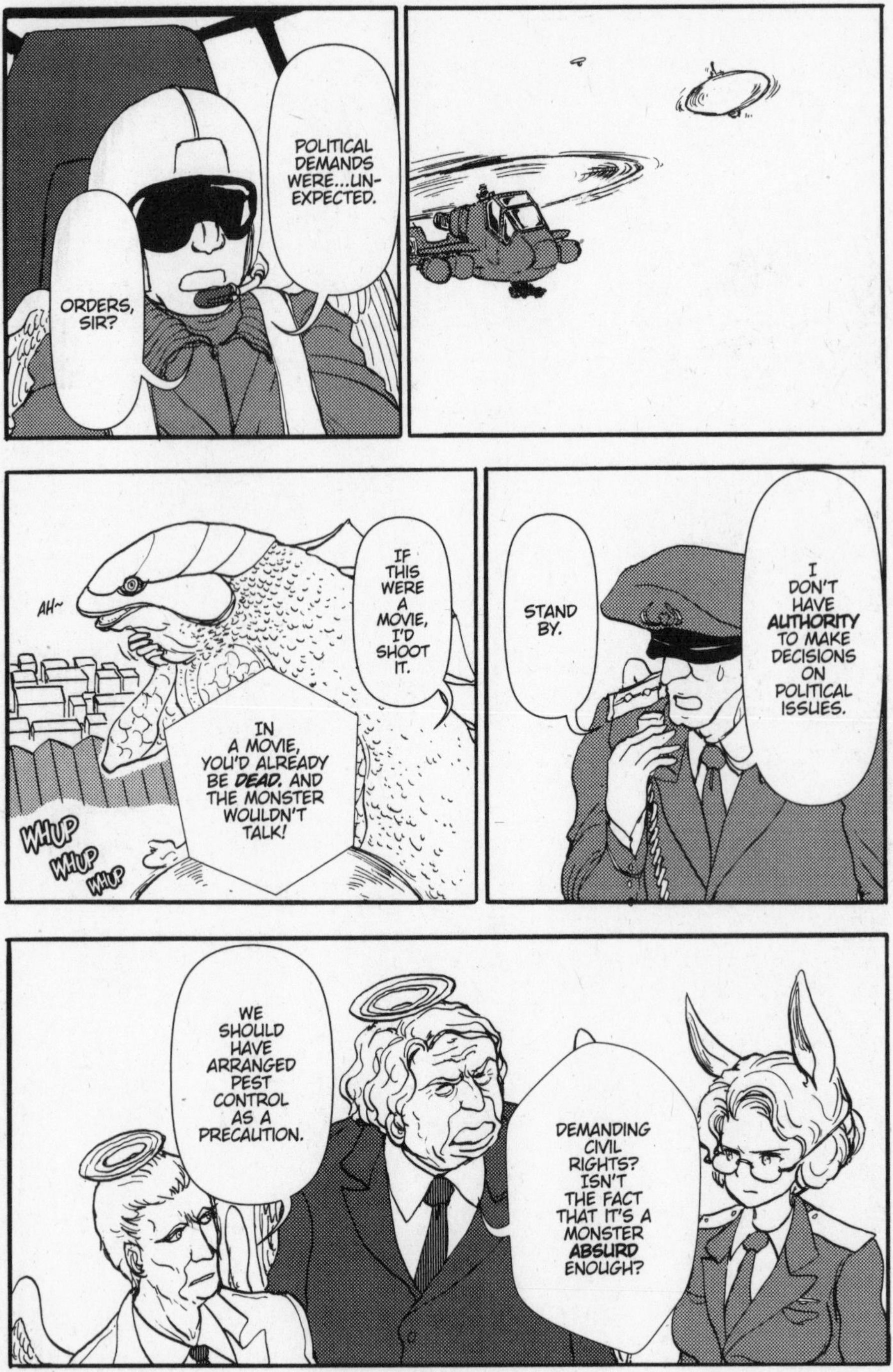
POLITICAL DEMANDS WERE...UN-EXPECTED.
ORDERS, SIR?
I DON'T HAVE **AUTHORITY** TO MAKE DECISIONS ON POLITICAL ISSUES.
STAND BY.
IF THIS WERE A MOVIE, I'D SHOOT IT.
IN A MOVIE, YOU'D ALREADY BE ***DEAD.*** AND THE MONSTER WOULDN'T TALK!
AH~
WHUP WHUP WHUP
DEMANDING CIVIL RIGHTS? ISN'T THE FACT THAT IT'S A MONSTER **ABSURD** ENOUGH?
WE SHOULD HAVE ARRANGED PEST CONTROL AS A PRECAUTION.

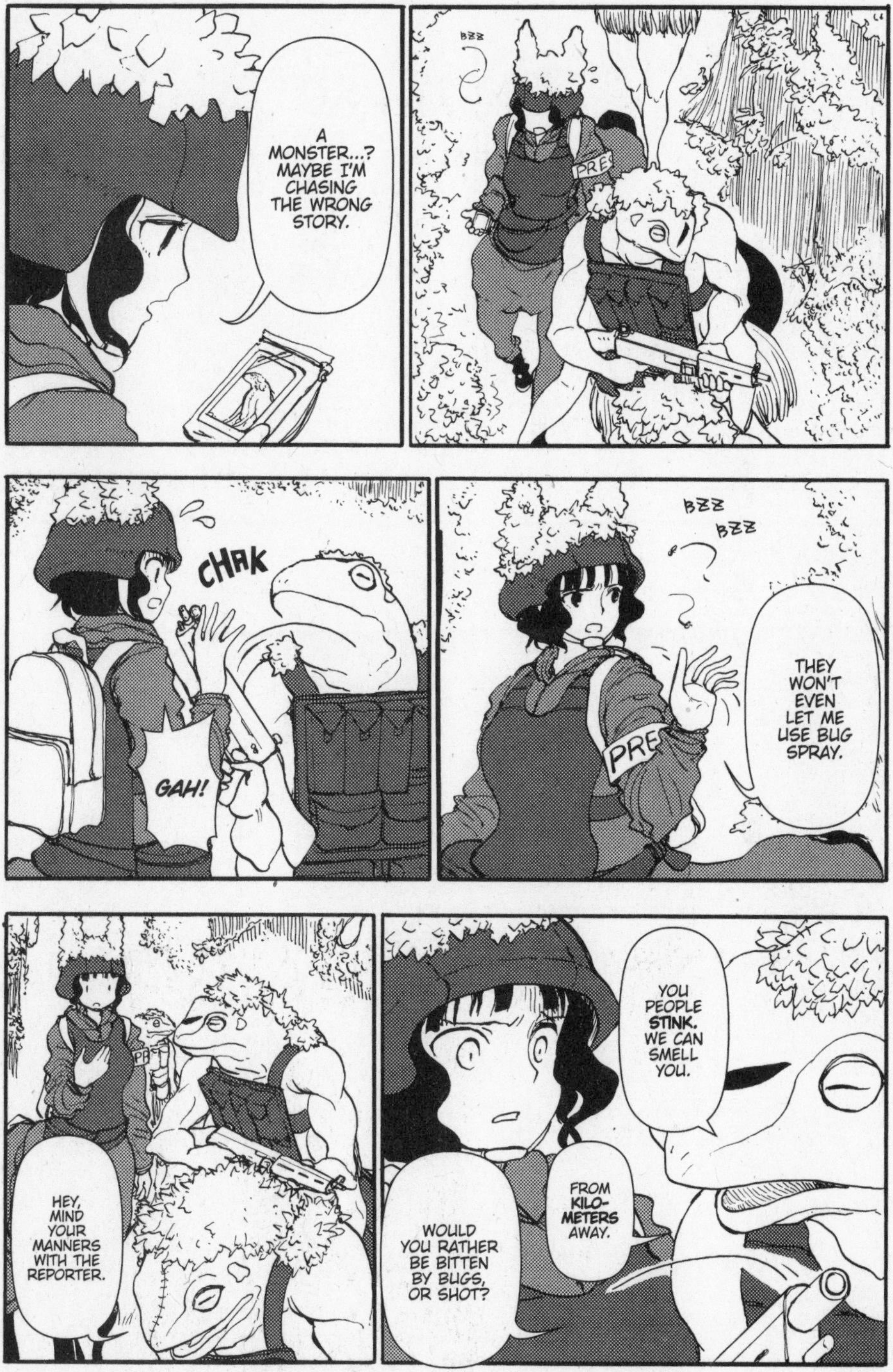
BZZ
A MONSTER...? MAYBE I'M CHASING THE WRONG STORY.
BZZ
BZZ
THEY WON'T EVEN LET ME USE BUG SPRAY.
CHAK
GAH!
YOU PEOPLE STINK. WE CAN SMELL YOU.
FROM KILO-METERS AWAY.
WOULD YOU RATHER BE BITTEN BY BUGS, OR SHOT?
HEY, MIND YOUR MANNERS WITH THE REPORTER.

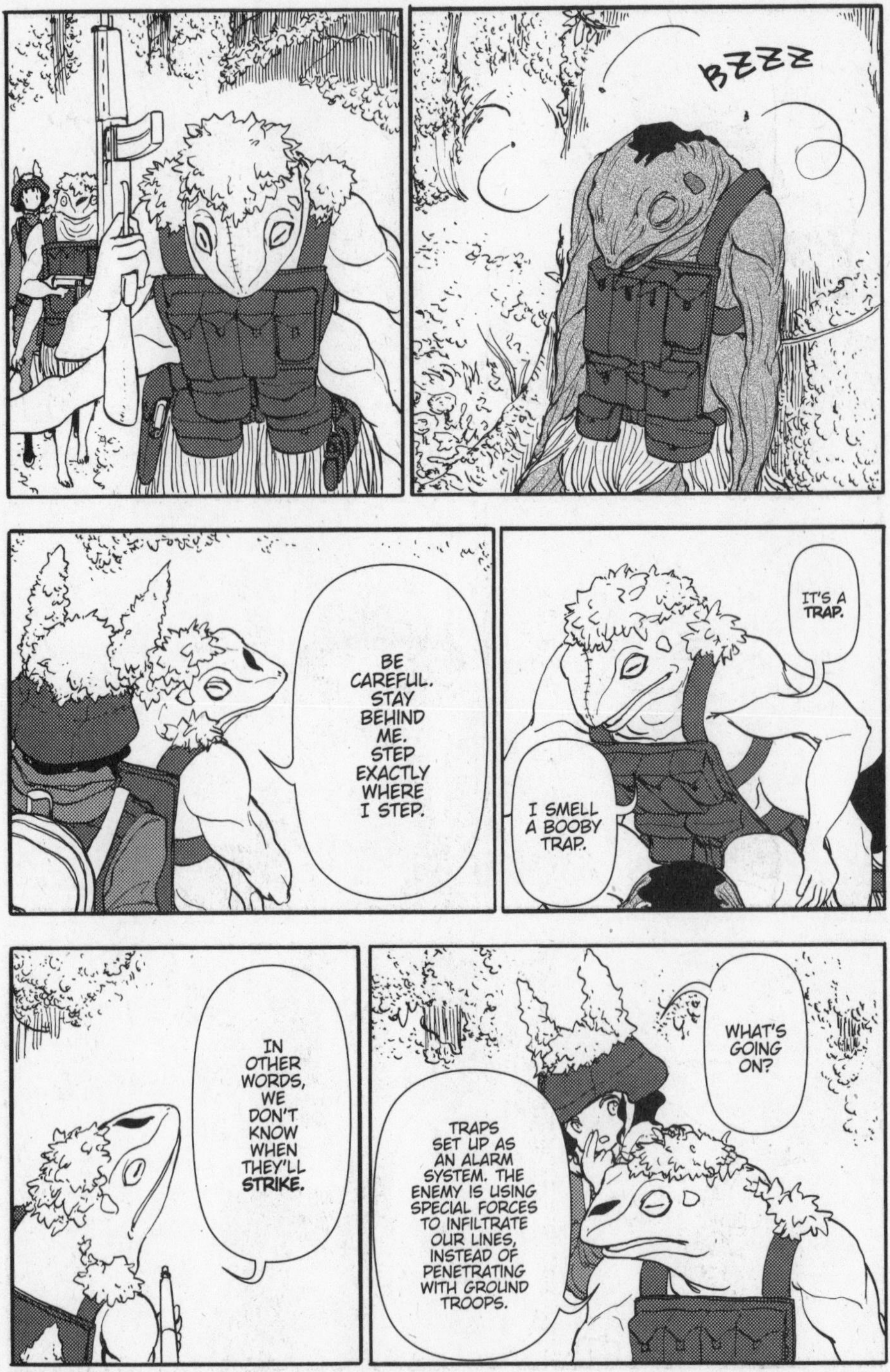
BZZZ
IT'S A TRAP.
I SMELL A BOOBY TRAP.
BE CAREFUL. STAY BEHIND ME. STEP EXACTLY WHERE I STEP.
WHAT'S GOING ON?
TRAPS SET UP AS AN ALARM SYSTEM. THE ENEMY IS USING SPECIAL FORCES TO INFILTRATE OUR LINES, INSTEAD OF PENETRATING WITH GROUND TROOPS.
IN OTHER WORDS, WE DON'T KNOW WHEN THEY'LL STRIKE.

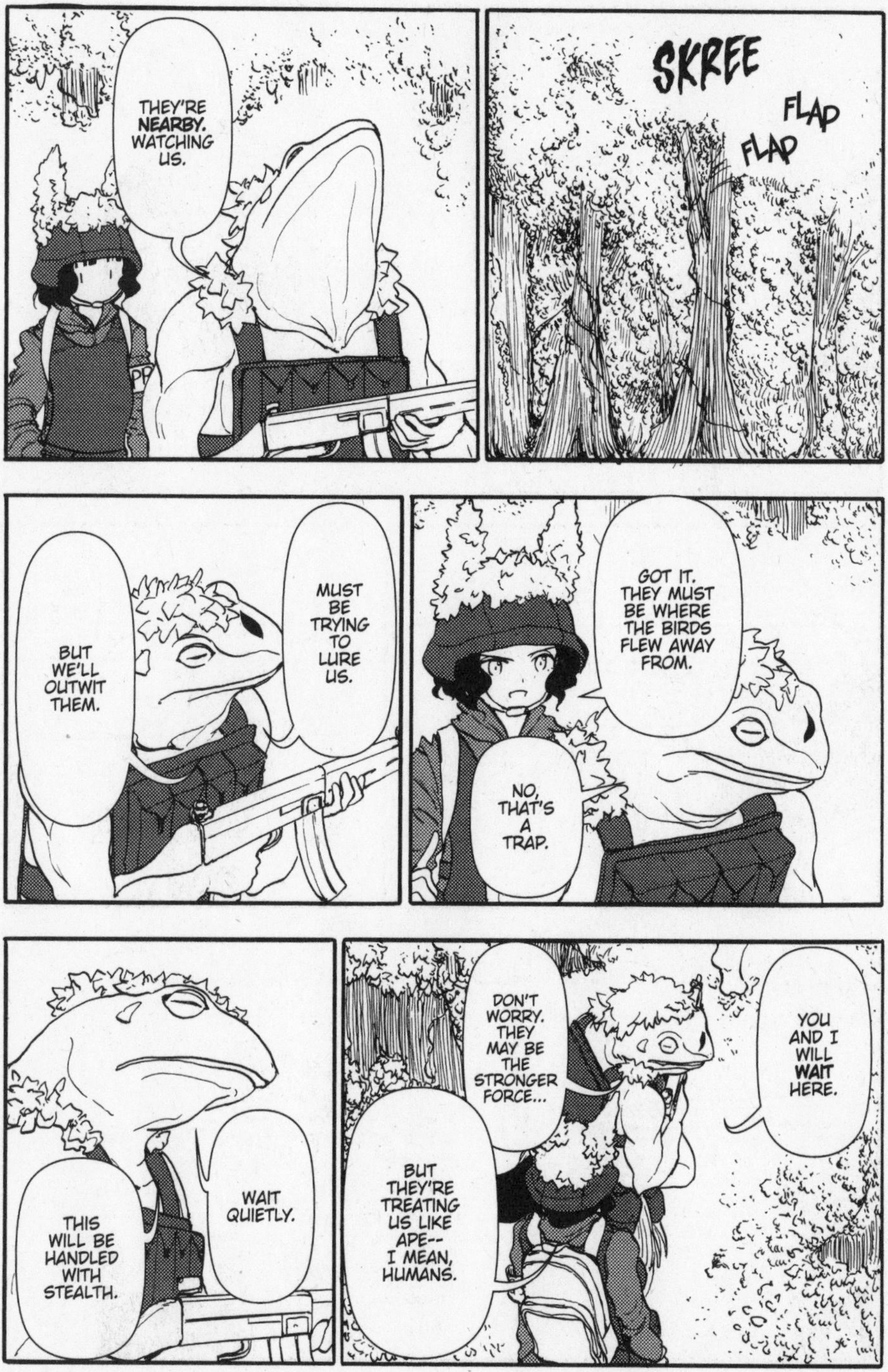
SKREE
FLAP
FLAP
THEY'RE NEARBY. WATCHING US.
GOT IT. THEY MUST BE WHERE THE BIRDS FLEW AWAY FROM.
NO, THAT'S A TRAP.
MUST BE TRYING TO LURE US.
BUT WE'LL OUTWIT THEM.
YOU AND I WILL WAIT HERE.
DON'T WORRY. THEY MAY BE THE STRONGER FORCE...
BUT THEY'RE TREATING US LIKE APE-- I MEAN, HUMANS.
WAIT QUIETLY.
THIS WILL BE HANDLED WITH STEALTH.

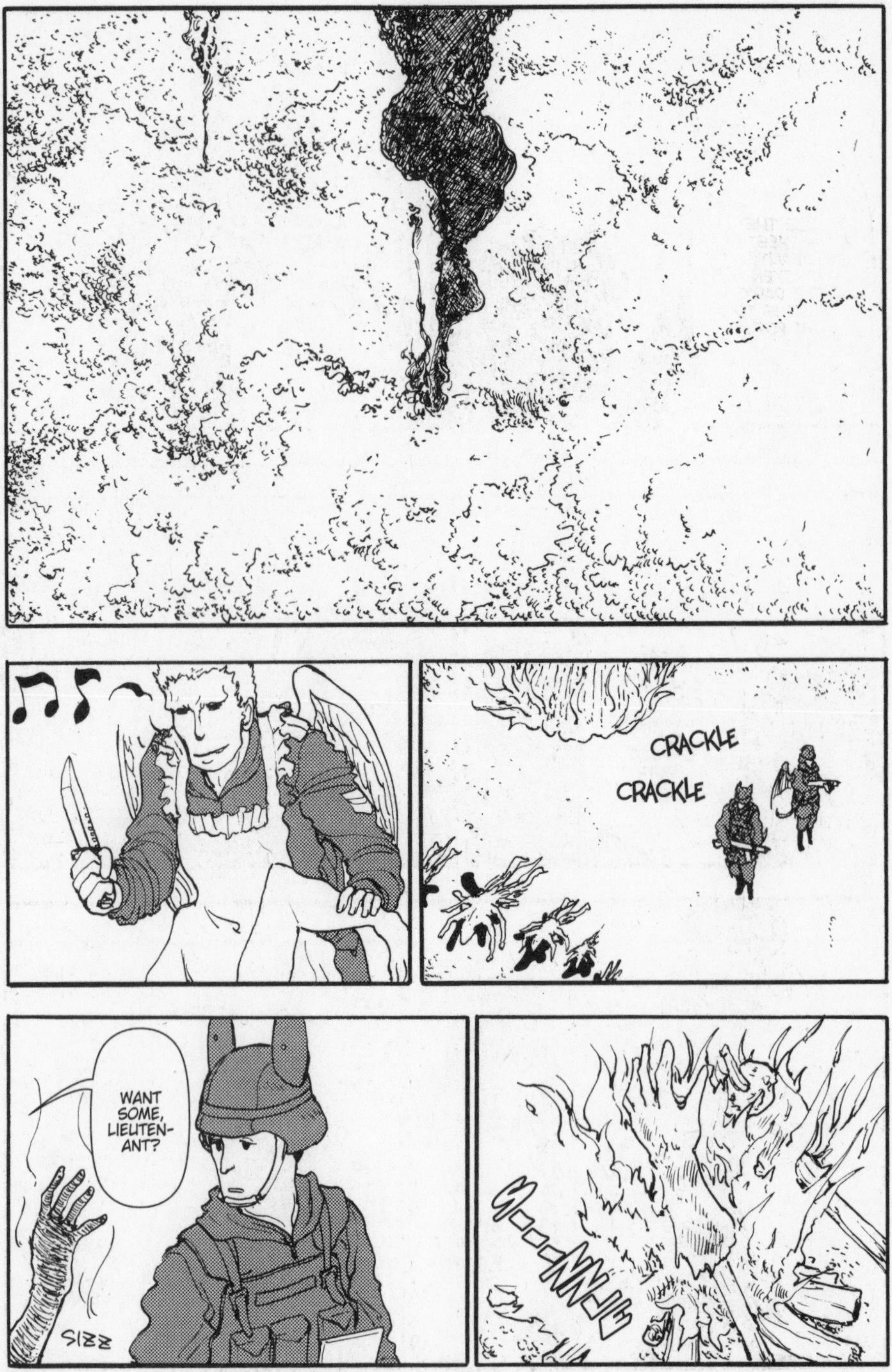
CRACKLE
CRACKLE
WANT SOME, LIEUTEN-ANT?
SIZZ

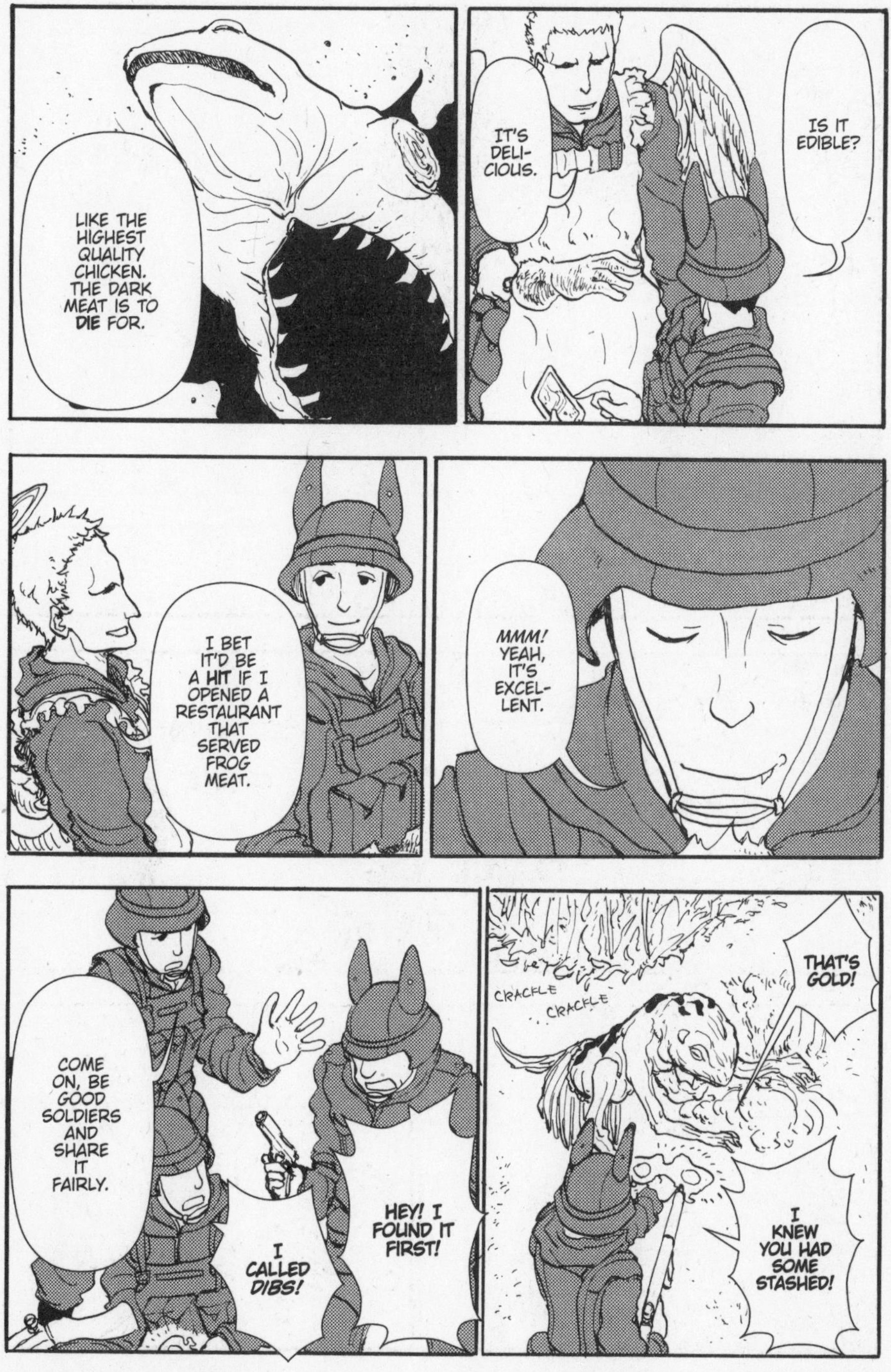
IS IT EDIBLE?
IT'S DELICIOUS.
LIKE THE HIGHEST QUALITY CHICKEN. THE DARK MEAT IS TO DIE FOR.
MMM! YEAH, IT'S EXCELLENT.
I BET IT'D BE A HIT IF I OPENED A RESTAURANT THAT SERVED FROG MEAT.
THAT'S GOLD!
CRACKLE CRACKLE
I KNEW YOU HAD SOME STASHED!
HEY! I FOUND IT FIRST!
I CALLED DIBS!
COME ON, BE GOOD SOLDIERS AND SHARE IT FAIRLY.

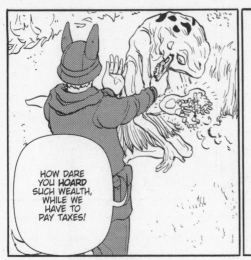

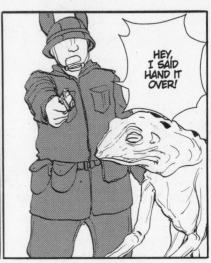

HEY, I SAID HAND IT OVER!
HOW DARE YOU HOARD SUCH WEALTH, WHILE WE HAVE TO PAY TAXES!
COME ON, HAND IT OVER!
CLICK
BWOOM

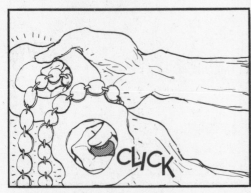

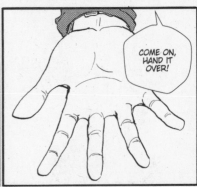

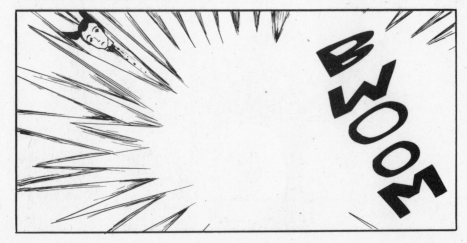

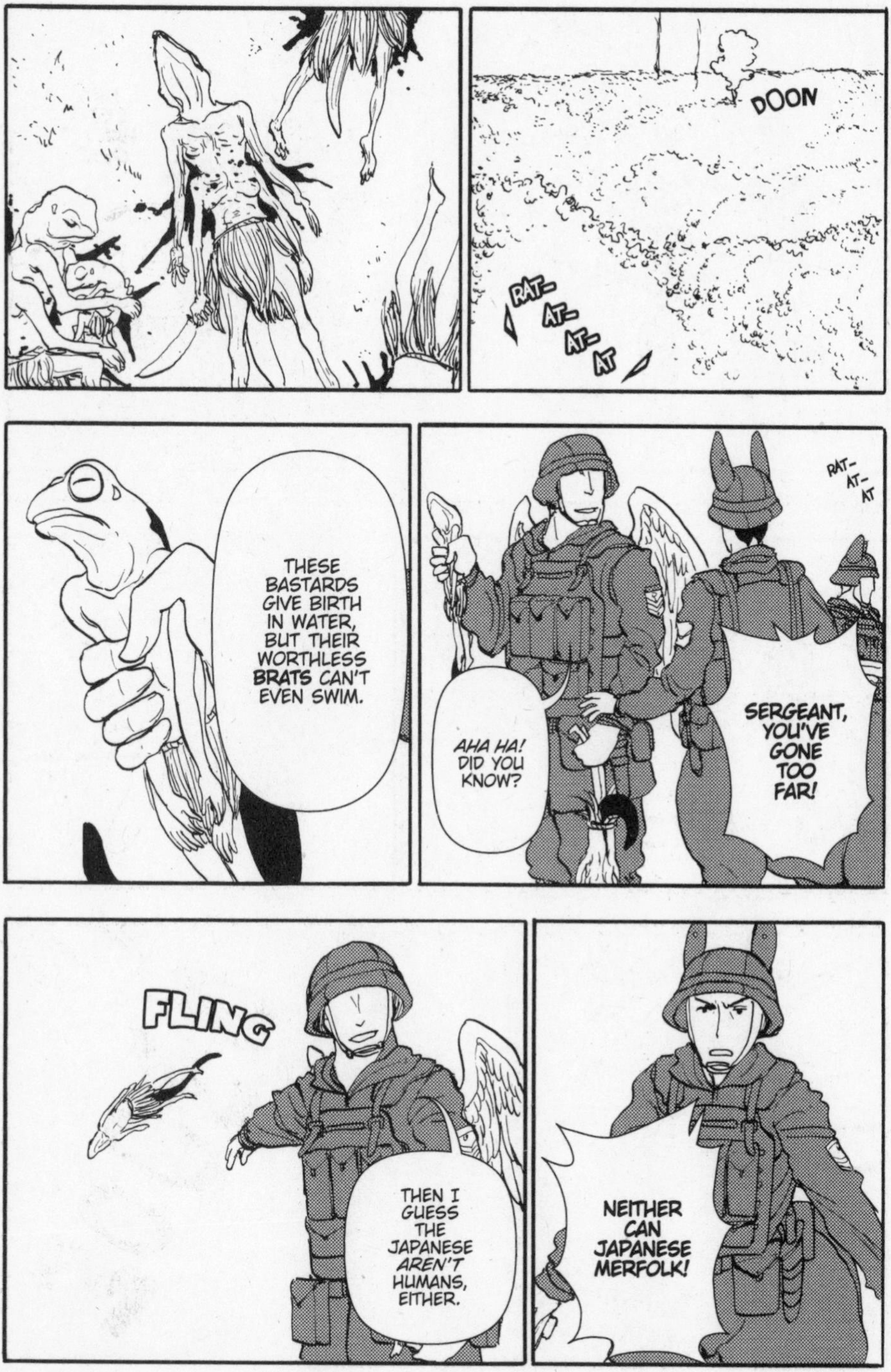
DOON
RAT-AT-AT-AT
RAT-AT-AT
SERGEANT, YOU'VE GONE TOO FAR!
AHA HA! DID YOU KNOW?
THESE BASTARDS GIVE BIRTH IN WATER, BUT THEIR WORTHLESS BRATS CAN'T EVEN SWIM.
NEITHER CAN JAPANESE MERFOLK!
FLING
THEN I GUESS THE JAPANESE AREN'T HUMANS, EITHER.

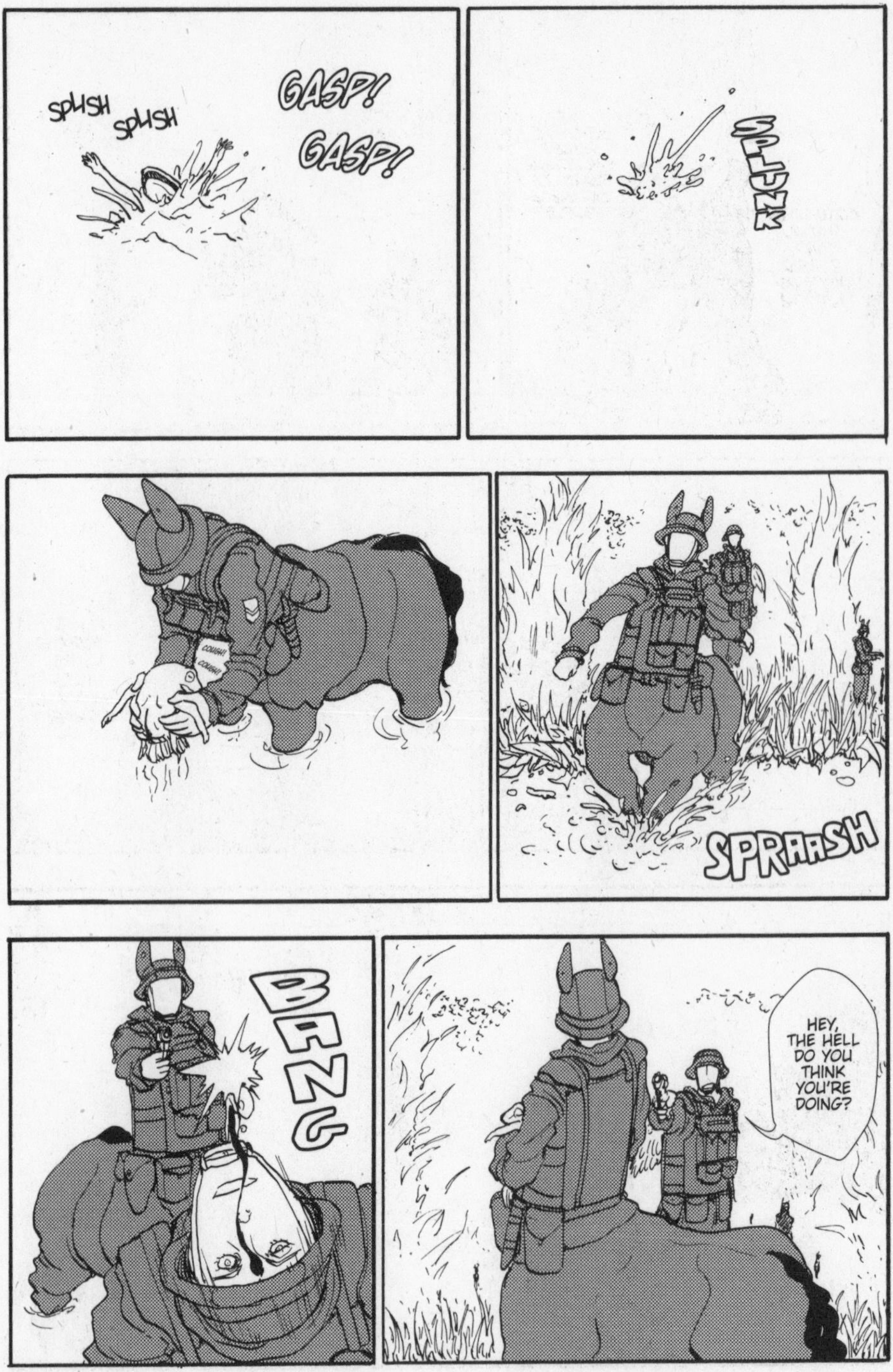
SPLISH
SPLISH
GASP!
GASP!
SPLUNK
COUGH!
COUGH!
SPRAASH
BANG
HEY, THE HELL DO YOU THINK YOU'RE DOING?

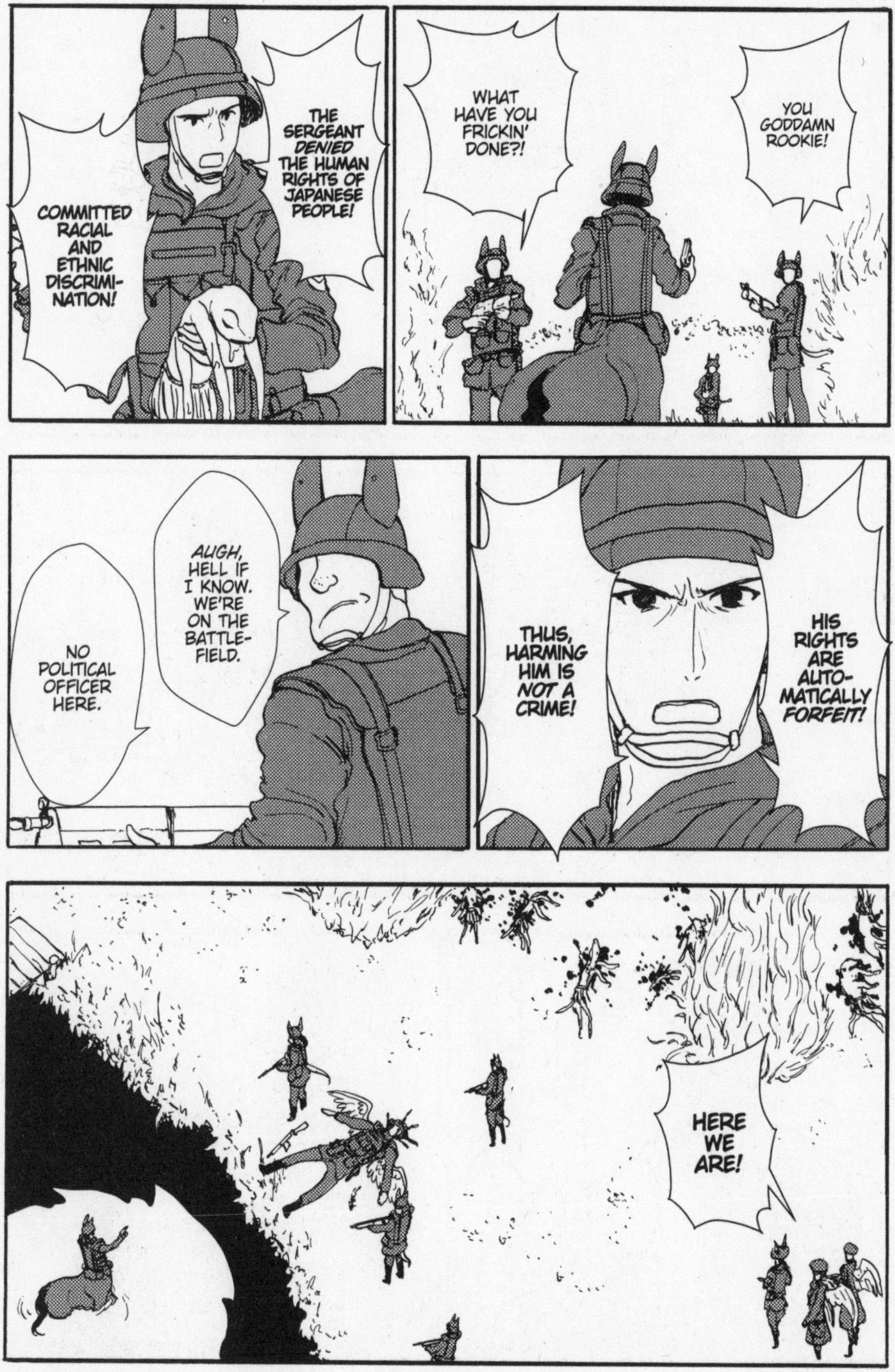
YOU GODDAMN ROOKIE!
WHAT HAVE YOU FRICKIN' DONE?!
THE SERGEANT *DENIED* THE HUMAN RIGHTS OF JAPANESE PEOPLE!
COMMITTED RACIAL AND ETHNIC DISCRIMINATION!
HIS RIGHTS ARE AUTOMATICALLY *FORFEIT!*
THUS, HARMING HIM IS *NOT* A CRIME!
AUGH, HELL IF I KNOW. WE'RE ON THE BATTLEFIELD.
NO POLITICAL OFFICER HERE.
HERE WE ARE!

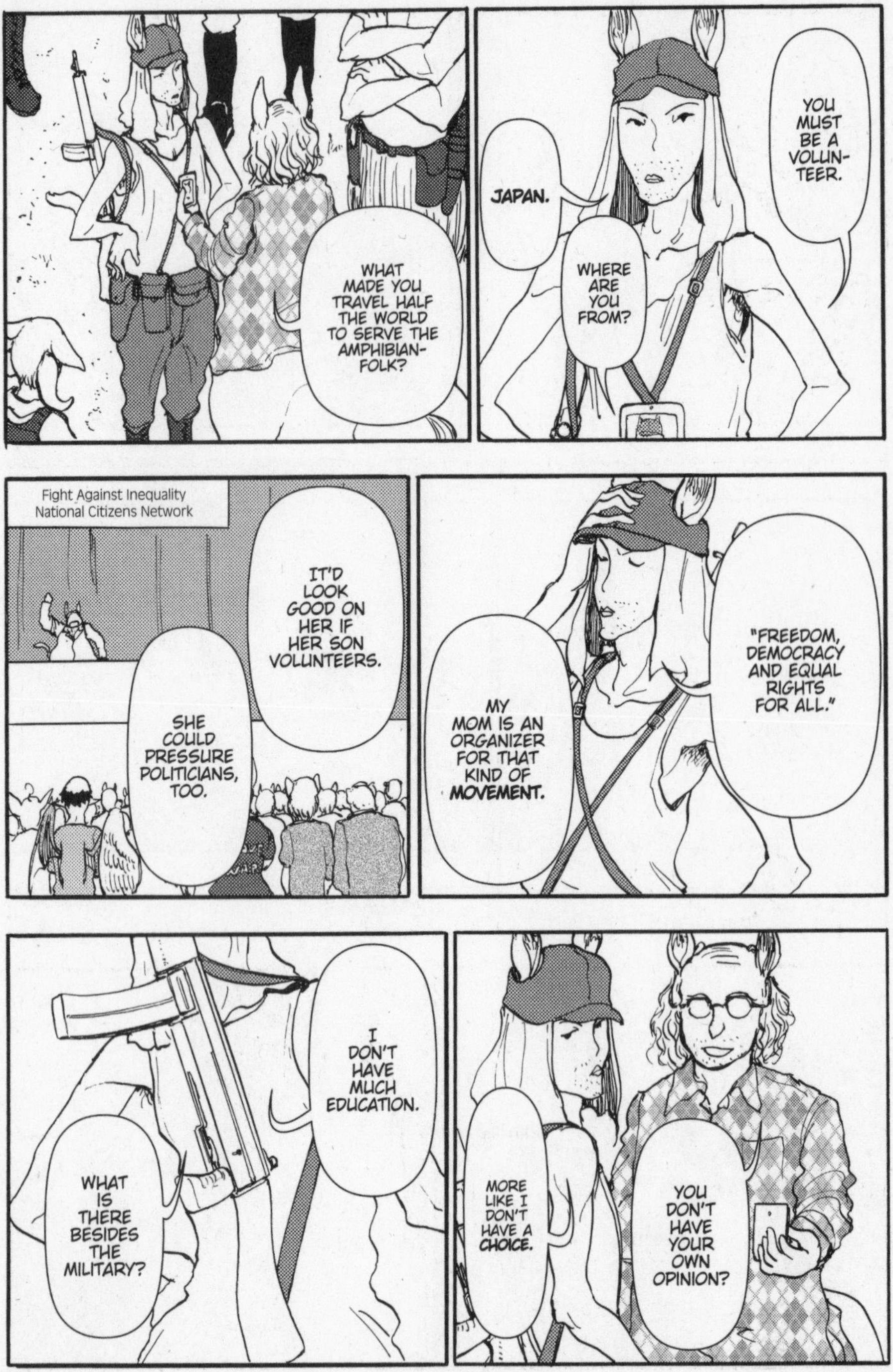
YOU MUST BE A VOLUNTEER.
WHERE ARE YOU FROM?
JAPAN.
WHAT MADE YOU TRAVEL HALF THE WORLD TO SERVE THE AMPHIBIAN-FOLK?
"FREEDOM, DEMOCRACY AND EQUAL RIGHTS FOR ALL."
MY MOM IS AN ORGANIZER FOR THAT KIND OF MOVEMENT.
Fight Against Inequality National Citizens Network
IT'D LOOK GOOD ON HER IF HER SON VOLUNTEERS.
SHE COULD PRESSURE POLITICIANS, TOO.
YOU DON'T HAVE YOUR OWN OPINION?
MORE LIKE I DON'T HAVE A CHOICE.
I DON'T HAVE MUCH EDUCATION.
WHAT IS THERE BESIDES THE MILITARY?

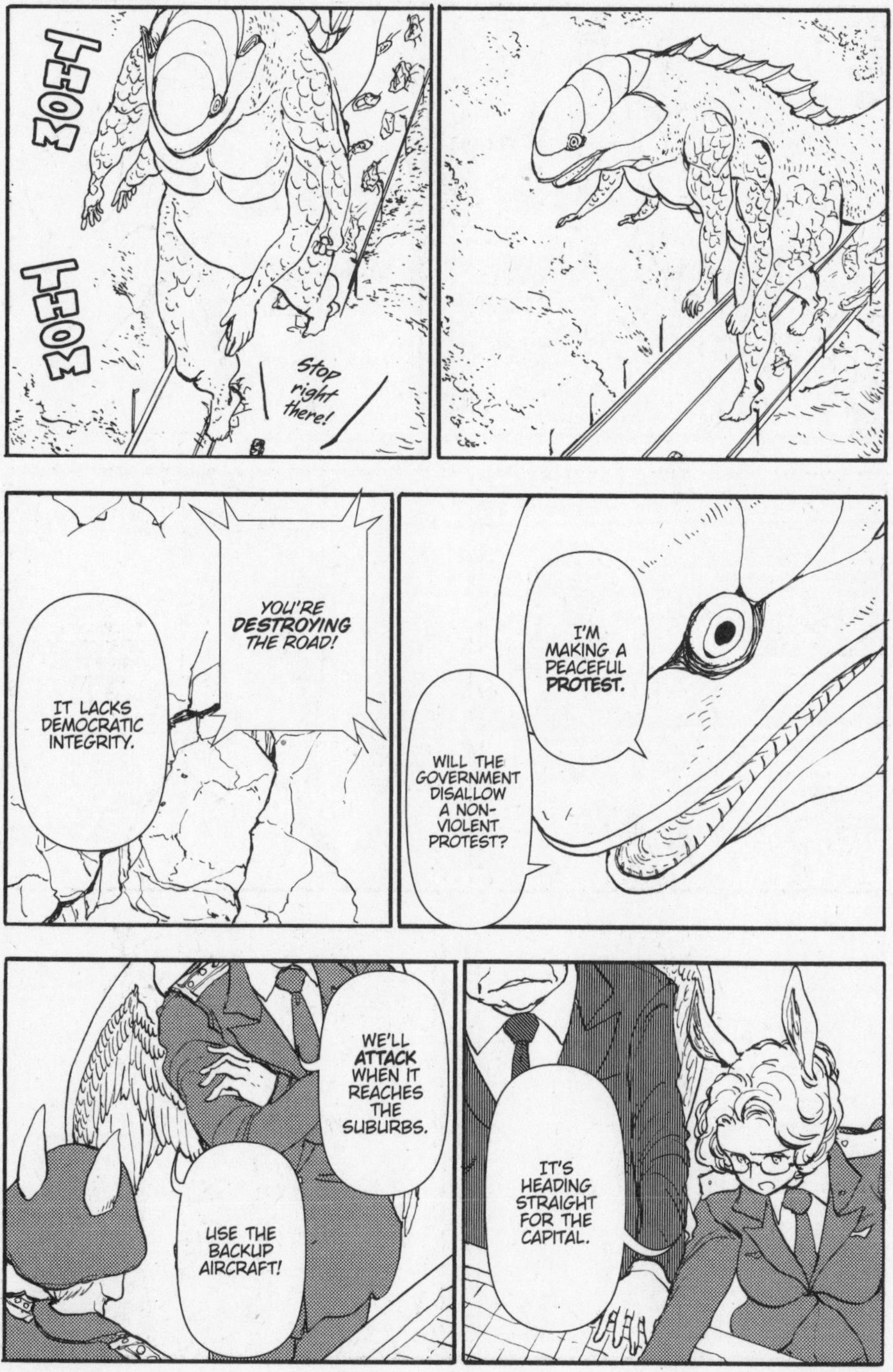
THOM
THOM
Stop right there!
I'M MAKING A PEACEFUL **PROTEST.**
WILL THE GOVERNMENT DISALLOW A NON-VIOLENT PROTEST?
*YOU'RE **DESTROYING** THE ROAD!*
IT LACKS DEMOCRATIC INTEGRITY.
IT'S HEADING STRAIGHT FOR THE CAPITAL.
WE'LL **ATTACK** WHEN IT REACHES THE SUBURBS.
USE THE BACKUP AIRCRAFT!

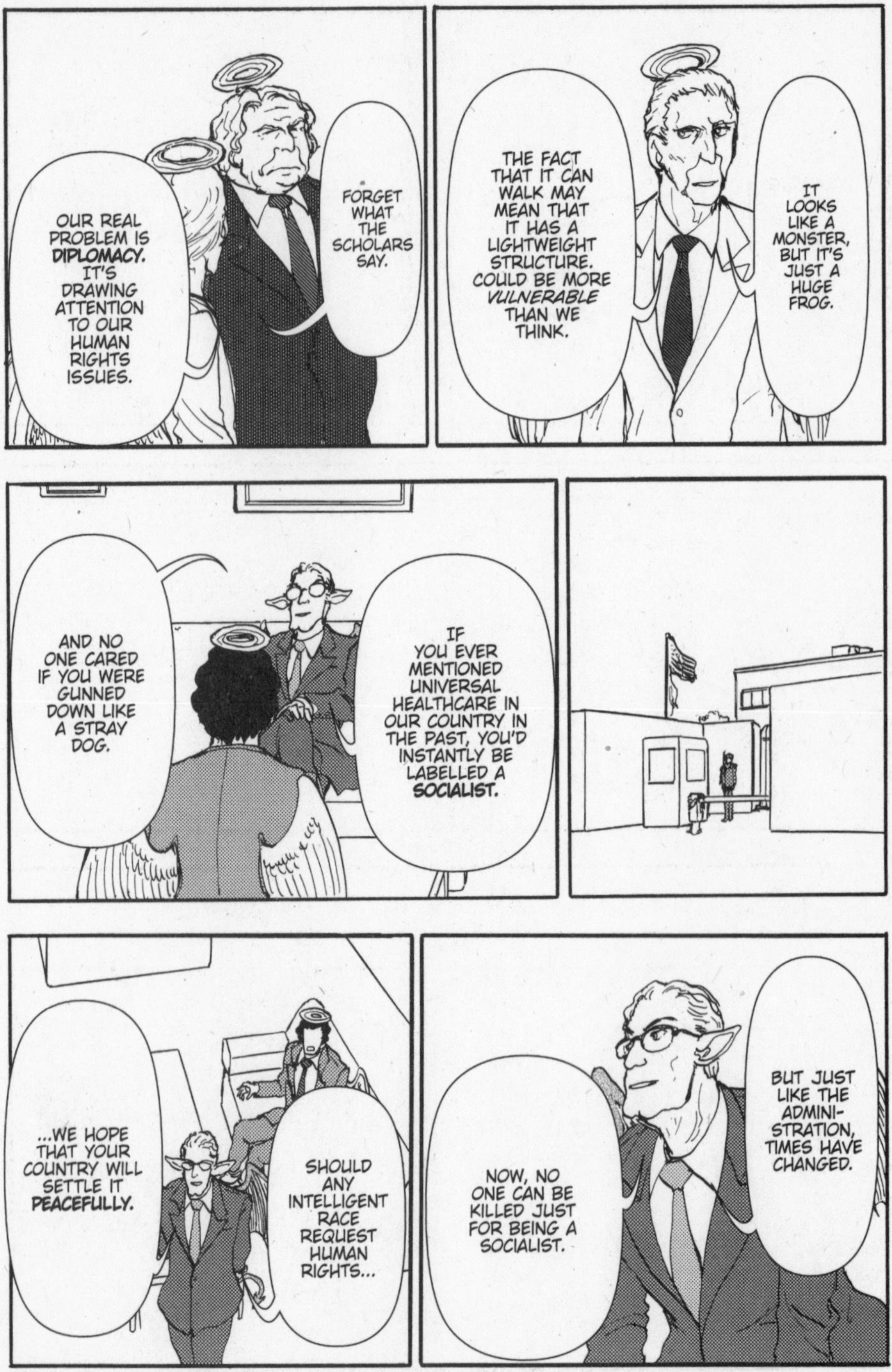
IT LOOKS LIKE A MONSTER, BUT IT'S JUST A HUGE FROG.
THE FACT THAT IT CAN WALK MAY MEAN THAT IT HAS A LIGHTWEIGHT STRUCTURE. COULD BE MORE VULNERABLE THAN WE THINK.
FORGET WHAT THE SCHOLARS SAY.
OUR REAL PROBLEM IS DIPLOMACY. IT'S DRAWING ATTENTION TO OUR HUMAN RIGHTS ISSUES.
IF YOU EVER MENTIONED UNIVERSAL HEALTHCARE IN OUR COUNTRY IN THE PAST, YOU'D INSTANTLY BE LABELLED A SOCIALIST.
AND NO ONE CARED IF YOU WERE GUNNED DOWN LIKE A STRAY DOG.
BUT JUST LIKE THE ADMINI-STRATION, TIMES HAVE CHANGED.
NOW, NO ONE CAN BE KILLED JUST FOR BEING A SOCIALIST.
SHOULD ANY INTELLIGENT RACE REQUEST HUMAN RIGHTS...
...WE HOPE THAT YOUR COUNTRY WILL SETTLE IT PEACEFULLY.

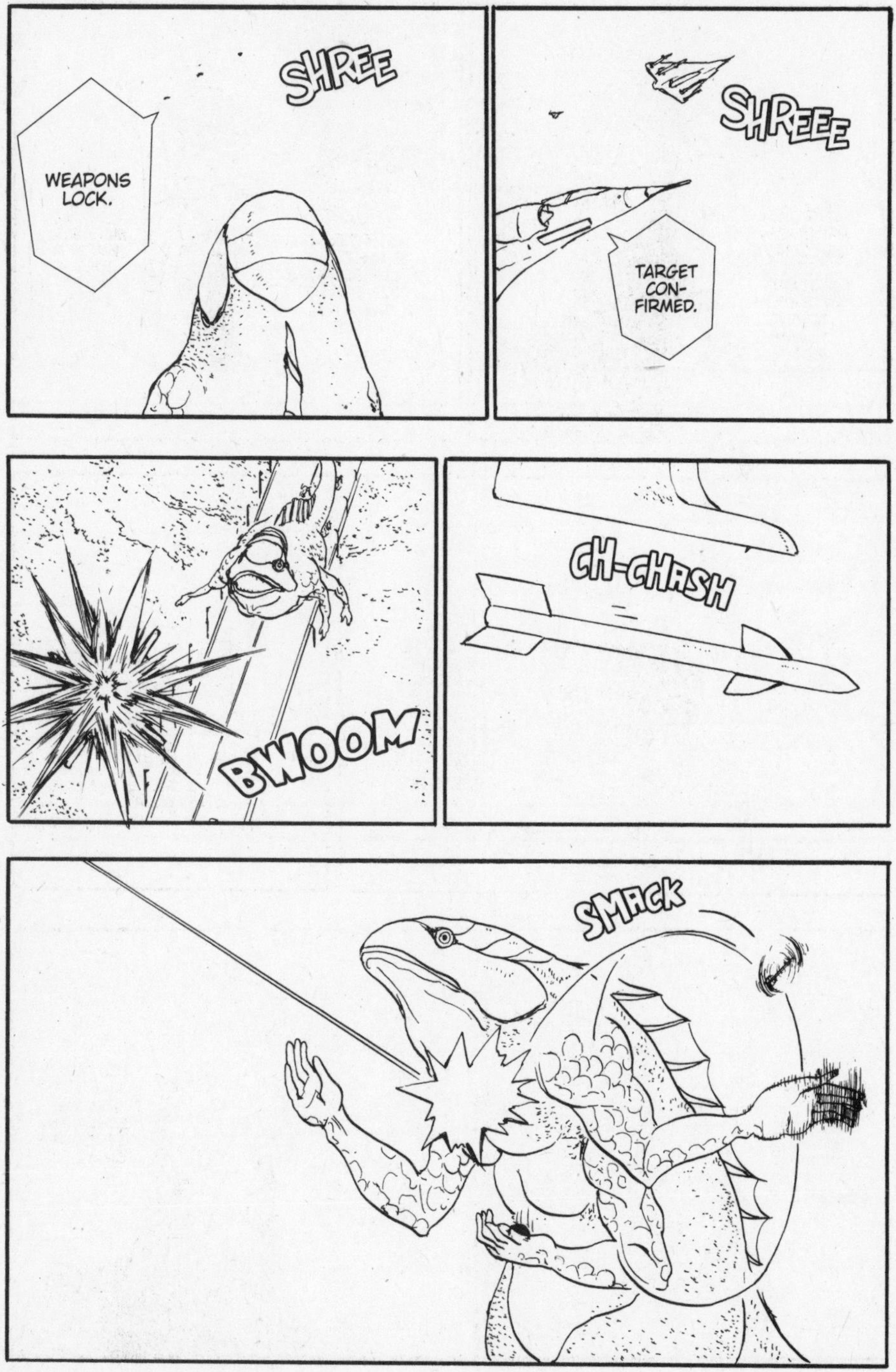
SHREEE
TARGET CONFIRMED.
SHREE
WEAPONS LOCK.
CH-CHASH
BWOOM
SMACK

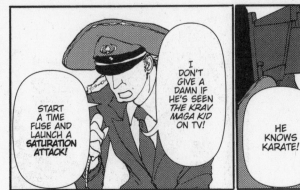

THAT'S A KARATE MOVE.
HE KNOWS KARATE!
I DON'T GIVE A DAMN IF HE'S SEEN *THE KRAV MAGA KID* ON TV!
START A TIME FUSE AND LAUNCH A **SATURATION ATTACK!**

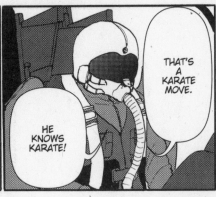

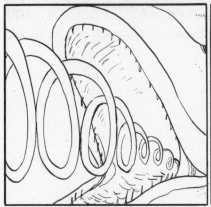

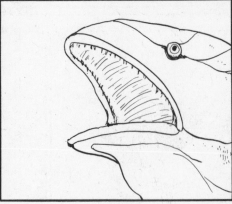

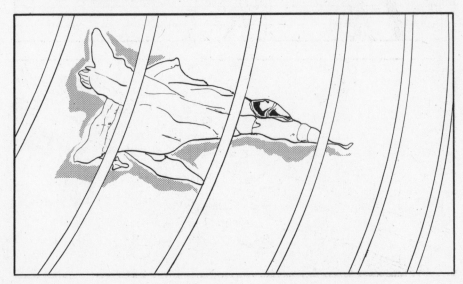

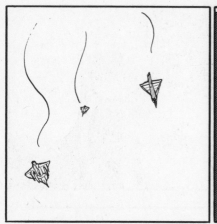

WHA--?! THE SYSTEM'S MALFUNC-TIONING!

I'VE LOST CON-TROL!

I--! I CAN'T EJECT!

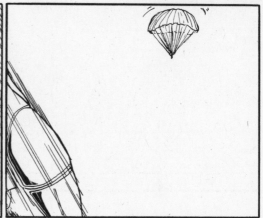

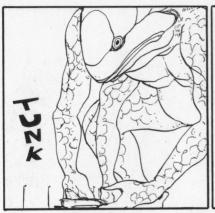

TUNK

I WANT RIGHTS. INCLUDING THE RIGHT TO **EXIST**.

SO, I'M PROTECTING YOUR RIGHT TO LIVE, TOO.

WHY?

COULD MY COUNTRY BE... **WRONG** ABOUT YOU?

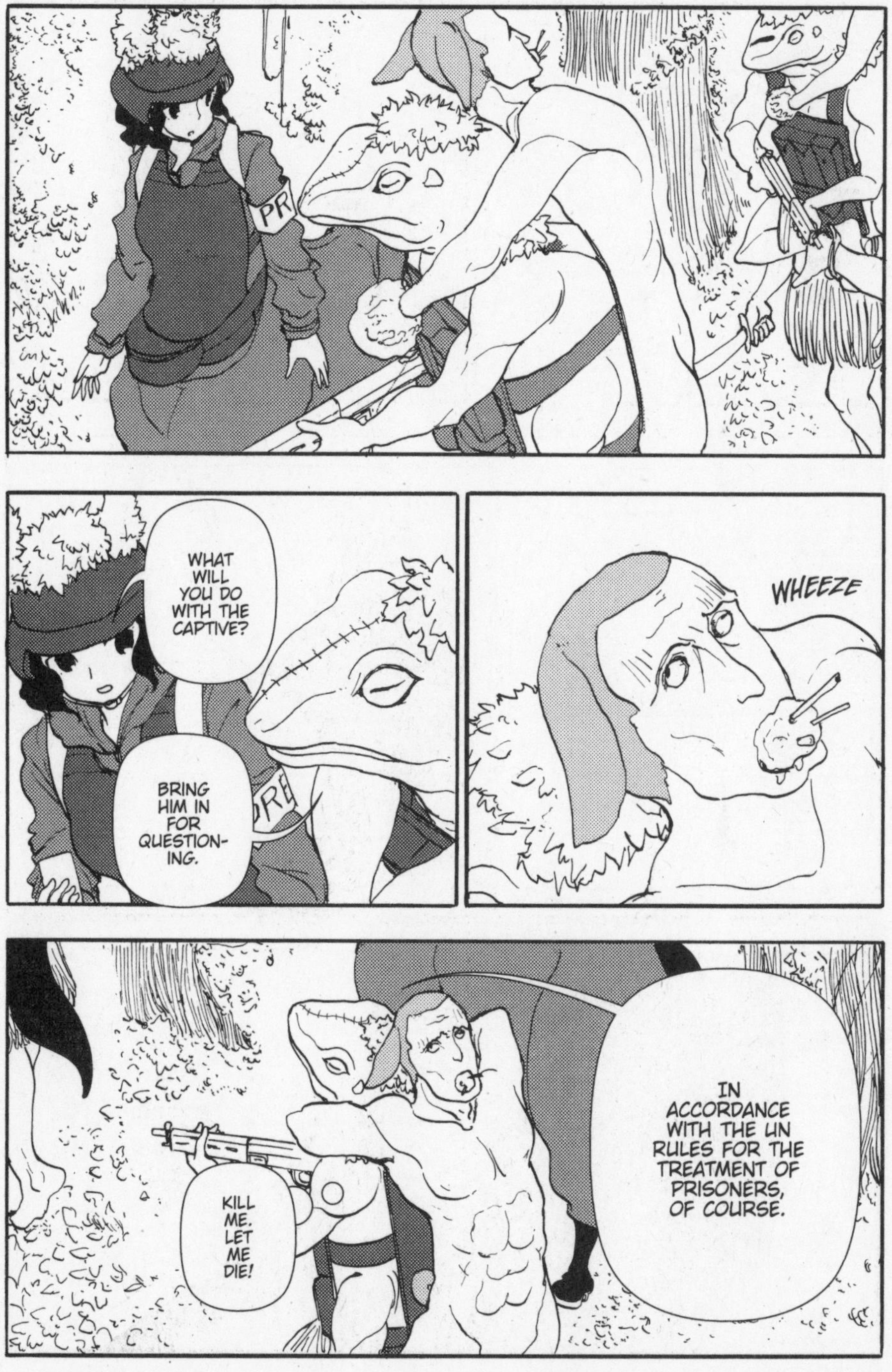
WHEEZE
WHAT WILL YOU DO WITH THE CAPTIVE?
BRING HIM IN FOR QUESTION-ING.
IN ACCORDANCE WITH THE UN RULES FOR THE TREATMENT OF PRISONERS, OF COURSE.
KILL ME. LET ME DIE!

The mysterious giant creature...

WHO'D WANT TO MISS THIS?

EVERYONE'S INTO MONSTERS NOW.

TAMA-CHAN LEFT AS SOON AS SHE FOUND OUT WE HAD A FREE PERIOD.

I'LL BET THE WORLD HISTORY TEACHER TOOK THE DAY OFF TO WATCH THIS.

	Monday	Tuesday	...day
1	Modern Japanese		
2	Physics		
3	Chemistry		
4	Phys. Ed.	Ph	
5	Govt/Econ	Japanese History	Chemistry
6	World History	Geopolitics	Health

IS IT TRUE THAT ANTARCTICA IS INVOLVED?

ANY RIGHTEOUS PERSON WILL BE SAVED.

PRIESTESS, IS THIS THE END OF THE WORLD?

SO MANY PAYING VISITORS. I SHOULD THANK THE MONSTER.

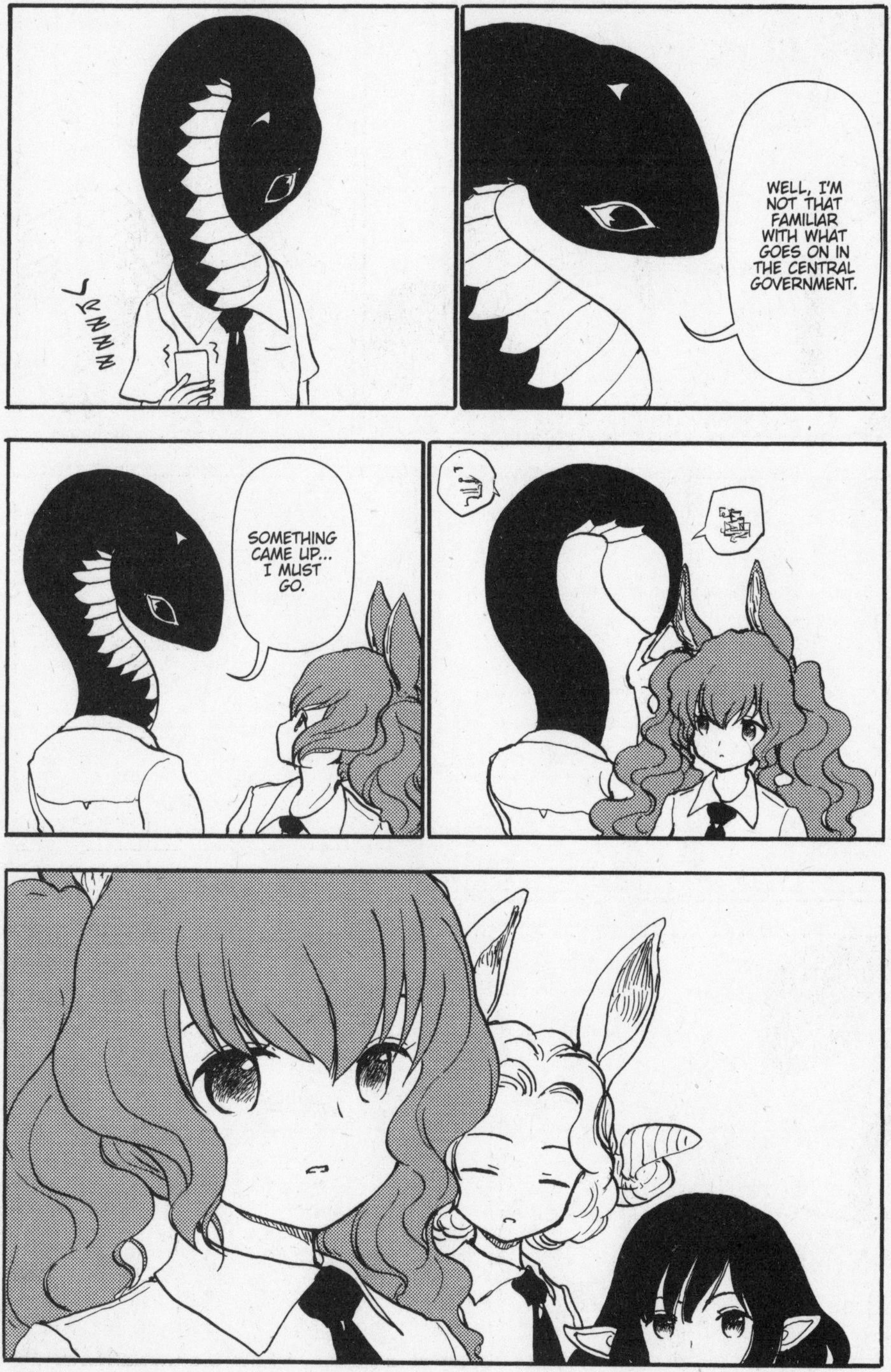
WELL, I'M NOT THAT FAMILIAR WITH WHAT GOES ON IN THE CENTRAL GOVERNMENT.
SOMETHING CAME UP... I MUST GO.

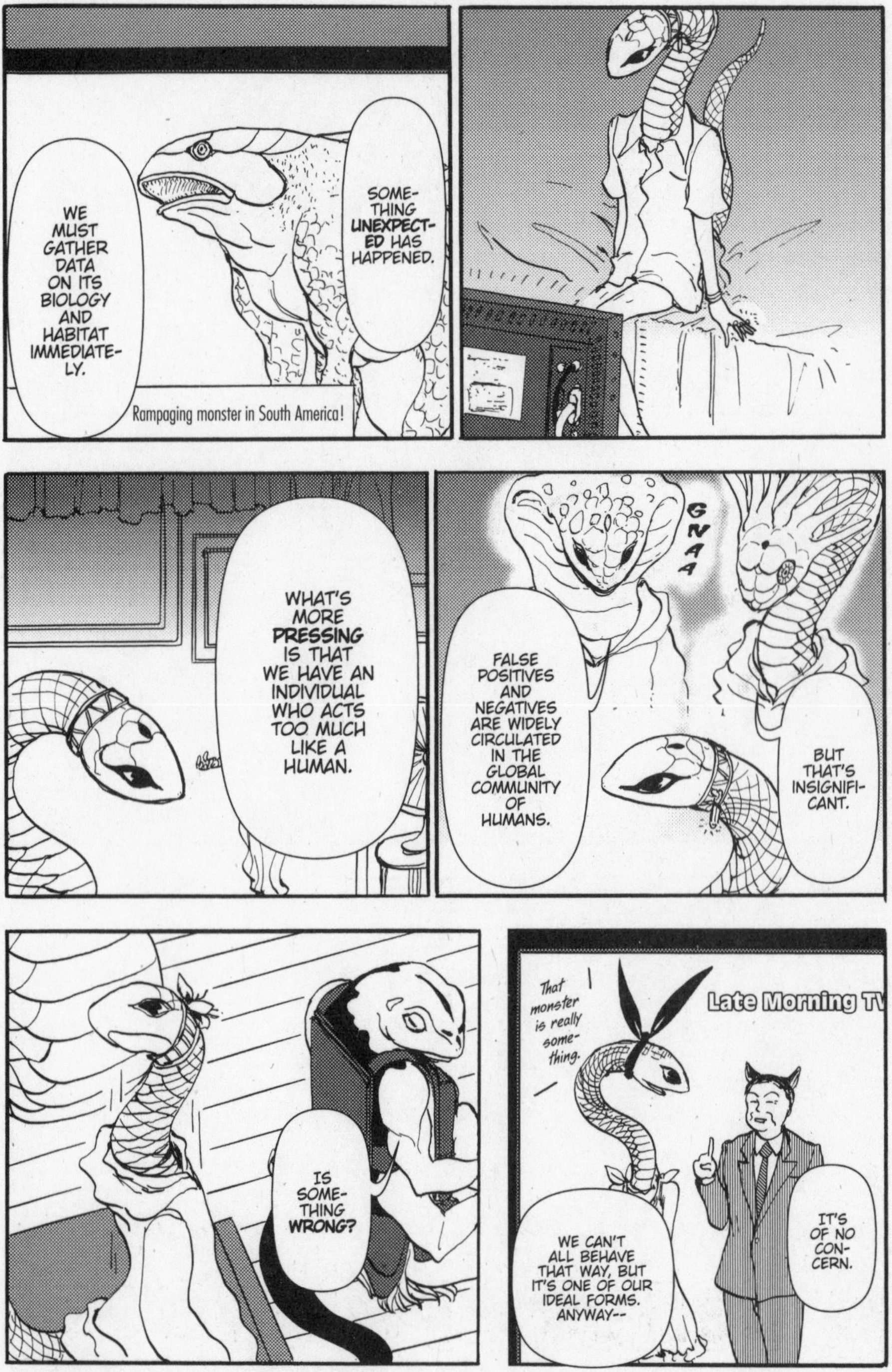
SOMETHING UNEXPECTED HAS HAPPENED.
WE MUST GATHER DATA ON ITS BIOLOGY AND HABITAT IMMEDIATELY.
Rampaging monster in South America!
GNAA
FALSE POSITIVES AND NEGATIVES ARE WIDELY CIRCULATED IN THE GLOBAL COMMUNITY OF HUMANS.
BUT THAT'S INSIGNIFICANT.
WHAT'S MORE PRESSING IS THAT WE HAVE AN INDIVIDUAL WHO ACTS TOO MUCH LIKE A HUMAN.
Late Morning TV
That monster is really something.
IT'S OF NO CONCERN.
WE CAN'T ALL BEHAVE THAT WAY, BUT IT'S ONE OF OUR IDEAL FORMS. ANYWAY--
IS SOMETHING WRONG?

A Centaur's Life

SOLDIERS AROUND THE WORLD:

AMPHIBIANFOLK GUERRILLA

HISTORICALLY, THE AMPHIBIANFOLK LIVED IN NUMEROUS TRIBES WITH PRIMITIVE LIFESTYLES, BUT THEY HAVE RECENTLY BECOME MORE ORGANIZED, AND HAVE EVEN STAGED ARMED UPRISINGS. WITHIN THE PAST YEAR, THEY HAVE ESTABLISHED A TERRITORY LARGE ENOUGH TO BE CONSIDERED AN INDEPENDENT NATION.

IF PROMINENT AMPHIBIANFOLK ENTREPRENEUR JEAN ROUSSEAU CAN BE SEEN AS A TYPICAL EXAMPLE, THEN AMPHIBIANFOLK ARE LIKELY TO HAVE AN INTELLECTUAL CAPACITY COMPARABLE TO THAT OF MAMMALIAN HUMANS. IT'S IMPORTANT TO NOTE THAT MR. ROUSSEAU WAS INTRODUCED TO HUMAN SOCIETY AT A YOUNG AGE AND RECEIVED A HIGH-QUALITY MODERN EDUCATION, BUT THE READINESS WITH WHICH THE OTHER AMPHIBIANFOLK HAVE TAKEN TO MODERN TECHNOLOGY HAS SHOCKED THE WORLD. DESPITE THEIR LACK OF EDUCATION AND SCIENTIFIC LITERACY, AMPHIBIANFOLK HAVE BEEN ABLE TO FULLY UTILIZE EVERYTHING FROM COMMUNICATIONS TECHNOLOGY LIKE THE INTERNET, SMARTPHONES, AND SOCIAL NETWORKING, TO MODERN WEAPONRY LIKE ADVANCED FIREARMS AND PORTABLE MISSILES.

AS SCIENCE AND TECHNOLOGY HAVE CHANGED AND FACILITATED WARFARE FOR MAMMALIAN SOCIETY, SO TOO WILL IT CHANGE AND FACILITATE WARFARE FOR THE AMPHIBIANFOLK.

CHAPTER 107

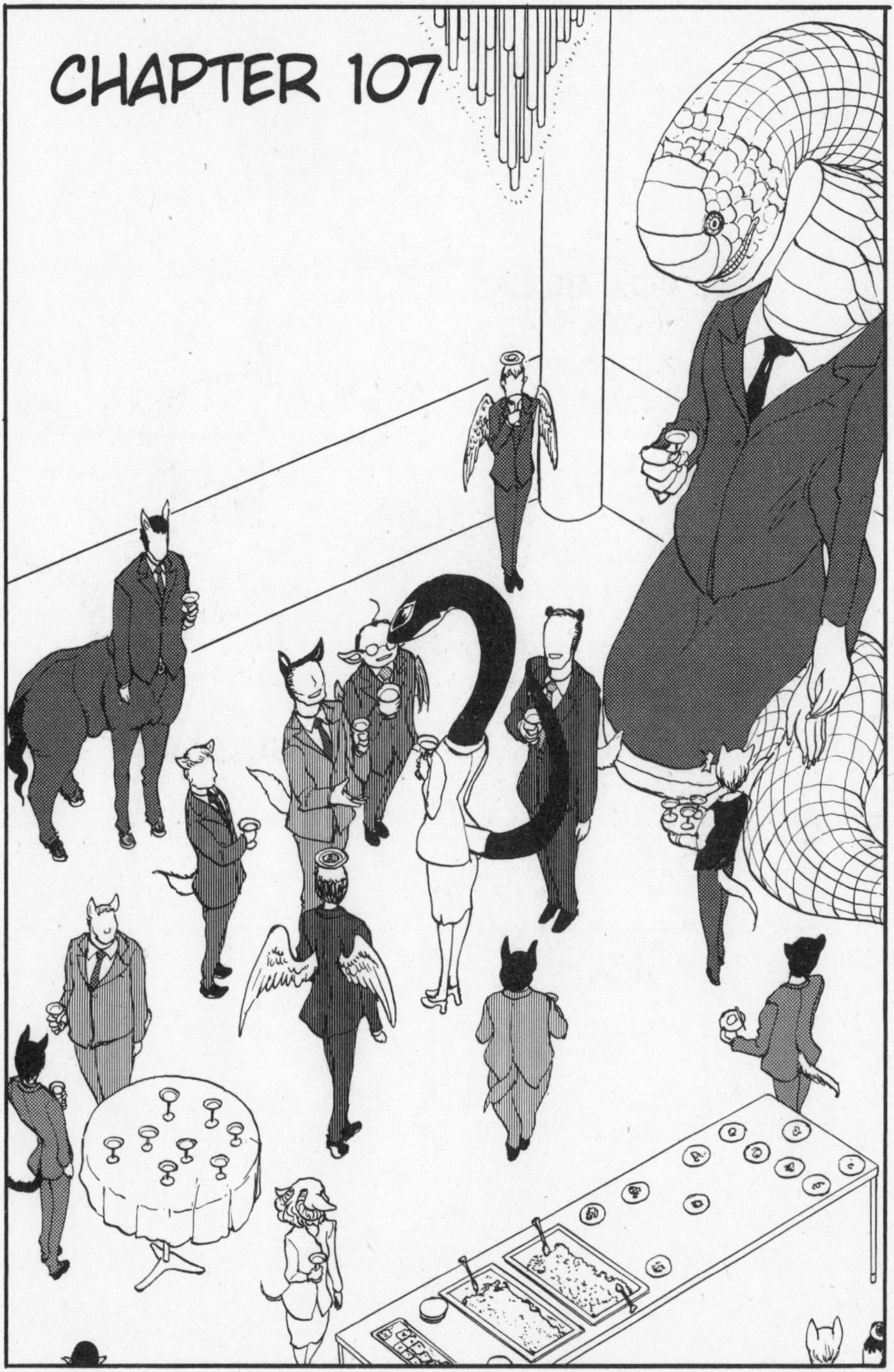

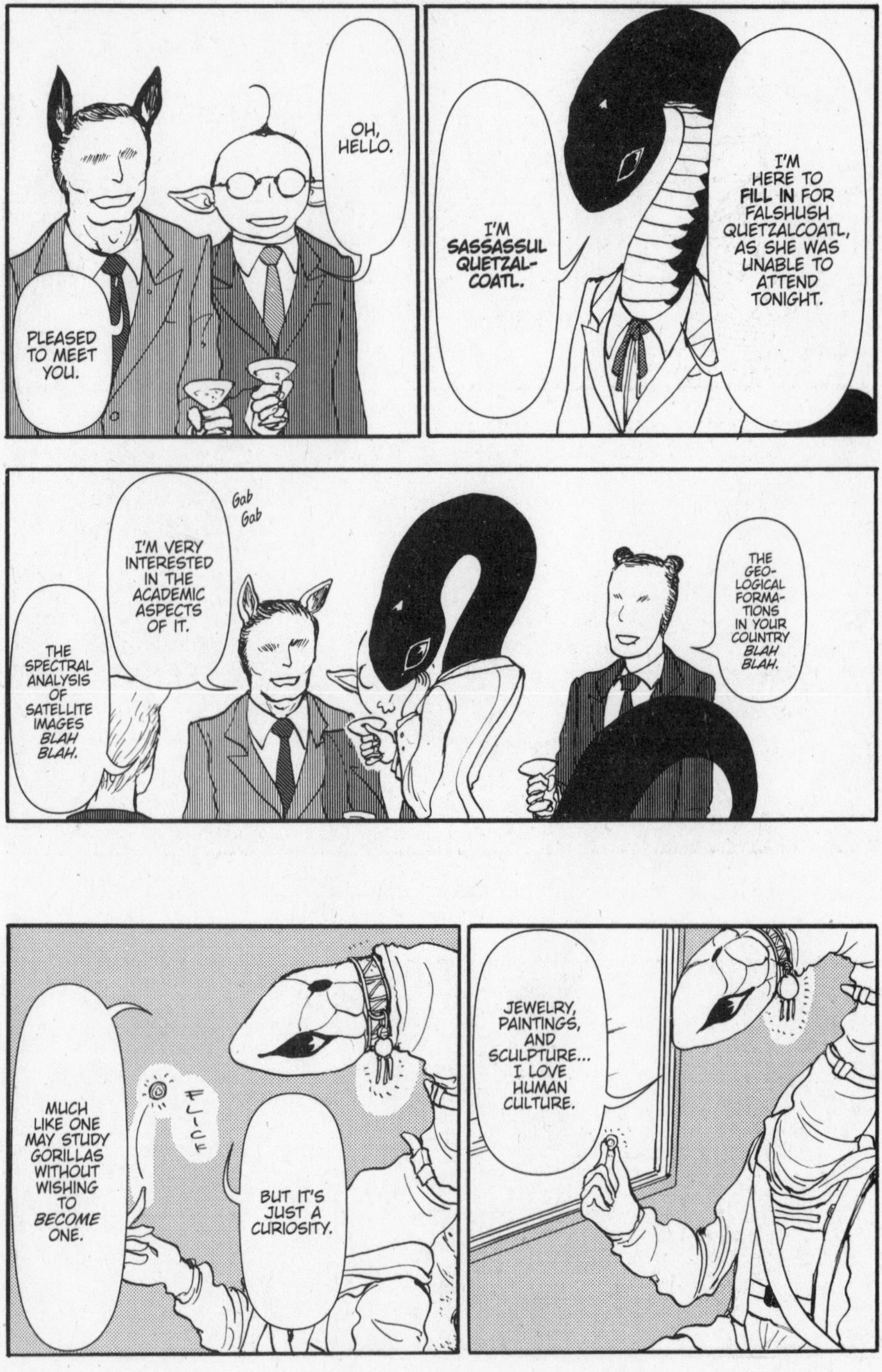
I'M HERE TO **FILL IN** FOR FALSHUSH QUETZALCOATL, AS SHE WAS UNABLE TO ATTEND TONIGHT.
I'M SASSASSUL QUETZALCOATL.
OH, HELLO.
PLEASED TO MEET YOU.
THE GEOLOGICAL FORMATIONS IN YOUR COUNTRY *BLAH BLAH.*
Gab Gab
I'M VERY INTERESTED IN THE ACADEMIC ASPECTS OF IT.
THE SPECTRAL ANALYSIS OF SATELLITE IMAGES *BLAH BLAH.*
JEWELRY, PAINTINGS, AND SCULPTURE... I LOVE HUMAN CULTURE.
FLICK
BUT IT'S JUST A CURIOSITY.
MUCH LIKE ONE MAY STUDY GORILLAS WITHOUT WISHING TO *BECOME* ONE.

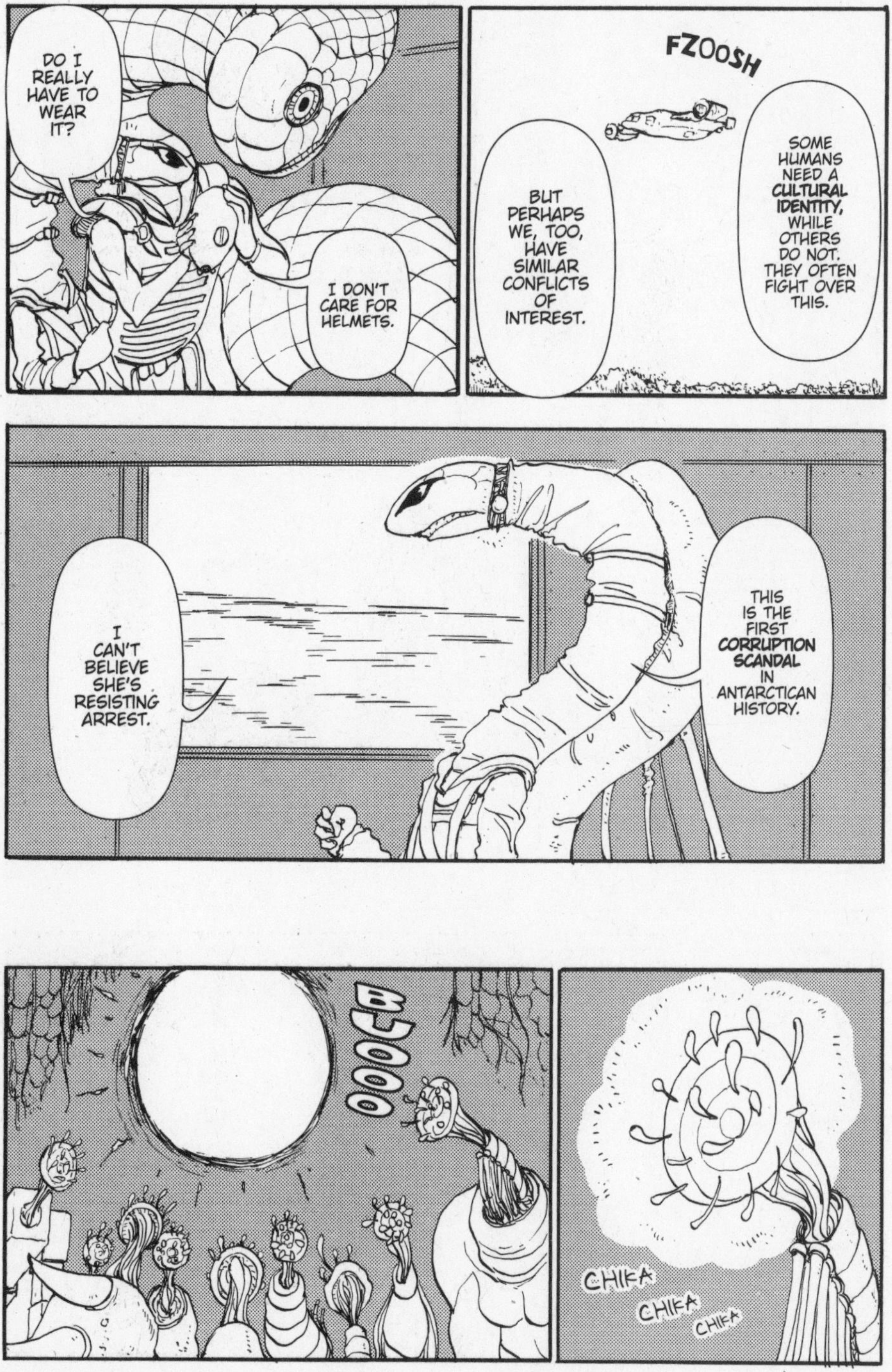
FZOOSH
SOME HUMANS NEED A **CULTURAL IDENTITY,** WHILE OTHERS DO NOT. THEY OFTEN FIGHT OVER THIS.
BUT PERHAPS WE, TOO, HAVE SIMILAR CONFLICTS OF INTEREST.
DO I REALLY HAVE TO WEAR IT?
I DON'T CARE FOR HELMETS.
THIS IS THE FIRST **CORRUPTION SCANDAL** IN ANTARCTICAN HISTORY.
I CAN'T BELIEVE SHE'S RESISTING ARREST.
CHIKA
CHIKA
CHIKA
BJOOOO

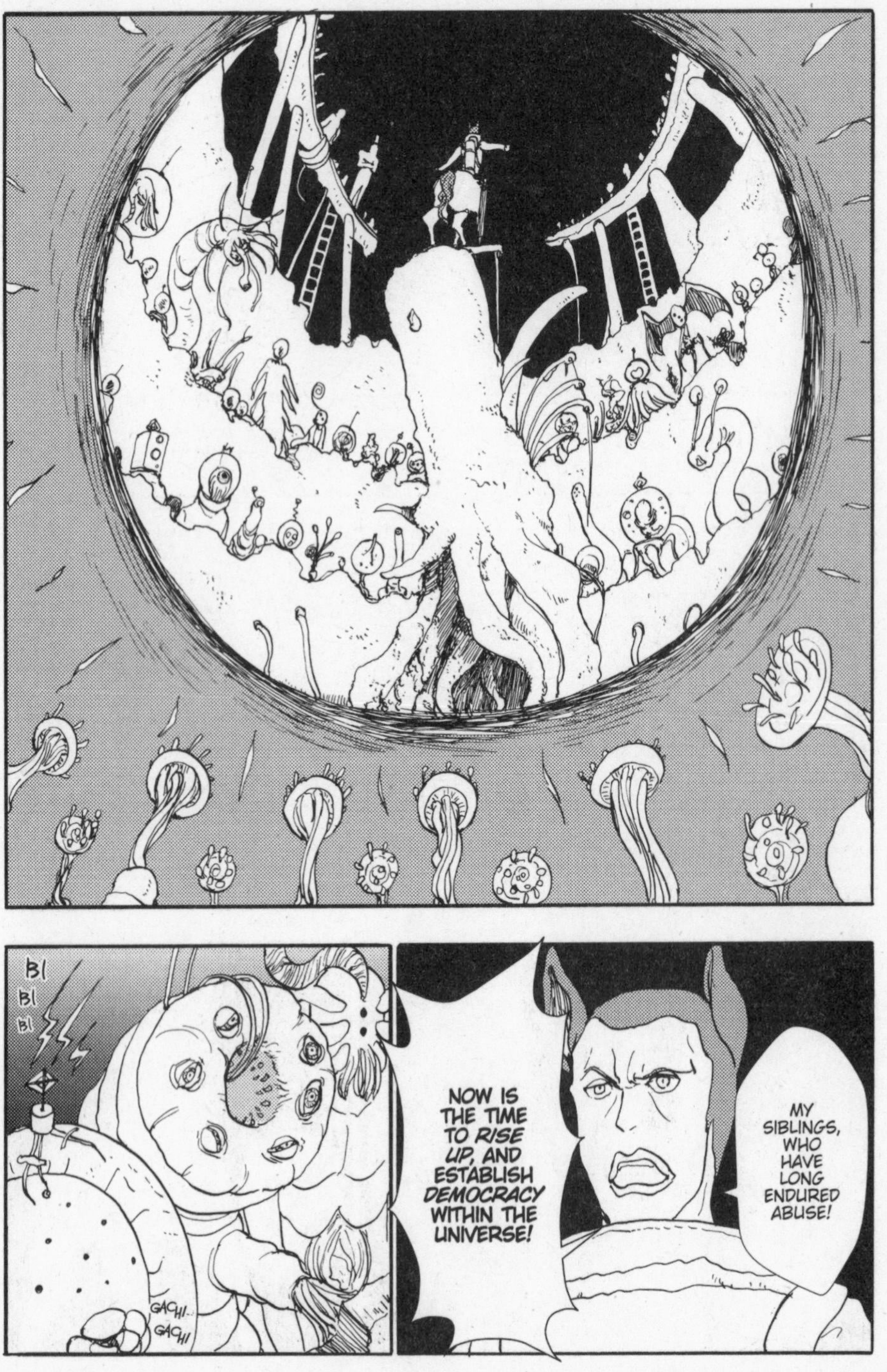
MY SIBLINGS, WHO HAVE LONG ENDURED ABUSE!
NOW IS THE TIME TO *RISE UP*, AND ESTABLISH *DEMOCRACY* WITHIN THE UNIVERSE!
BI BI BI
GACHI GACHI

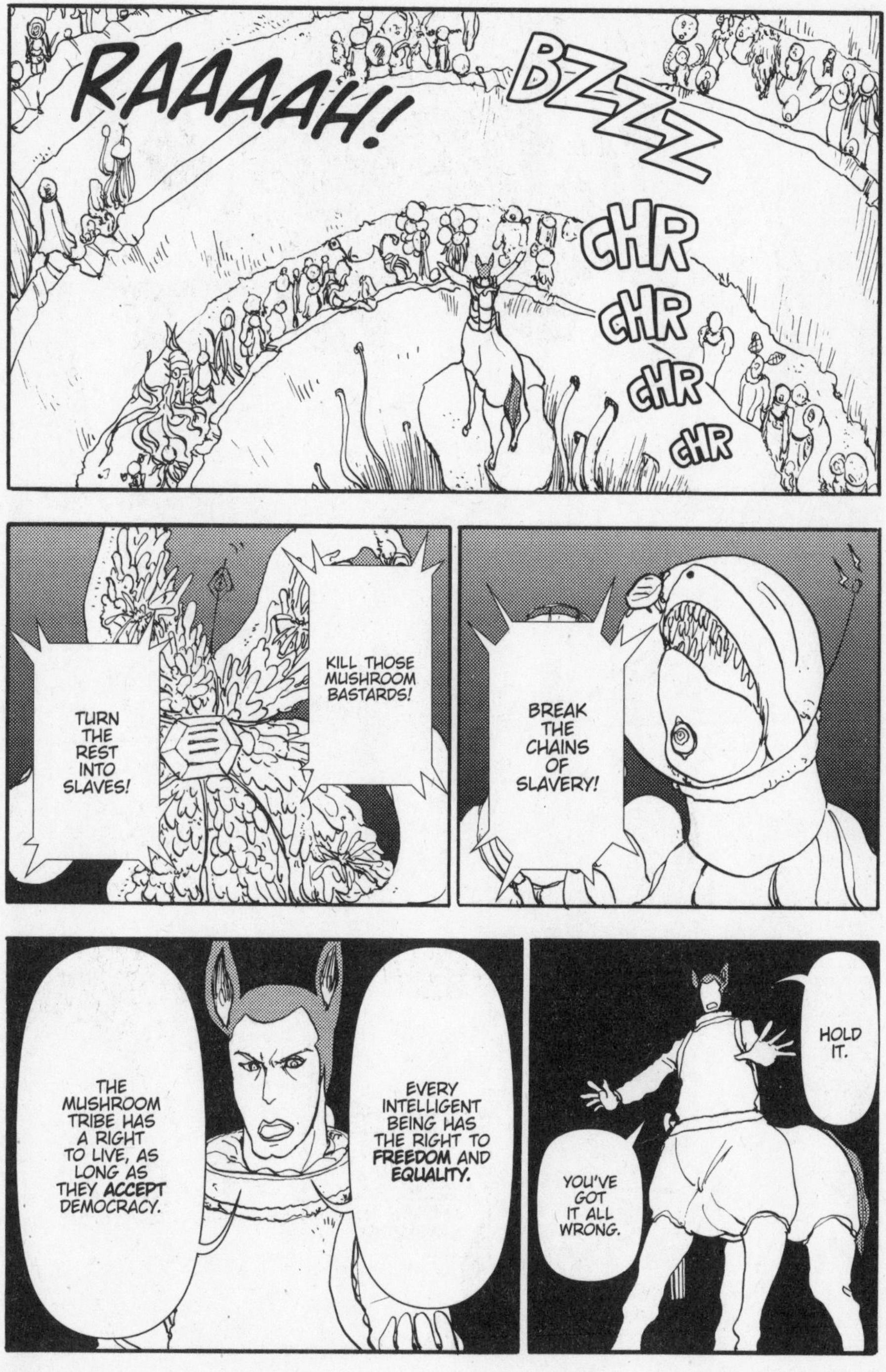
BZZZ
CHR CHR CHR CHR
RAAAAH!
BREAK THE CHAINS OF SLAVERY!
KILL THOSE MUSHROOM BASTARDS!
TURN THE REST INTO SLAVES!
HOLD IT.
YOU'VE GOT IT ALL WRONG.
EVERY INTELLIGENT BEING HAS THE RIGHT TO **FREEDOM** AND **EQUALITY.**
THE MUSHROOM TRIBE HAS A RIGHT TO LIVE, AS LONG AS THEY **ACCEPT** DEMOCRACY.

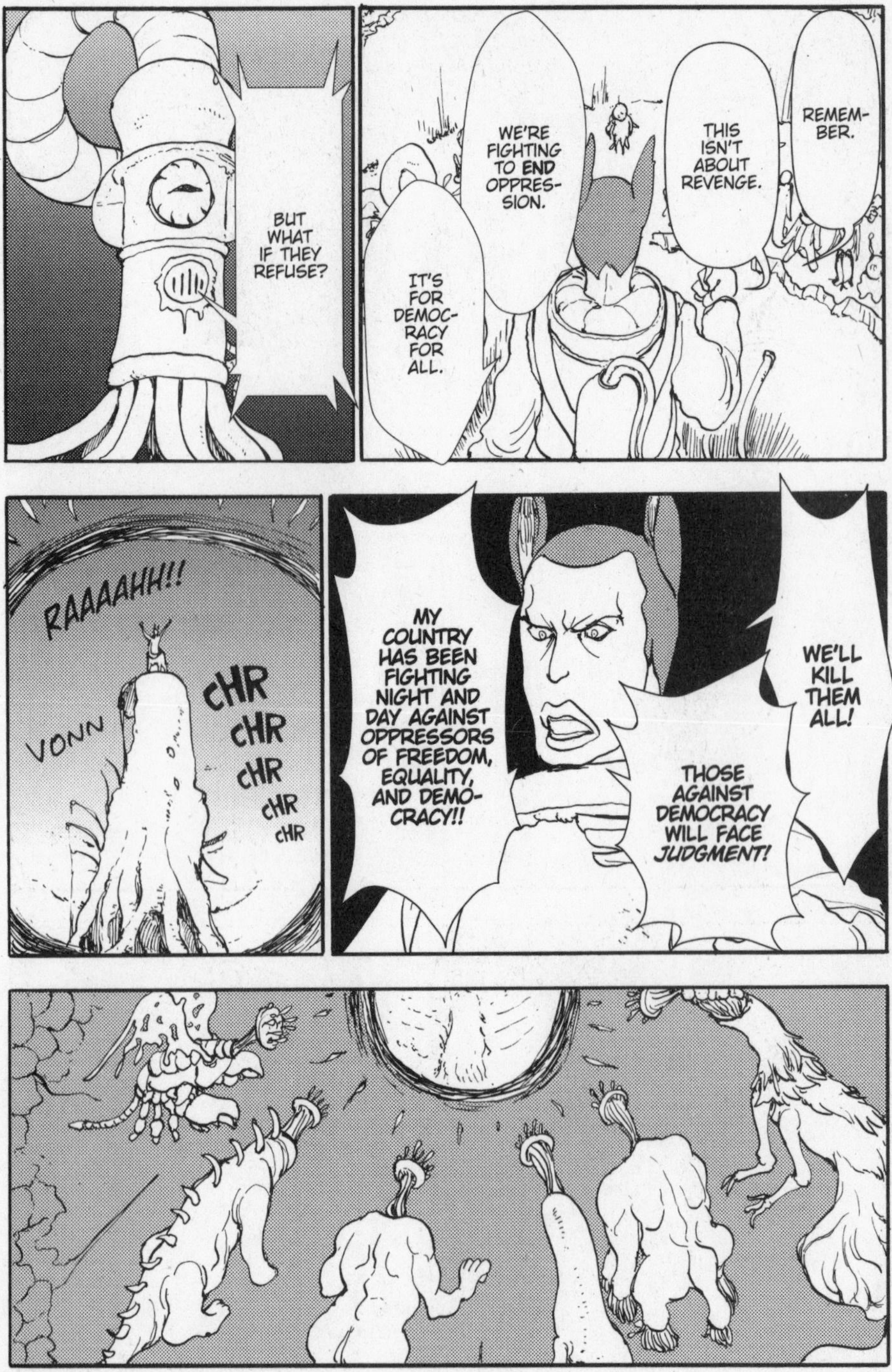
REMEMBER.
THIS ISN'T ABOUT REVENGE.
WE'RE FIGHTING TO END OPPRESSION.
IT'S FOR DEMOCRACY FOR ALL.
BUT WHAT IF THEY REFUSE?
WE'LL KILL THEM ALL!
MY COUNTRY HAS BEEN FIGHTING NIGHT AND DAY AGAINST OPPRESSORS OF FREEDOM, EQUALITY, AND DEMOCRACY!!
THOSE AGAINST DEMOCRACY WILL FACE JUDGMENT!
RAAAAHH!!
CHR CHR CHR CHR CHR
VONN

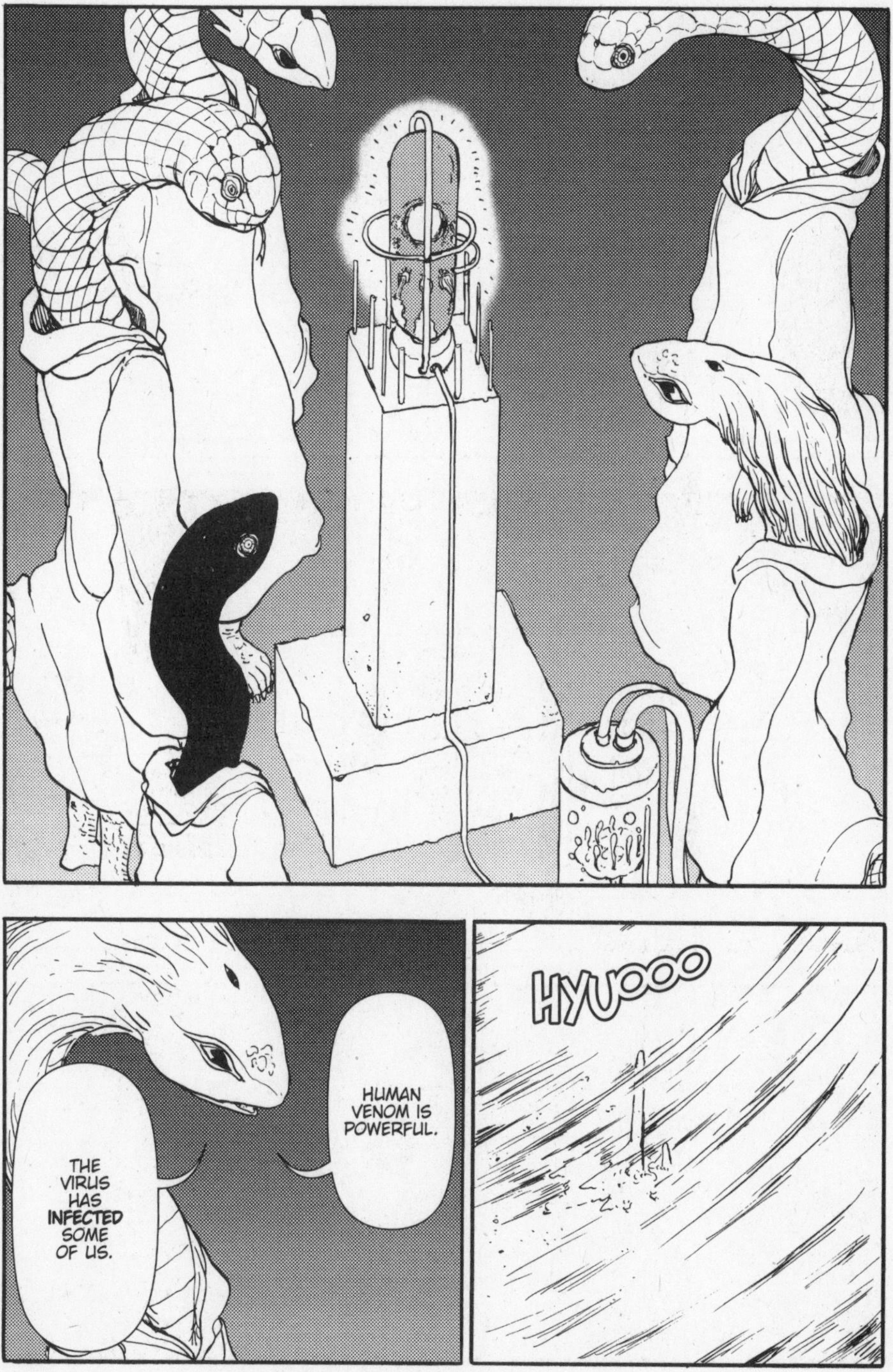
HYUOOO
HUMAN VENOM IS POWERFUL.
THE VIRUS HAS INFECTED SOME OF US.

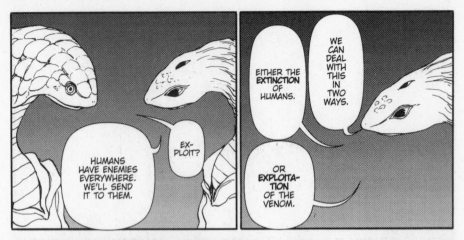

WE CAN DEAL WITH THIS IN TWO WAYS.
EITHER THE **EXTINCTION** OF HUMANS.
OR **EXPLOITATION** OF THE VENOM.
EXPLOIT?
HUMANS HAVE ENEMIES EVERYWHERE. WE'LL SEND IT TO THEM.
THIS SOUNDS LIKE BIOLOGICAL WARFARE.
BUT HUMANS ARE SELF-SUFFICIENT.
WE'RE MORE DEPENDENT ON *THEM*, IF ANYTHING.
FOR THIS REASON, WE NEED THEM TO RETAIN THEIR **UNIQUENESS.**
SHUD
SHUD

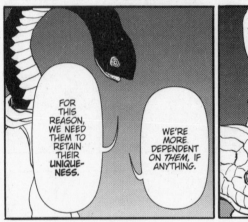

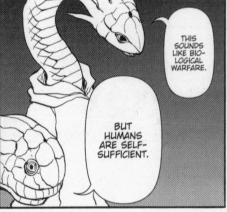

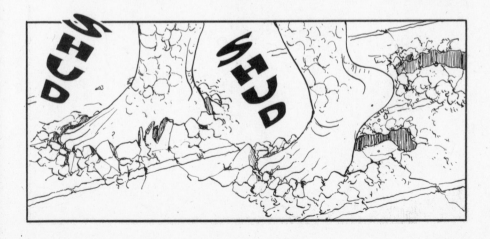

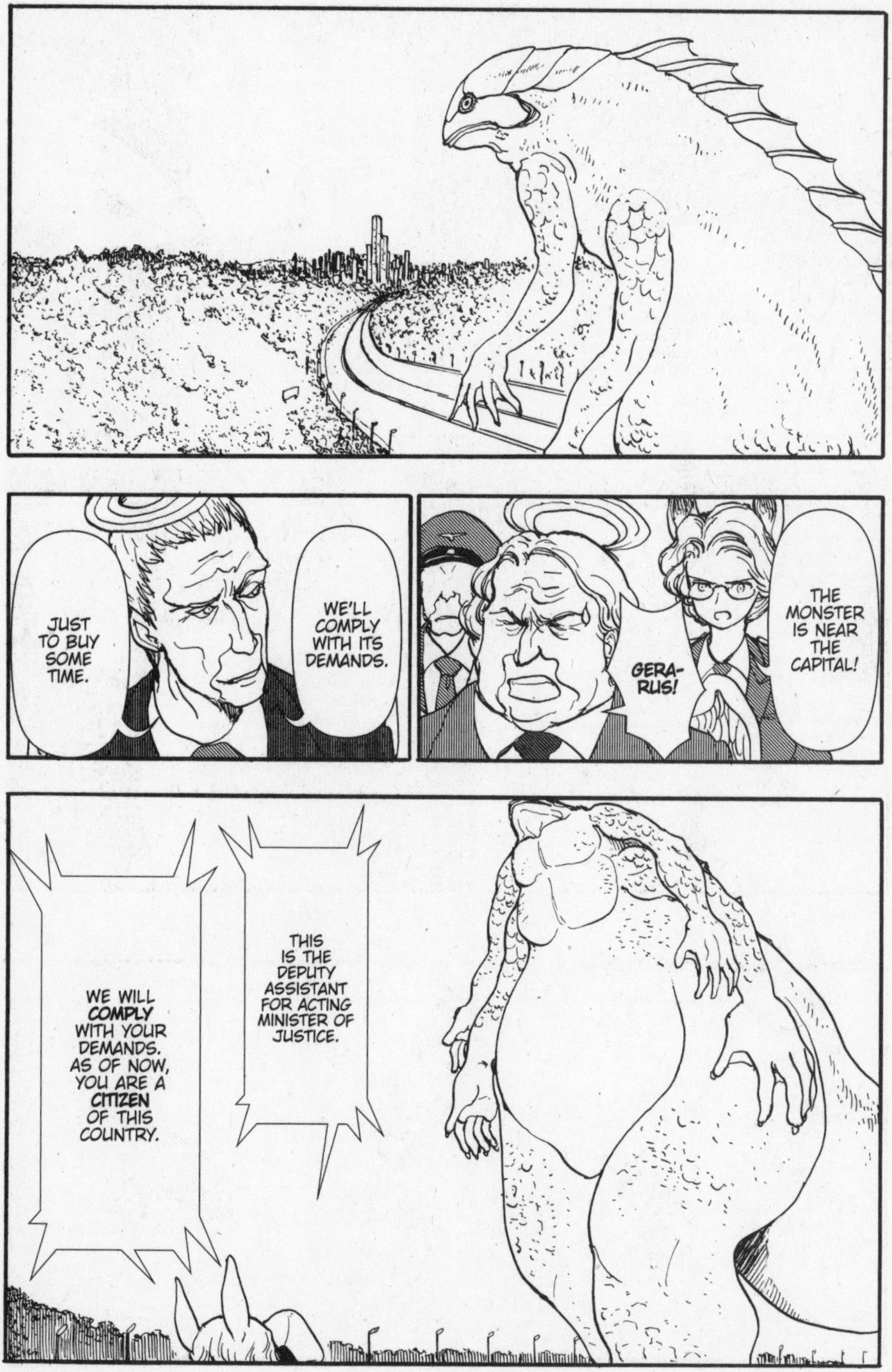
THE MONSTER IS NEAR THE CAPITAL!
GERA-RUS!
WE'LL COMPLY WITH ITS DEMANDS.
JUST TO BUY SOME TIME.
THIS IS THE DEPUTY ASSISTANT FOR ACTING MINISTER OF JUSTICE.
WE WILL **COMPLY** WITH YOUR DEMANDS. AS OF NOW, YOU ARE A **CITIZEN** OF THIS COUNTRY.

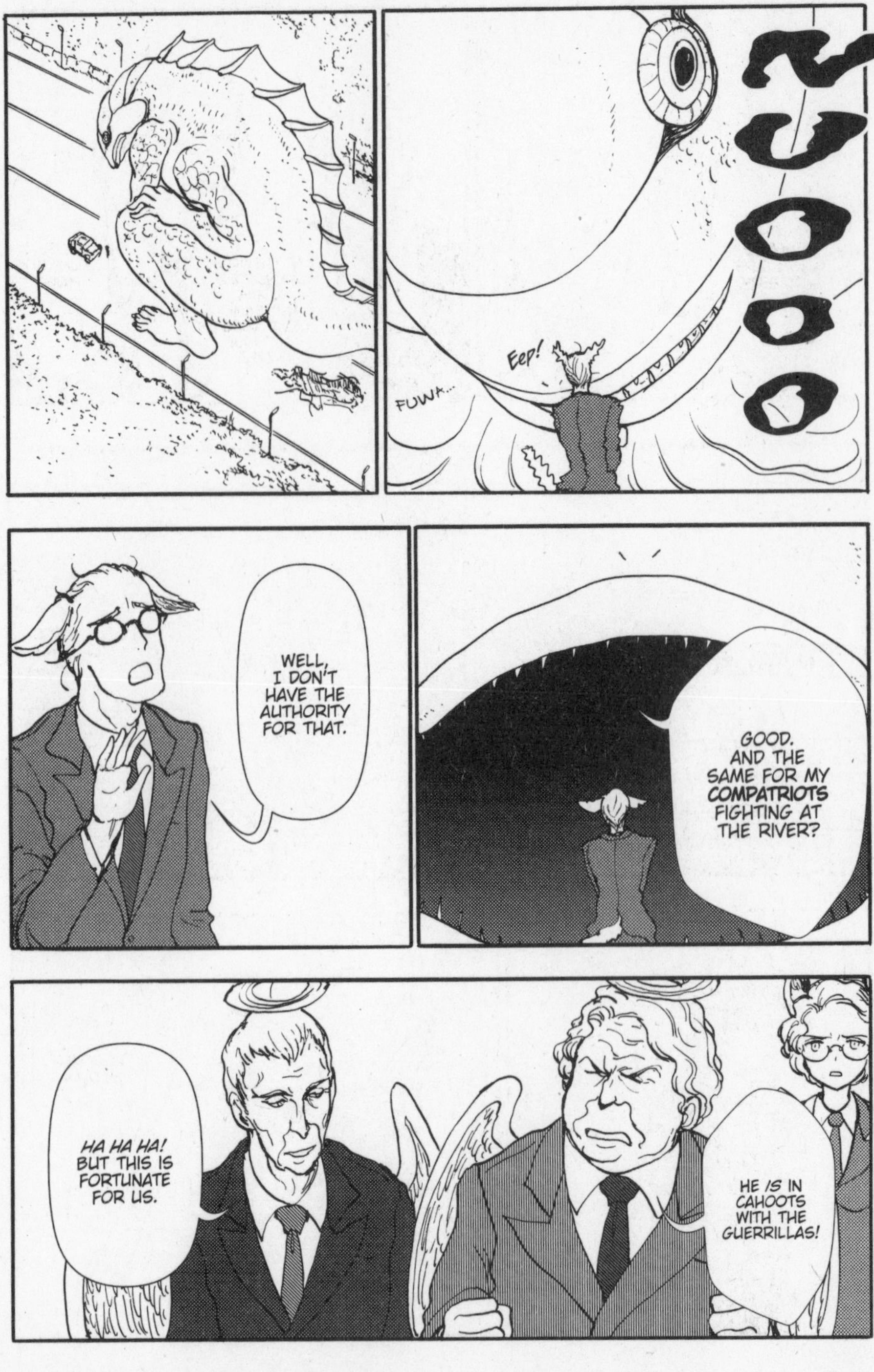
NUOOOO
Eep!
FUWA...
GOOD. AND THE SAME FOR MY **COMPATRIOTS** FIGHTING AT THE RIVER?
WELL, I DON'T HAVE THE AUTHORITY FOR THAT.
HE *IS* IN CAHOOTS WITH THE GUERRILLAS!
HA HA HA! BUT THIS IS FORTUNATE FOR US.

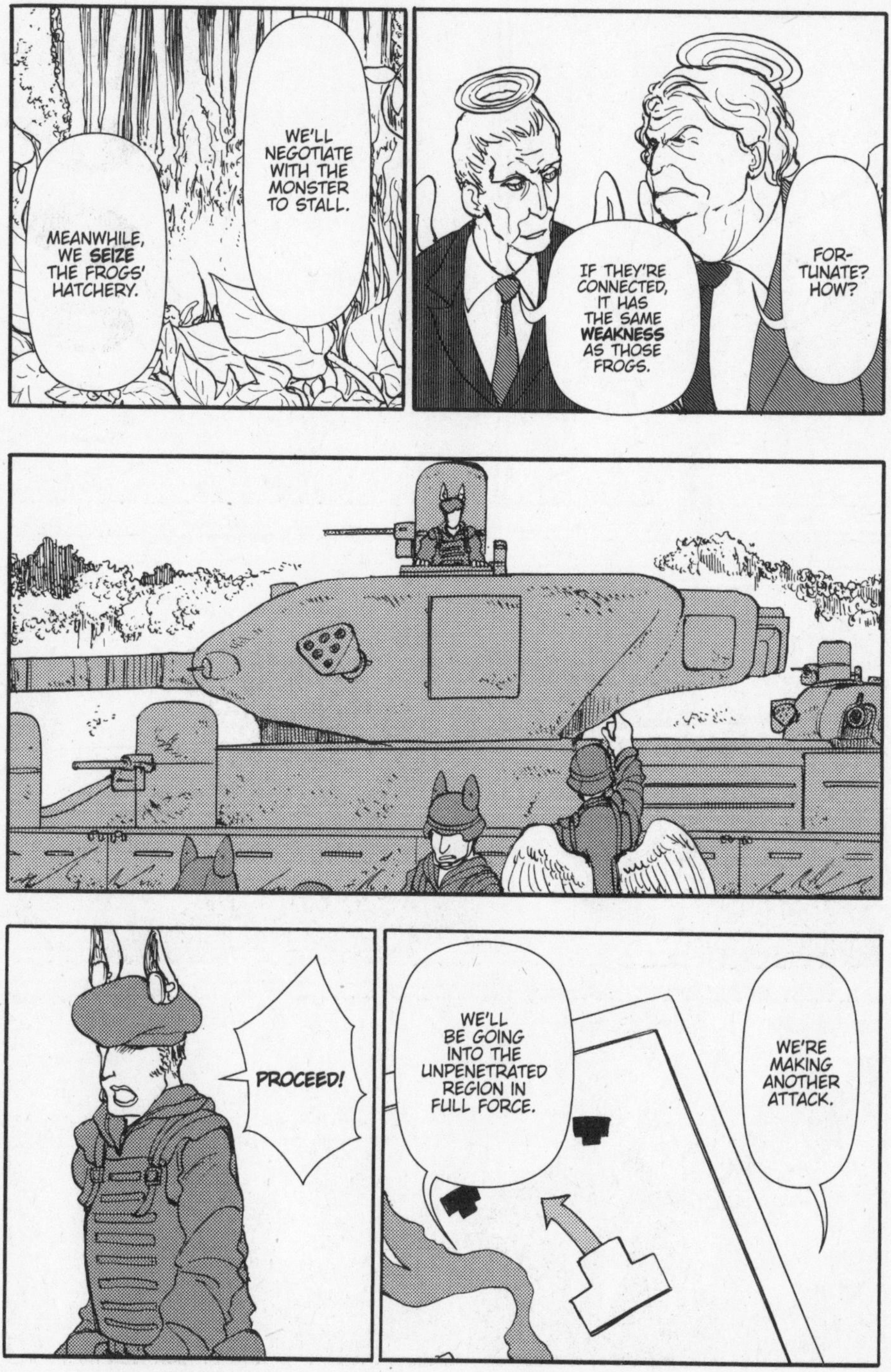
FOR-TUNATE? HOW?
IF THEY'RE CONNECTED, IT HAS THE SAME **WEAKNESS** AS THOSE FROGS.
WE'LL NEGOTIATE WITH THE MONSTER TO STALL.
MEANWHILE, WE **SEIZE** THE FROGS' HATCHERY.
WE'RE MAKING ANOTHER ATTACK.
WE'LL BE GOING INTO THE UNPENETRATED REGION IN FULL FORCE.
PROCEED!

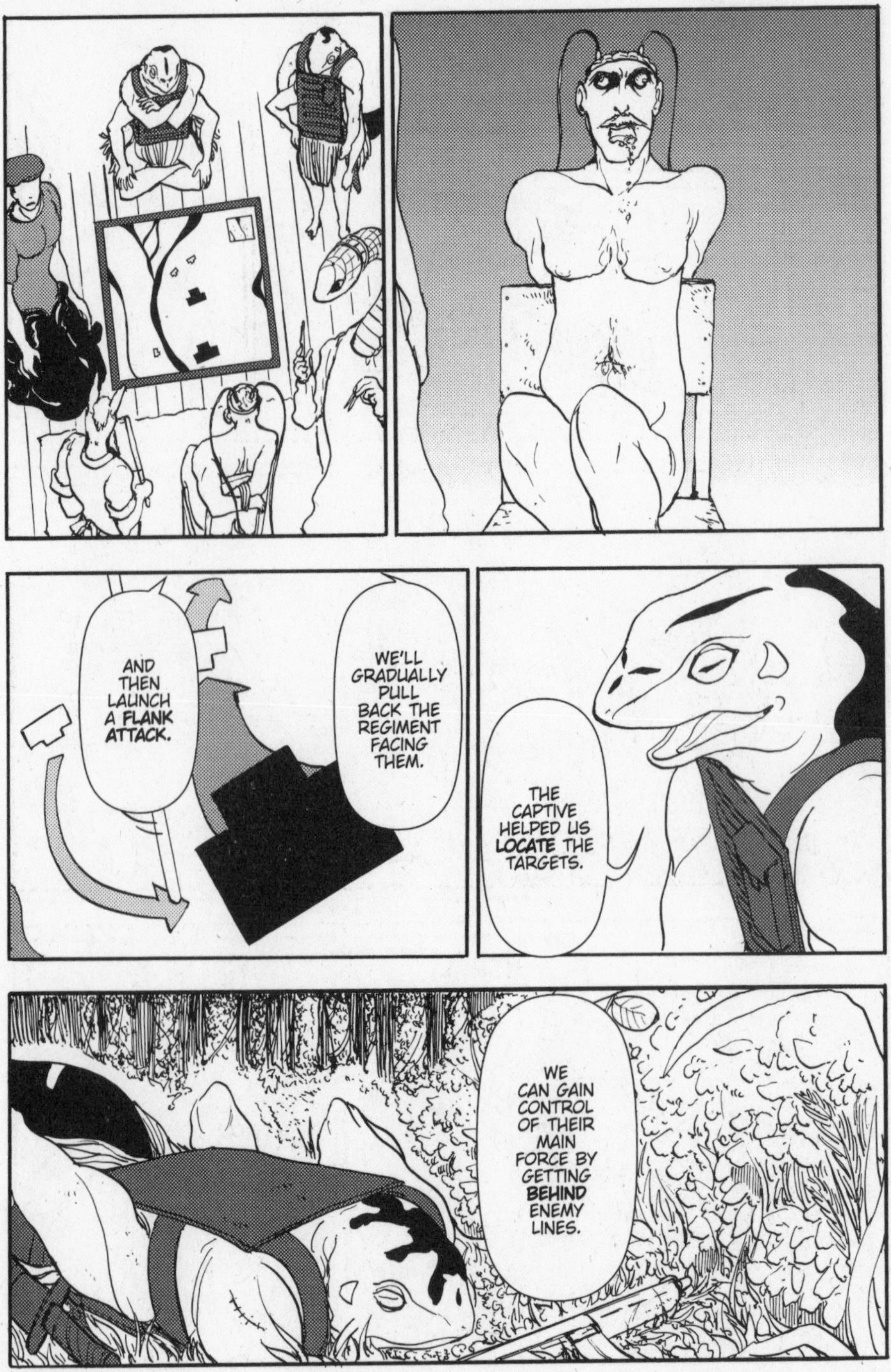
THE CAPTIVE HELPED US LOCATE THE TARGETS.
WE'LL GRADUALLY PULL BACK THE REGIMENT FACING THEM.
AND THEN LAUNCH A FLANK ATTACK.
WE CAN GAIN CONTROL OF THEIR MAIN FORCE BY GETTING BEHIND ENEMY LINES.

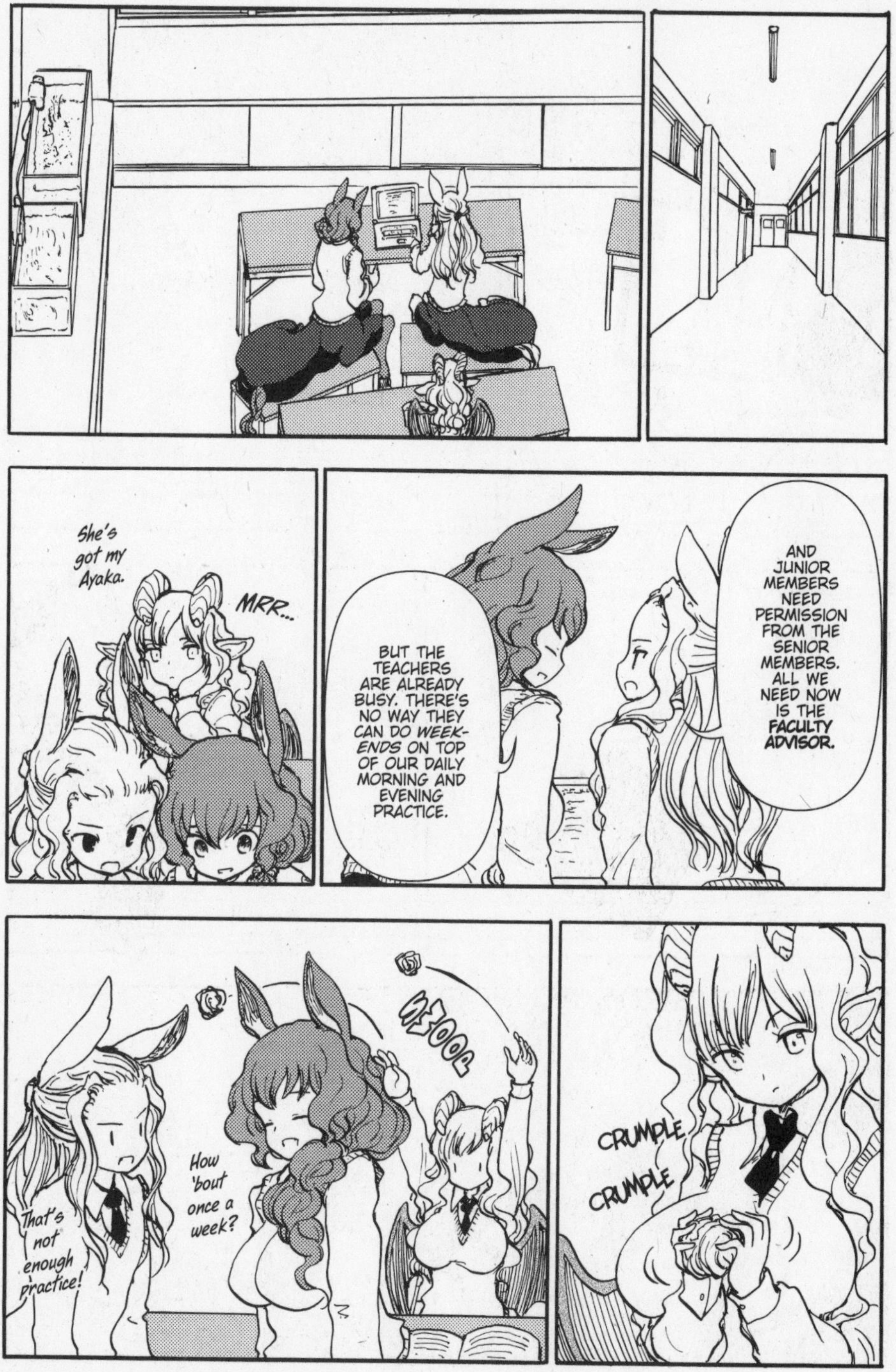
AND JUNIOR MEMBERS NEED PERMISSION FROM THE SENIOR MEMBERS. ALL WE NEED NOW IS THE **FACULTY ADVISOR.**
BUT THE TEACHERS ARE ALREADY BUSY. THERE'S NO WAY THEY CAN DO *WEEKENDS* ON TOP OF OUR DAILY MORNING AND EVENING PRACTICE.
MRR...
She's got my Ayaka.
CRUMPLE
CRUMPLE
WHOOP
How 'bout once a week?
That's not enough practice!

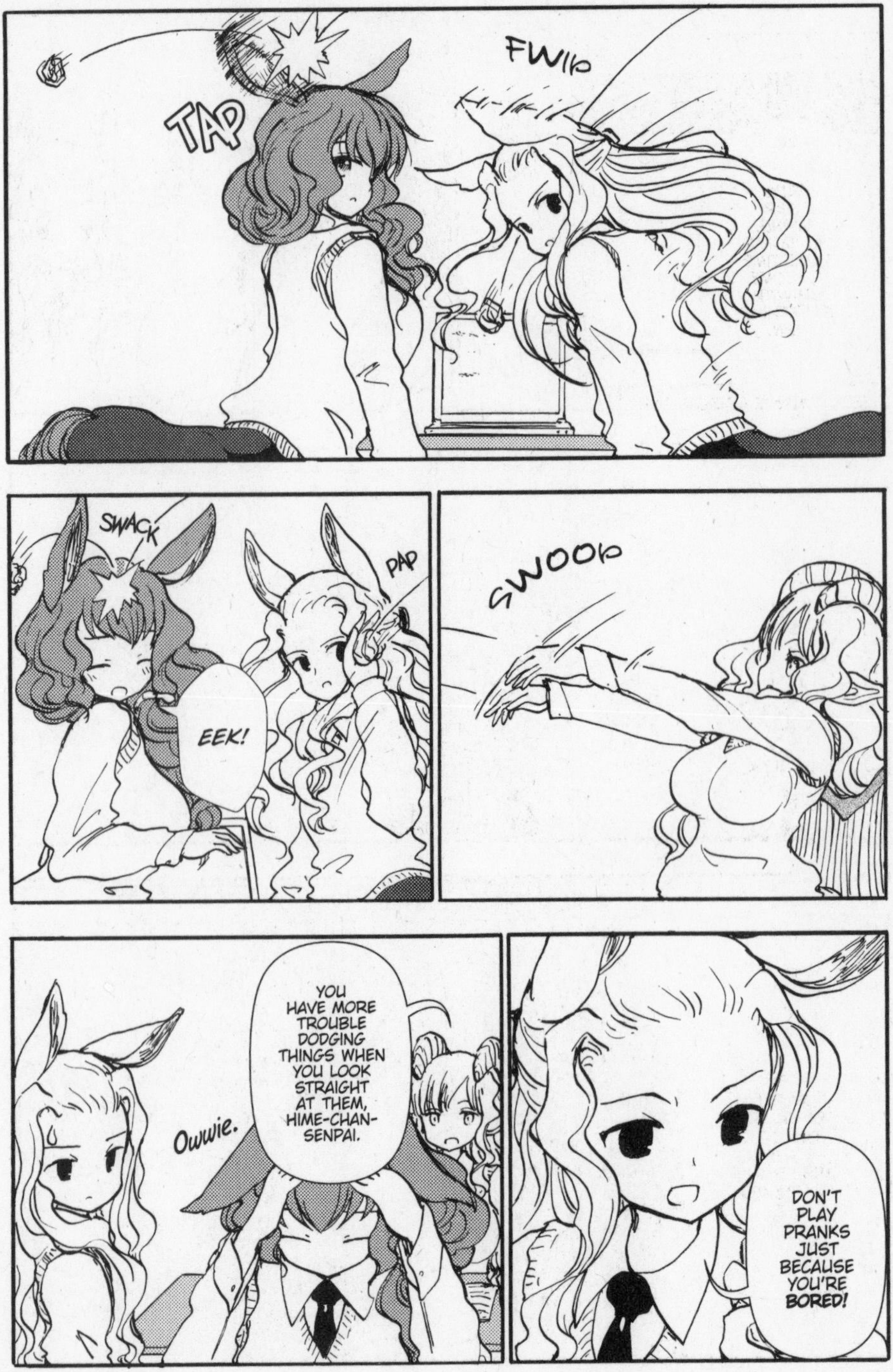
FWIP
TAP
SWOOP
PAP
SWACK
EEK!
DON'T PLAY PRANKS JUST BECAUSE YOU'RE BORED!
YOU HAVE MORE TROUBLE DODGING THINGS WHEN YOU LOOK STRAIGHT AT THEM, HIME-CHAN-SENPAI.
Owwie.

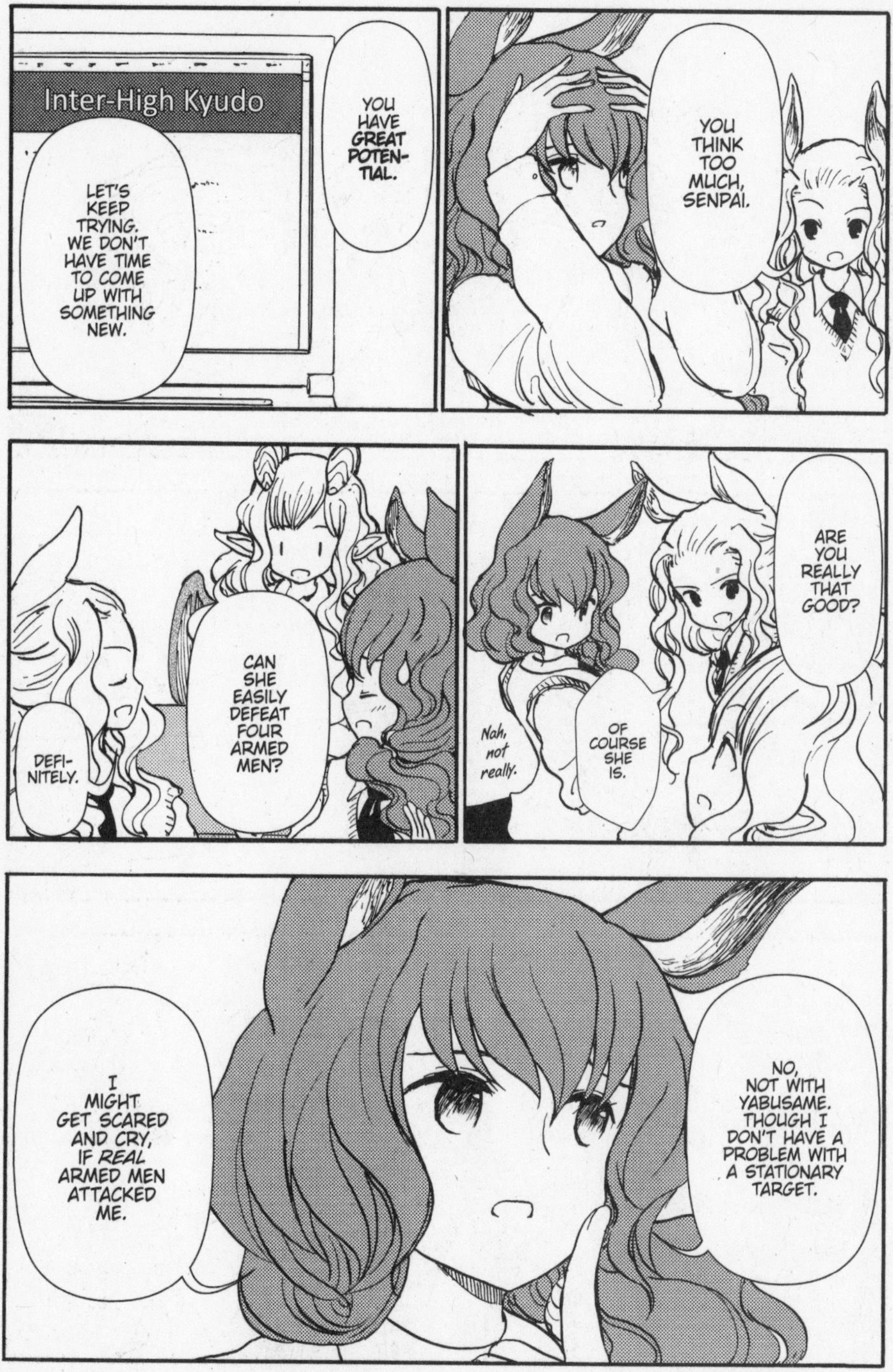
YOU THINK TOO MUCH, SENPAI.
YOU HAVE GREAT POTEN-TIAL.
Inter-High Kyudo
LET'S KEEP TRYING. WE DON'T HAVE TIME TO COME UP WITH SOMETHING NEW.
ARE YOU REALLY THAT GOOD?
OF COURSE SHE IS.
Nah, not really.
CAN SHE EASILY DEFEAT FOUR ARMED MEN?
DEFI-NITELY.
NO, NOT WITH YABUSAME. THOUGH I DON'T HAVE A PROBLEM WITH A STATIONARY TARGET.
I MIGHT GET SCARED AND CRY, IF REAL ARMED MEN ATTACKED ME.

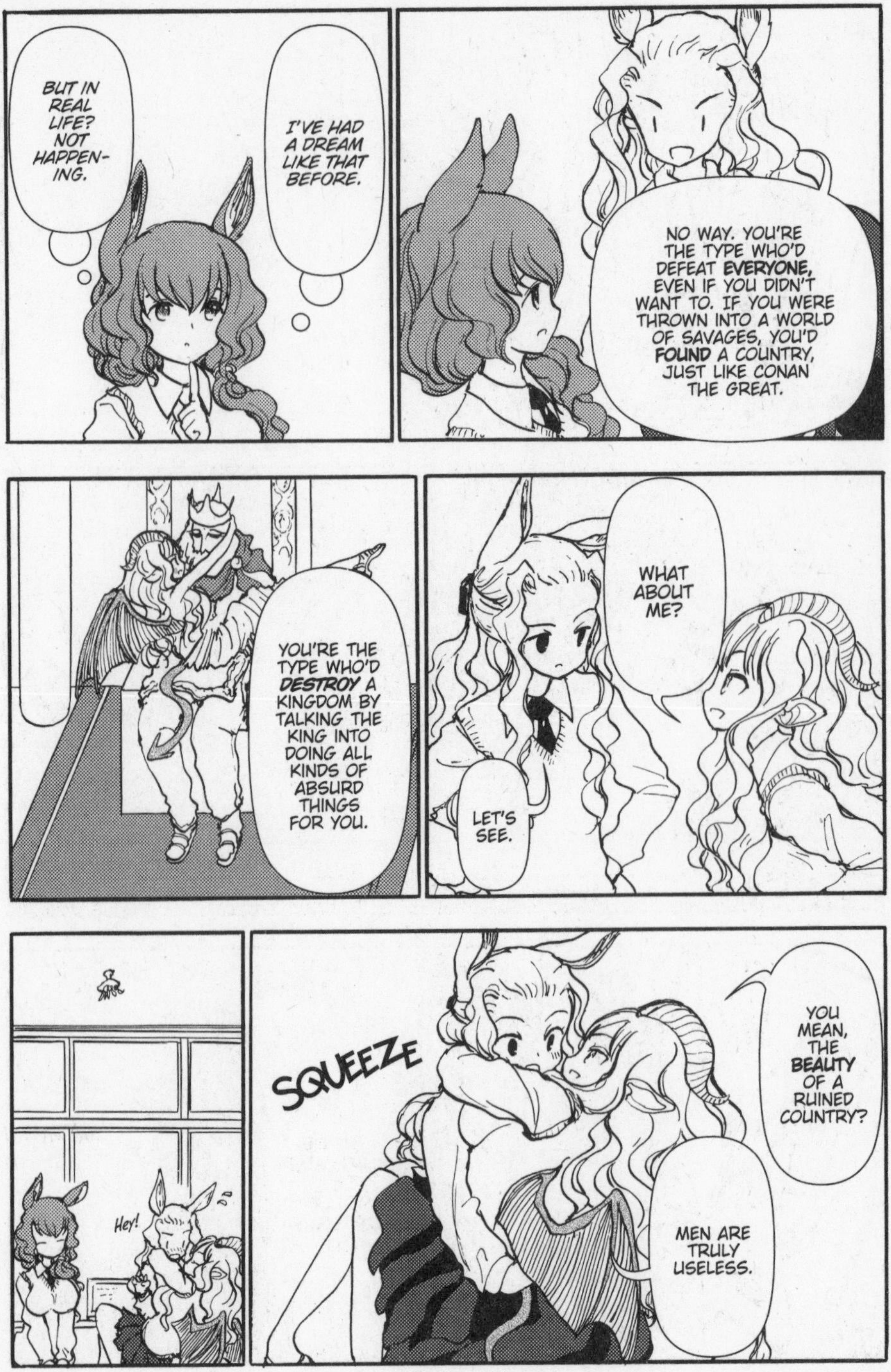
NO WAY. YOU'RE THE TYPE WHO'D DEFEAT **EVERYONE**, EVEN IF YOU DIDN'T WANT TO. IF YOU WERE THROWN INTO A WORLD OF SAVAGES, YOU'D **FOUND** A COUNTRY, JUST LIKE CONAN THE GREAT.
I'VE HAD A DREAM LIKE THAT BEFORE.
BUT IN REAL LIFE? NOT HAPPEN-ING.
WHAT ABOUT ME?
LET'S SEE.
YOU'RE THE TYPE WHO'D ***DESTROY*** A KINGDOM BY TALKING THE KING INTO DOING ALL KINDS OF ABSURD THINGS FOR YOU.
YOU MEAN, THE **BEAUTY** OF A RUINED COUNTRY?
MEN ARE TRULY USELESS.
SQUEEZE
Hey!

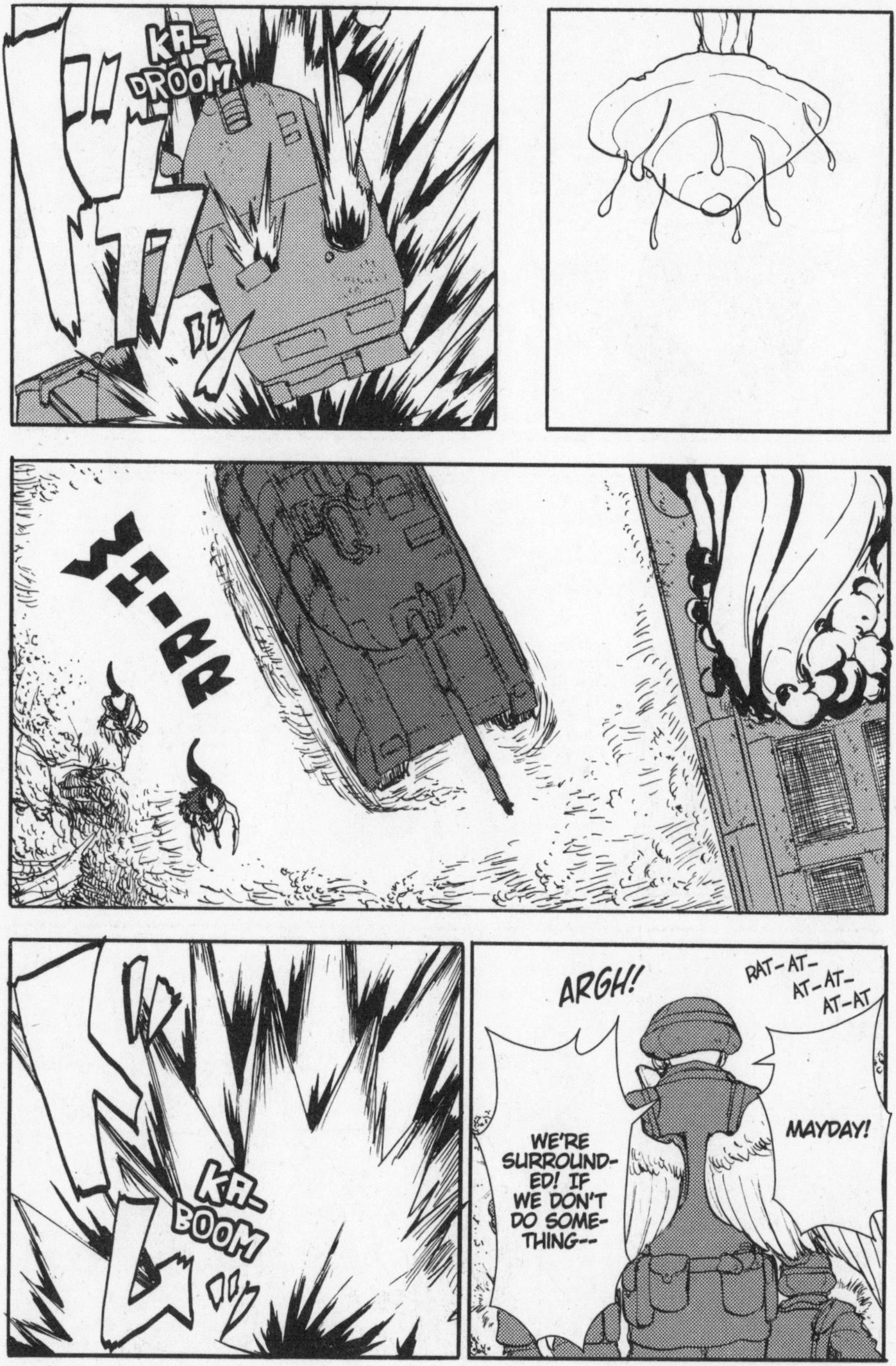
KA-DROOM
WHIRR
RAT-AT-AT-AT-AT-AT
ARGH!
MAYDAY!
WE'RE SURROUNDED! IF WE DON'T DO SOMETHING--
KA-BOOM

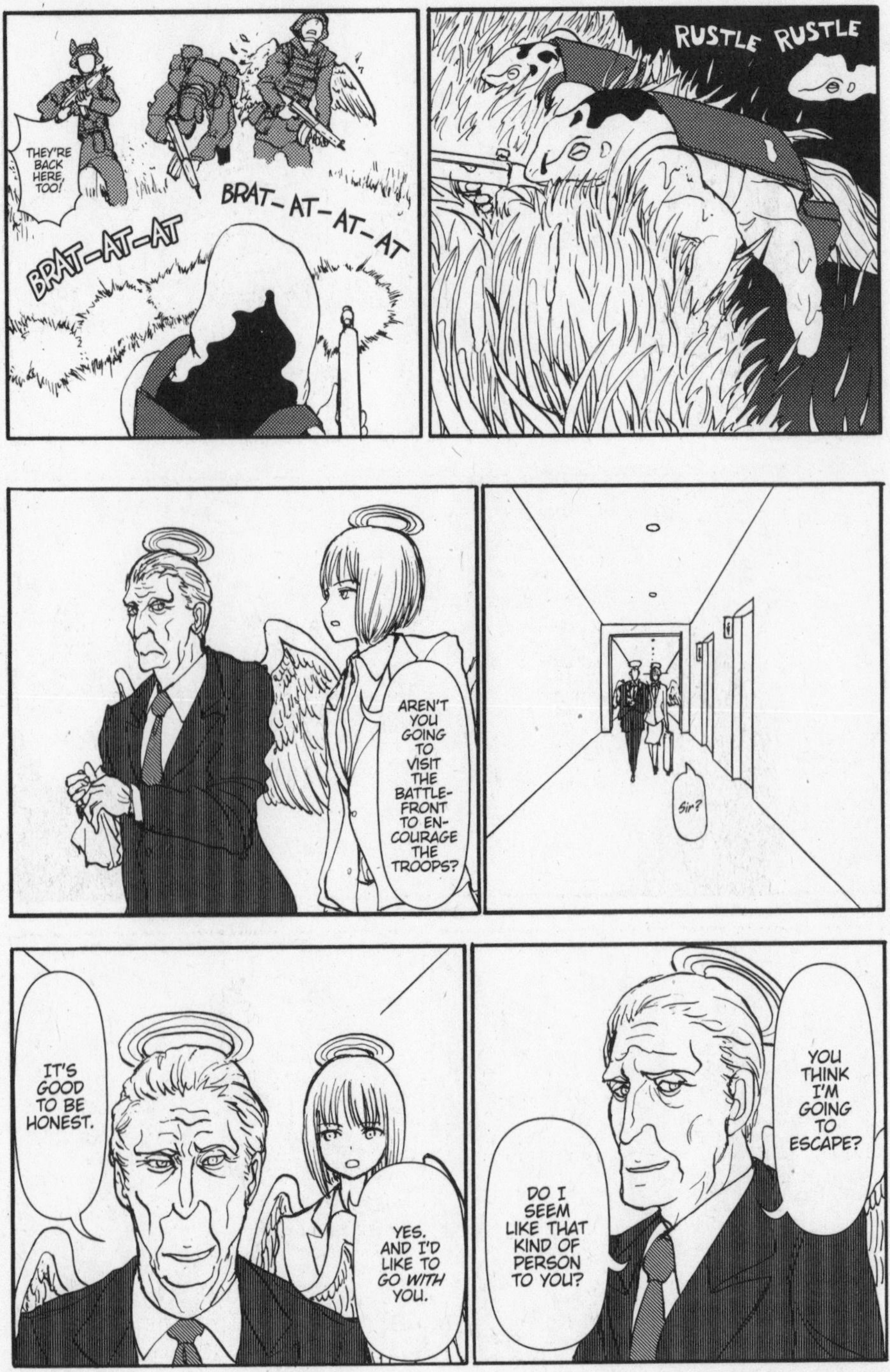
RUSTLE RUSTLE
THEY'RE BACK HERE, TOO!
BRAT-AT-AT-AT
BRAT-AT-AT
Sir?
AREN'T YOU GOING TO VISIT THE BATTLE-FRONT TO EN-COURAGE THE TROOPS?
YOU THINK I'M GOING TO ESCAPE?
DO I SEEM LIKE THAT KIND OF PERSON TO YOU?
YES. AND I'D LIKE TO GO *WITH* YOU.
IT'S GOOD TO BE HONEST.

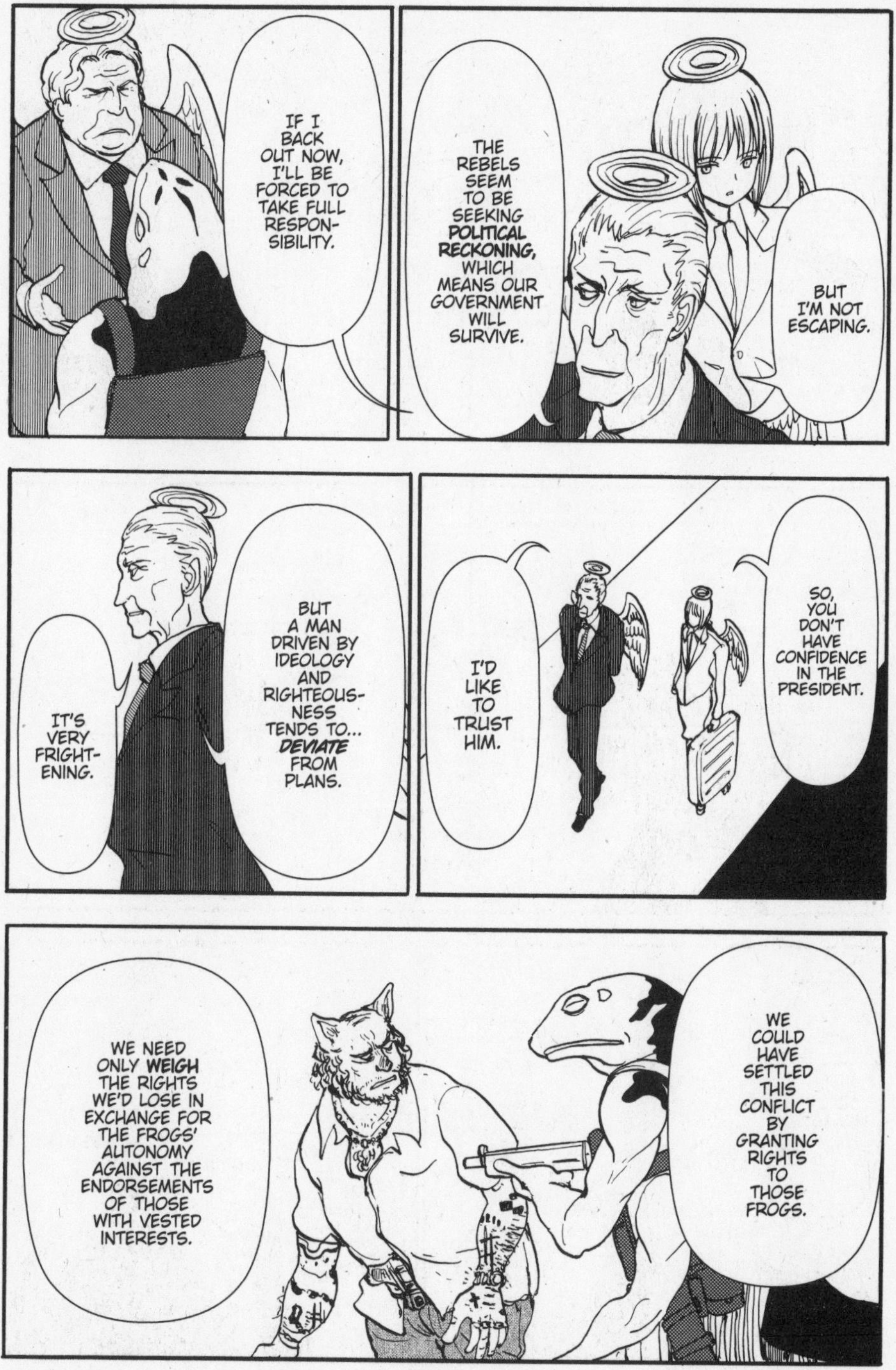
THE REBELS SEEM TO BE SEEKING **POLITICAL RECKONING,** WHICH MEANS OUR GOVERNMENT WILL SURVIVE.
BUT I'M NOT ESCAPING.
IF I BACK OUT NOW, I'LL BE FORCED TO TAKE FULL RESPONSIBILITY.
SO, YOU DON'T HAVE CONFIDENCE IN THE PRESIDENT.
I'D LIKE TO TRUST HIM.
BUT A MAN DRIVEN BY IDEOLOGY AND RIGHTEOUSNESS TENDS TO... ***DEVIATE*** FROM PLANS.
IT'S VERY FRIGHTENING.
WE COULD HAVE SETTLED THIS CONFLICT BY GRANTING RIGHTS TO THOSE FROGS.
WE NEED ONLY **WEIGH** THE RIGHTS WE'D LOSE IN EXCHANGE FOR THE FROGS' AUTONOMY AGAINST THE ENDORSEMENTS OF THOSE WITH VESTED INTERESTS.

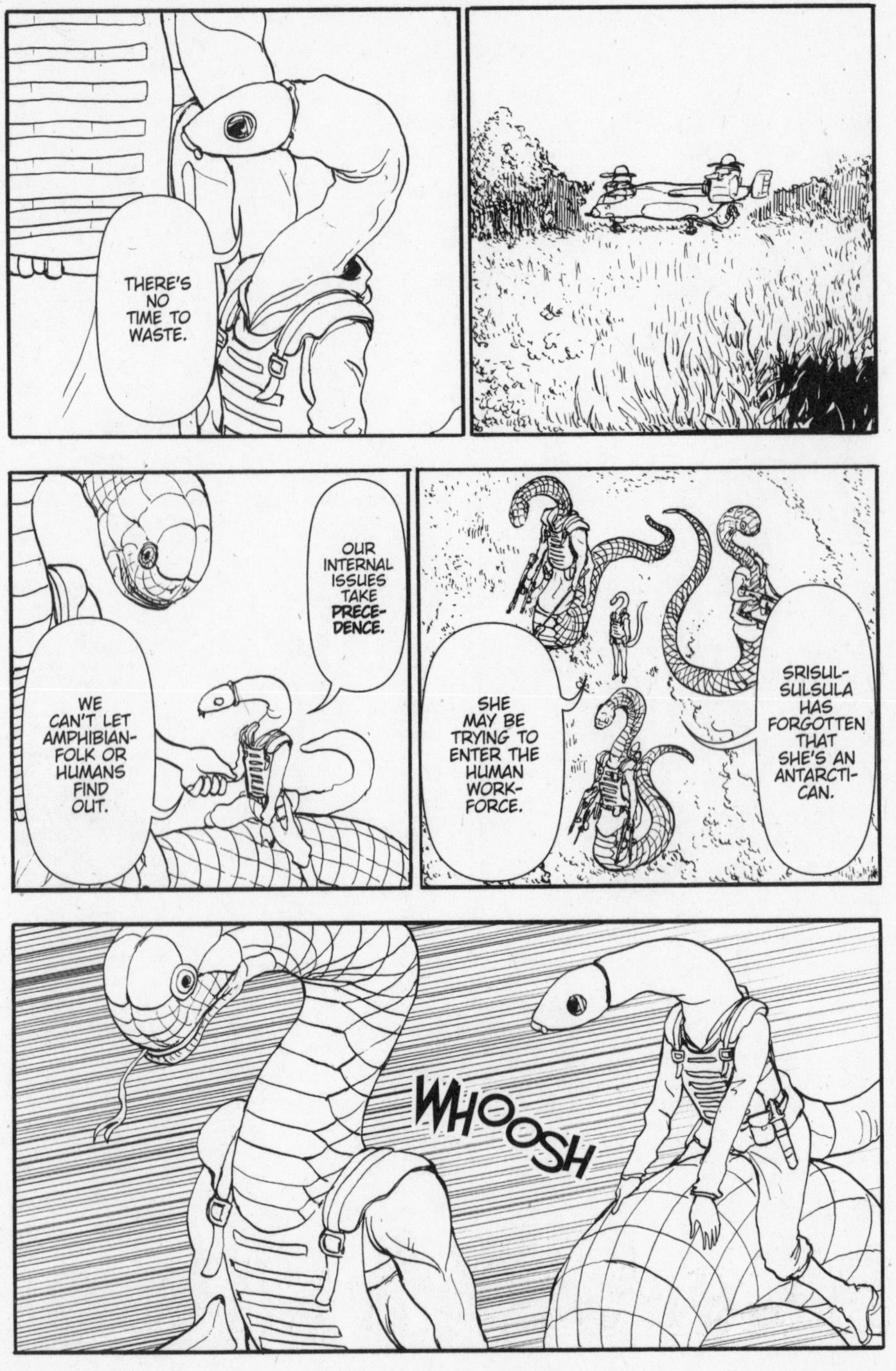
THERE'S NO TIME TO WASTE.
SRISULSULSULA HAS FORGOTTEN THAT SHE'S AN ANTARCTICAN.
SHE MAY BE TRYING TO ENTER THE HUMAN WORKFORCE.
OUR INTERNAL ISSUES TAKE **PRECEDENCE**.
WE CAN'T LET AMPHIBIAN-FOLK OR HUMANS FIND OUT.
WHOOSH

A CentaUr's Life

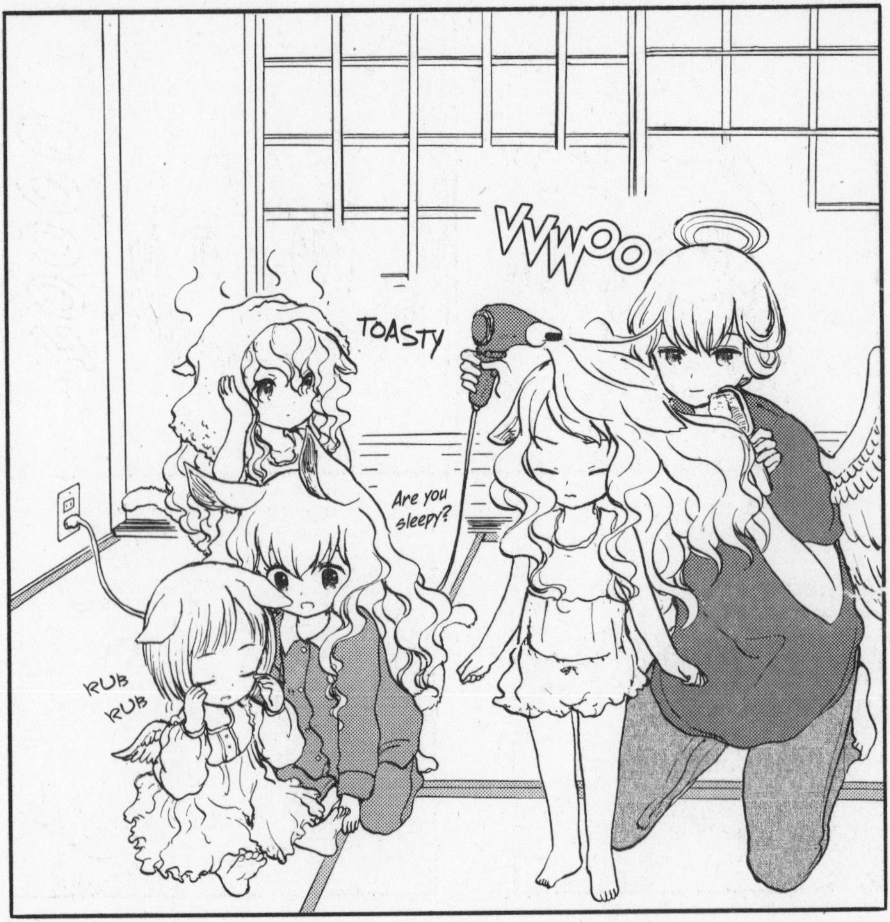
VVWOO
TOASTY
Are you sleepy?
RUB RUB

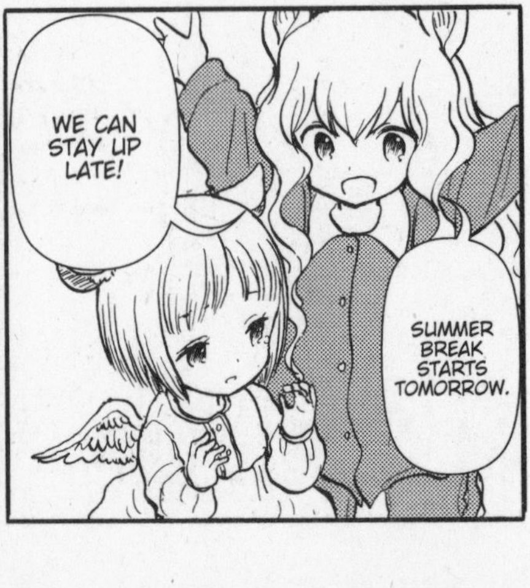
SUMMER BREAK STARTS TOMORROW.
WE CAN STAY UP LATE!

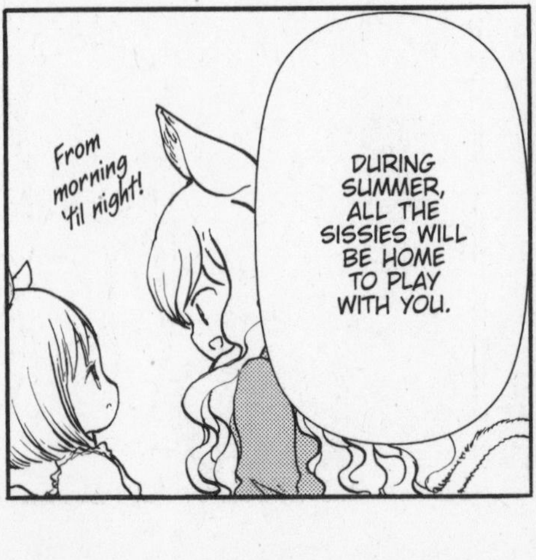
DURING SUMMER, ALL THE SISSIES WILL BE HOME TO PLAY WITH YOU.
From morning 'til night!

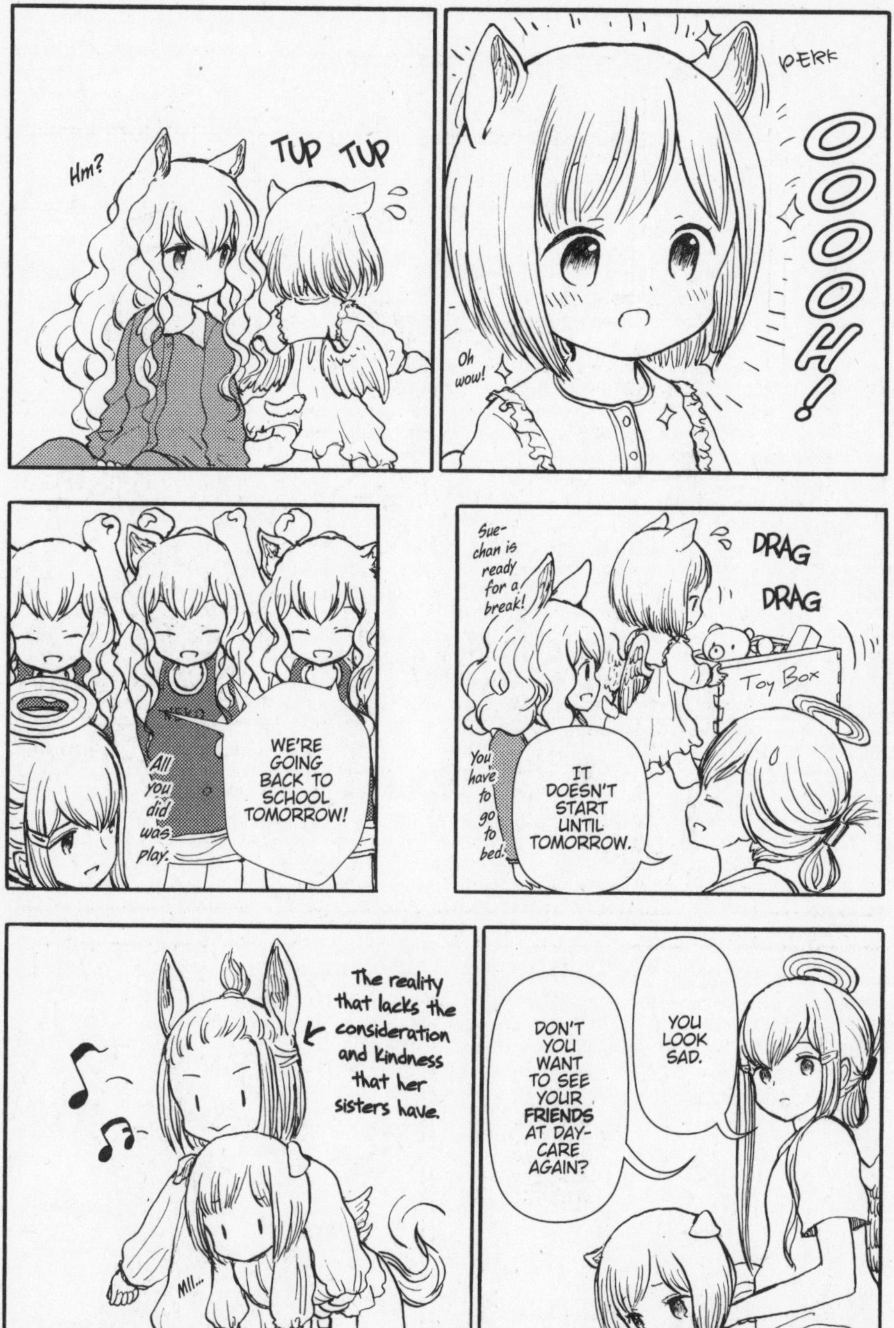
PERK
OOOOOH!
Oh wow!
TUP TUP
Hm?
DRAG DRAG
Sue-chan is ready for a break!
Toy Box
IT DOESN'T START UNTIL TOMORROW.
You have to go to bed.
WE'RE GOING BACK TO SCHOOL TOMORROW!
All you did was play.
YOU LOOK SAD.
DON'T YOU WANT TO SEE YOUR FRIENDS AT DAY-CARE AGAIN?
The reality that lacks the consideration and kindness that her sisters have.
MII...

FREEDOM AND CAPITALIST SOCIETY

After gaining control of the anti-government movement (led by former samurai) and achieving victory in foreign wars, the Meiji government aspired to enhance the nation's wealth and military power while forging ahead with modernization. In this context, modernization referred to westernization, which meant moving to a capitalist economy based on free competition. Since they were no longer bound by feudal restrictions, the people gained freedoms like the ability to buy or sell land, visit a town, go to the capital, run a business, establish a new industry in another prefecture, or even run in an election and become a statesman. Writers often enjoyed luxurious lifestyles, eating Western cuisine and buying foreign books in the capital. Even farmers began to see some improvements to their lifestyles, including access to newspapers. Lifestyle enhancements were available to anyone who could afford them.

Hitachi Prefecture wasn't known for any industries other than natto. It was, however, where many industrialists were produced, and where a considerable number of new industries flourished. Those industries included tea, konnyaku jelly, chestnuts, wine, soy sauce, sericulture, stone, finance, energy, and even the manufacturing of firearms. Although there were many successful people who earned their place in history, there were even more people who were not successful. Most wealthy farmers were major landowners, or held leadership positions in the region. From a historical perspective, the social class of wealthy farmers was made up of villains that had imposed cruel and unjust taxes on the peasants. In the Saviet Union, they were considered enemies of the people, meant to become extinct. In Japan, however, a considerable number of them represented other farmers (as they did in the Bakyuu Riot) and brought in new industries to enhance their villages' success in a rapidly changing world.

One of the new industries chosen in Kanata was sericulture, which coincided with the government's support for the increase of raw silk production. Centaurs, who couldn't work in rice fields, found a new economic opportunity in breeding silkworms. The first silkworm breeders were wealthy farmers, but the practice eventually spread, first to independent farmers and then to lower-income people, such as sharecroppers. In an attempt to expand the industry, some entrepreneurs imported equipment and opened silk thread factories, but many people who made large investments ultimately went bankrupt and left the region. This may have been because these industry pioneers had poor sericultural skills and a lack of sericultural education, or because making profit at market was difficult due to competition, causing prices to fluctuate severely. But an even more fundamental problem may have been that the wealthy farmers of the Edo period lacked the proper mindset to be industrialists or capitalists in the new world of free competition. These farmers, who owned many acres of land, acted as magnanimous landlords and often overlooked workers who had stolen rice or firewood. Only their fellow workers condemned such petty thefts.

The rent for farmland may have been considered expensive by today's standards, but it was common for land-owners to be lenient to workers who were behind on their rent. In the Edo period, many of them acted as officials and mediated between samurai and villagers, only to be driven to financial ruin by giving advances on settlements. Such a patriarchal management style would not be wise in a capitalist society. Forgiving irresponsible management by relatives and refusing to listen to their workers' grievances also made it impossible to survive in a free society.

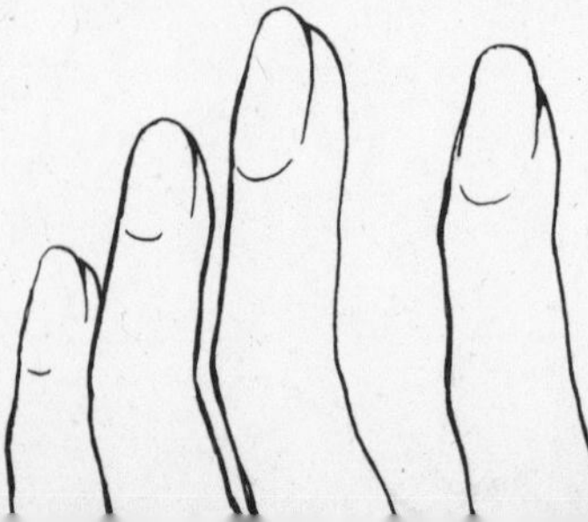

RURAL COMMUNITY UNDER THE INFLUENCE OF THE MARKET

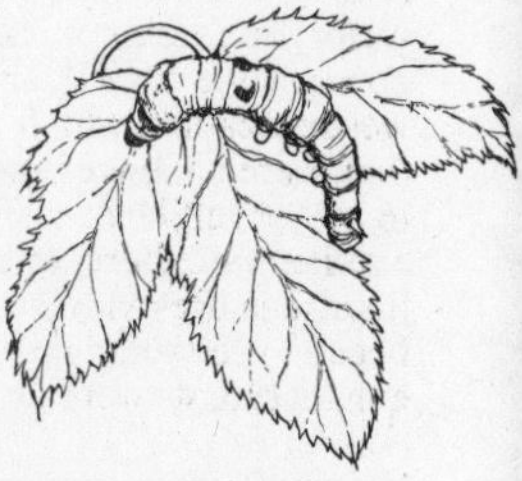

Making profit from sericultural business was still difficult, even with proper education. Silkworms didn't always survive; some of them died of silkworm rot before spinning their cocoons. If the growers were unable to grow enough mulberry leaves, they had to be purchased from elsewhere instead. Even having cocoons to sell didn't necessarily mean that farmers were able to earn enough to cover their expenses. Roads were paved with tax money, which made it possible for buses to transport people and goods to towns. Although significant profit could have been earned at an auction market in town (as opposed to local bargain hunters), farmers would then have to pay selling fees and transportation costs. The greater availability of goods in towns put even more pressure on local markets. If the farmers were devoted solely to cultivation, then they couldn't expect a large enough harvest to make a living without the use of increasingly expensive fertilizers. A village like Kanata (that didn't produce any particular specialty products) had no opportunities for earning a substantial income other than sericulture. Since the farmers had already used their lands as collateral, taking out a loan or putting things on credit was not an option. They were forced to use their profits from the cocoons as collateral.

Rice, which was a major crop, was influenced by the market as well, and its price soared due to the deployment of troops to Siberia during the Russo-Japanese War. Housewives rioted in Toyama as a direct result of the rising cost of rice; however, this incident worked in the favor of farmers in Kanata, who were shocked at the prices offered by rice buyers. But even though they sold at a high price, the proceeds were quickly spent on their daily expenses or uneducated investments, which meant that the rural economy continued to struggle. Naturally, when the market worked to their disadvantage, they suffered even more. After tenant farmers finished paying their rent and fees, there wasn't enough rice left for themselves, and they were forced to buy cheap, imported rice that smelled like oil.

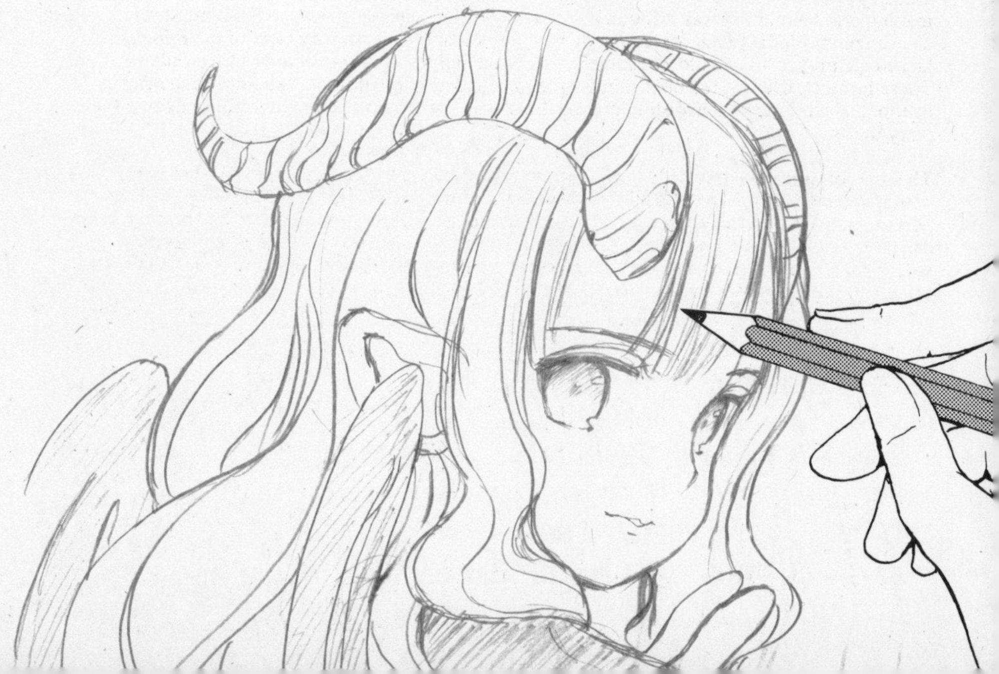

SEVEN SEAS ENTERTAINMENT PRESENTS *anya*

A Centaur's Life

story and art by KEI MURAYAMA

VOLUME 14

TRANSLATION
Elina Ishikawa

ADAPTATION
Holly Kolodziejczak

LETTERING AND RETOUCH
Jennifer Skarupa

LOGO DESIGN
Courtney Williams

COVER DESIGN
Nicky Lim

PROOFREADER
Janet Houck

ASSISTANT EDITOR
Jenn Grunigen

PRODUCTION ASSISTANT
CK Russell

PRODUCTION MANAGER
Lissa Pattillo

EDITOR-IN-CHIEF
Adam Arnold

PUBLISHER
Jason DeAngelis

CENTAUR NO NAYAMI VOLUME 14
© KEI MURAYAMA 2016
Originally published in Japan in 2016 by TOKUMA SHOTEN PUBLISHING
CO., LTD., Tokyo. English translation rights arranged with TOKUMA SHOTEN
PUBLISHING CO., LTD., Tokyo, through TOHAN CORPORATION, Tokyo.

Seven Seas books may be purchased in bulk for promotional, educational, or
business use. Please contact your local bookseller or the Macmillan Corporate
and Premium Sales Department at 1-800-221-7945, extension 5442, or by
e-mail at MacmillanSpecialMarkets@macmillan.com.

Seven Seas and the Seven Seas logo are trademarks of
Seven Seas Entertainment, LLC. All rights reserved.

ISBN: 978-1-626927-18-6

Printed in Canada

First Printing: April 2018

10 9 8 7 6 5 4 3 2 1

FOLLOW US ONLINE: www.gomanga.com

READING DIRECTIONS

This book reads from **right to left**, Japanese style. If
this is your first time reading manga, you start
reading from the top right panel on each page and
take it from there. If you get lost, just follow the
numbered diagram here. It may seem backwards at
first, but you'll get the hang of it! Have fun!!

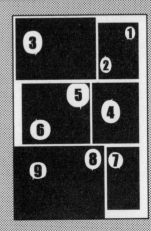